SHAKESPEARE,

SHAMANS,

AND

SHOW BIZ

Books by David Kaplan

Shakespeare, Shamans, and Show Biz: An Impolite Guide to Theater History, (2021)

Lorca in Lubbock: A Photographic Essay (2018)

Tenn Years: Tennessee Williams on Stage (2016)

Tenn at One Hundred: The Reputation of Tennessee Williams (2011)

Tennessee Williams in Provincetown (2007)

Five Approaches to Acting Series (2001, 2007)

SHAKESPEARE, SHAMANS AND SHOW BIZ

An Impolite Guide to Theater History

David Kaplan

HANSEN PUBLISHING GROUP

Shakespeare, Shamans, and Show Biz: An Impolite Guide to Theater History
Copyright © 2021, 2014 David Kaplan
All rights reserved. Published 2021
Preview Edition published 2014.
Printed in the United States

26, 25, 24, 23, 22, 21   1 2 3 4 5 6 7 8 9

ISBN: 978-1-60182-208-6 (Cloth)
ISBN: 978-1-60182-209-3 (Paper)
ISBN: 978-1-60182-210-9 (E-book)

Book interior and cover design by Jon Hansen

Cover Art: Ilya Repin, *The Unexpected Return* (1884–1888)

Author Photograph: Courtesy of Julia Cumes

Hansen Publishing Group, LLC
302 Ryders Lane,
East Brunswick, NJ 08816

https://hansenpublishing.com

David Kaplan's web site:
http://www.davidkaplanteacher.com/

For the students who listened, who questioned,
and who developed ideas of their own.

"Maeterlinck has given us the most brilliant work of our time, …superior in beauty to what is most beautiful in Shakespeare."

—Octave Mirbeau, August 1890, reviewing Maeterlinck's *La Princesse Maleine* for *Le Figaro*

"Listen, Ibsen is no playwright…Ibsen just doesn't know life. In life it simply isn't like that."

—Anton Chekhov, 1899, speaking to Stanislavsky after seeing rehearsals for *Hedda Gabler* at the Moscow Art Theater

CONTENTS

INTRODUCTION

The most important essay in this collection is the last, Chapter Twenty-four "Missing from History," and you could read it first. It's an essay about the playwrights and plays that didn't survive in history (so far) or got dropped from history (so far). Rather than claiming to find what's lost or reviving what's forgotten, the last chapter points out that accident, taste, political power, and passing fads are responsible for what makes history. Chapter Twenty-four "Missing from History" suggests you should read history skeptically, keeping in mind that what passes for history is always—always—a point of view about the past that comes from the past. You could begin by reading the first chapter, too.

Every chapter tries to share what someone working in the theater should know about the past for context in understanding or creating work in the theater today—not everything they should know; what's here isn't up-to-date, and it couldn't be. The year I'm writing this introduction, new plays have arrived, onstage and in manuscript; the year after this, new plays will arrive, as will new ideas and new sources for ideas.

Even if what I've written can't be up to date, I'm hoping it has some value in the present moment. Knowing something of what came *before* the present moment—not just plays, but past standards of excellence, or importance, or beauty—is useful for creating new work now and in the future. Past standards of excellence, importance, and beauty might inspire you or leave you skeptical. To respect or reject the opinions of the past is a choice, and such choices can be based on knowledge rather than ignorance. To respect or reject the opinions of the present is also a choice and could be based on knowledge, rather than ignorance, that includes self-knowledge and a consideration of contemporary pieties. An exclusive insistence on the value of self-approval, self-worth, self-understanding, and self-reference can easily lead to forgetting or willfully ignoring that other values are possible. Questioning what passes for value in the world around you is a powerful way to achieve an understanding of what is of value to you.

My own sense of value includes the value of texts written to be performed for an audience. In my own experience in an audience, in a rehearsal studio, and in a classroom, texts take effect—on the page or on the stage—when they create relationships between those reading, listening, rehearsing, performing, and watching. Beyond my own experience, theater history makes the case that some texts from the past continue to resound with audiences, sometimes in ways unanticipated by their creators or by me—or by you.

There is no obvious or inevitable order to what might create value for you. The struggle for personal freedom that a feisty Norwegian playwright put onstage a hundred years ago is still an ongoing struggle moving forwards and sometimes backwards. You can read about it in Chapter Thirteen "Bad Boys Breaking the Rules." What a bored schoolboy in France found ridiculous about his pompous teacher still invites ridicule and sets off laughter to undo the charisma of power. That's in Chapter Thirteen, too. In Chapter Eighteen "Expressionism to Epic," you can read about Bertolt Brecht, a German chain-smoker inspired by Chinese acting. Brecht's realization of an audience's potential to think passionately has continuing potential to be explored and realized in further detail every time there is a new audience. You might be set off in our age of doubt by Chapter Five "Aeschylus—Writing in an Age of Certainty." The power of recited names to link the past with the present is as true now as it was among storytellers in precolonial Africa, the Old Testament, and the war stories of the ancient Greeks told by Aeschylus about the ancient Persians. You could start this collection with any of those chapters.

The first twelve chapters meander along a timeline that begins in the fifteenth century with plays performed in England.

Then they skip forward about two hundred years to consider what was performed in other parts of Western Europe during the Renaissance. Next, we track back a thousand years to ancient Greece and Rome. We retreat further, tracing what's claimed to be a 40,000-year-old tradition of shamanic ritual in Central Asia as the root of theater practiced in China under Mao Tse-tung and theater in post-World War II Japan. The book's first half concludes with the Neoclassical theater of the 1600s in Western Europe.

This meandering is meant to get to an idea shared by audience and performers in many different circumstances that certain forms of theater have been claimed as "classic," said to be forms significant in and of themselves: the literary and performance practices of, for example, tragedy, comedy, Noh theater, and Kabuki. Classic forms of gesture, movement, and language, whether in Asia or Europe, challenge performing artists to study given forms and embody their meaning. Classic form invites reinvention, reinterpretation, and universal participation. The process of achieving classic forms often negotiates collisions between different cultures and reconciles clashes within a culture. The achieved forms are classic, in part, because they balance diverse forces. Balance and harmony and the resolution of oppositions is something people seek throughout history. Sometimes classic form is rejected as old-fashioned; sometimes it is exalted as an eternal aim: the harmony of thesis and antithesis. Often classic rules are defined centuries after the creators of the work arrived at what they sought without thinking of any such rules.

Writing about classic forms, I've tried to undermine the sense that classic form is something to aspire to or to learn in order to obey. My idea has been, rather, to help you understand why there were rules, what they accomplished, where they had limits, and how they might inspire following or departing from such rules.

The second half of the book focuses on forms, defined as Romantic, with a capital *R*, upholding the aesthetic of tumult. Romantic forms share the aesthetic that forces at conflict are beau-

tiful in their lack of resolution. Romantic forms pass on the ongoing dynamic of unbalance, inspiring audiences with the thrill
or disquiet of coming to an end without a conclusion. The time
line of the second twelve chapters runs from Ibsen's *Peer Gynt*,
published in 1867 and stops (Chapter Twenty-three "Theater of
Identity") at the texts of the 1980s that began a sensibility that
has lasted three decades: time enough to be considered history,
and, even so, still current.

In the hundred-and-fifty-year progression of the book's second half, it's possible to see a repetition of themes found in the
first half of the book. Any period offers the potential for individual vision to overturn what's accepted practice. Whatever the
time or place, the use of crude materials to express sophisticated
ideas onstage is inevitable: breaking wind as expressions of an
inner life that cannot be repressed by social conventions begins
medieval theater and what we call modern theater, too. Clichés,
stock situations, and stock characters reappear onstage in different contexts. Inevitably creators strategically deploy conventional formulas to subvert expectations. Euripides mocked a general of the Trojan War as a pandering politician; Eugene O'Neill
imagined the same general as a tragic philosopher during the
American Civil War. There will always be, for better or worse, a
theater that seeks to improve the morals of its audience.

Among the continuities and repetition in every theater culture is a mix of storytelling and acting out, which is often how
theater begins on its own: when a community tells stories to
reinforce community identity. In Western Europe, the Catholic
Church arranged for the recitation and enactment of Bible stories
for people in the congregation who couldn't read. In the aisles of
an English church, or outside on the steps of an Italian cathedral,
or sometimes outdoors for passersby to see, plays were devised
and performed by priests and congregants unaware, it seems, of
any other theater, and so they found their own ways to share the
stories that inspired them and draw their community together.
Centuries later in America, August Wilson wrote an epic cycle of

ten plays, nine of them about the history of his African American neighborhood in Pittsburgh, unaware, at least at first, there were models for his work written by other playwrights. He invented his own strategies combining storytelling, music, and dance inspired by the lamentations of the blues and the pleasures of neighborhood gossip. The inclusion of Wilson's plays within the American theater's repertory has reinforced and broadened the American identity of its subject matter and audiences. The same might be said for the ancient Greek tragedies by Aeschylus, written more than two thousand years ago, that united disparate city-states celebrating their victory over the would-be invaders from Persia. The plays of Aeschylus or August Wilson are not reflections of Greek or American identity: they create such identities.

New theater might be created—and has been created—without knowing any of the old clichés, without the search for identity, without moral instruction. I'm willing to consider the value of starting fresh each time, and the value of pretending to start fresh that might lead to something fresh. The cul-de-sacs of intolerance and ignorance are there to be driven down and get stuck in again, too. Reimagining the past to make it more ethnically pure, or more diverse when it wasn't, or more realistic when it wasn't, are fantasies, undercut by knowledge of the evidence that performance in a foreign language inspires new ideas, that social circumstances prevented access to the majority of people who might have contributed to the theater in any place or time, and that realism was incomprehensible to audience used to centuries of stylization.

I have biases. If you think learning dates is important (I don't) learn them. Each chapter includes a list of characters discussed with their dates. I've kept out endnotes and tried to identify sources in the text. Rather than dates or sources, I'd rather readers understand the relationship between the audience and the performed text as an aspect of the society in which the text is performed. Start with the first chapter's title: "The Middle Ages as a State of Mind," not a set of dates. I've chosen to begin with the theater of the Middle Ages because I believe the people who were making theater in the Middle Ages did so without much (if any) knowledge of ancient Greek or Roman theater practice or literature.

For Americans, I think it's useful to know a variety of sources, not just the English language theater. English-language playwrights (the English Restoration playwrights chief among them) can be studied in other books. You can disagree, but I think it's more important for Americans to know something about Asian theater and shamans. See Chapter Nineteen "American Agitprop (Overt and Disguised)" for how Chinese theater inspired the "classic" American play *Our Town*. Artists whose work achieved commercial success and popular acclaim in American theater deserve attention, and so do Gertrude Stein, Marita Bonner and other visionary American writers who were ignored, or worse, condescended to by historians and critics. Even so, let's assess how and why Stein's influence was mighty, despite how little she was praised or how rarely her work is performed, and how Bonner's influence remains (so far) relatively weak and her plays unperformed despite her wide vision. In the last thirty years, there are new plays to consider from a much more diverse collection of writers than before. That's not what this book is about, but knowing about them, and seeing their plays in performance gives an opportunity to make your own theater history. Do.

In 1824, the French painter Eugène Delacroix recorded in his spattered journal what he was learning for himself by studying the work of great artists and writers from the past, from his own time, and from cultures other than his own. He wrote in his journal about Michelangelo, who had died in 1564, and Delacroix wrote in his journal about Jean Racine and playwrights of the 1660s (see Chapter Eleven "Neoclassic Theater and Why There is Such a Thing"). Delacroix wrote in his journal about the German genius Goethe, who was pistol hot in 1824 (again see Chapter Eleven), and Delacroix wrote about his predecessors among painters including Raphael (who died in 1520), and Delacroix wrote about his immediate contemporaries among painters, including Géricault, who had died on January 26, 1824.

In the spring of 1824 Delacroix wrote in his journal about the seventeenth century Spanish painter Velàzquez and the fourteenth century writer Dante, and Delacroix wrote down his thoughts about *Don Quixote*, a book written between 1605 and 1615, that Delacroix was about to illustrate.

On Saturday, May 15, 1824, Delacroix, wrote in his journal:

> What moves those of genius, what inspires their work is not new ideas, but their obsession with the idea that what has already been said is still not enough.

It will never be: that's the challenge and the opportunity. Every time we go to the theater or read a play, we're offered an opportunity to reshuffle another version of theater history, adding, omitting, rethinking.

Did knowing those dates help you? Not really.

SHAKESPEARE,
SHAMANS,
AND
SHOW BIZ

Chapter One

THE MIDDLE AGES AS A STATE OF MIND

Hroswitha (935–1002)
Terence (Publius Terentius Afer) (185–159 BC)

t's important to remember that history is not what happened. History is what was recorded and how we interpret
what we find as evidence of the past. When we speak of the
medieval mind, we are drawing inferences from what physically
survives from a time long ago, five hundred to fifteen hundred
years in the past: paintings, woodcuts, music, architecture, writing, bits of ivory, pieces of stone, embroidery, indentations in
the dirt, and scraps of sheepskin. These relics survive due to the
power of fate and, often, the power of politics and wealth.

When we read plays from the Middle Ages in which over and
over again there is the affirmation of faith and submission to God
as achieved through only one faith that described itself by the
Greek word *catholic*, meaning all-embracing, we must remember
that we have no records of any other points of view. From the
plays where debate is often the dramatic action, we know that dissent was common enough to be familiar to the audience. Doubt
was familiar to them, too. The blurred illusion of unanimity in
the Middle Ages was and is created by ignoring other points of
view. Protest wasn't so much omitted from the historical record
as erased. At a distance of hundreds of years, we have no way of
knowing what the illusion of unanimity hides or disguises.

What about the heretics? The doubters? The fringe? We can
deduce the existence of protest even though protest is unre-

corded in official or scholarly ways. The Church taught people to read, paid people to write, and maintained places to store writings. The Church did not devote resources to plays that attacked the faith.

We can look at times closer to our own to see how theater history is manufactured. In Soviet Russia, until the 1970s, mention of the greatest of Russian theater directors, Meyerhold, was omitted from history books after he denounced the government's artistic monopoly in 1939. Stanislavsky, Meyerhold's mentor, went along with the Soviet government's policies but at a price. The Stanislavsky system's roots in yoga went unmentioned because the Soviet censors maintained such practices were not part of the Soviet government's atheist aesthetic.

Just as you wouldn't know Stanislavsky's debt to yoga if you read the books published under his name, we must sometimes look beyond text and records to notice that medieval theater had other forms besides literally preaching to the choir. Aside from the historical record of medieval plays, there is evidence of a line of theatrical skills and experience passed down without writing: juggling, puppeteering, mime, and physical comedy.

There is a dissident tradition in medieval theater and evidence of it pops up in farts. Composed in the 1400s (maybe), the windy *Castle of Perseverance* has among its stage directions (some of the earliest in English theater history) the note to have a character named Mercy dressed in a white cape and a character named Righteousness in a red one, as well as the note to have firecrackers come out of the Devil's ass. Why is farting—rather than spitting or urinating—such a recurring part of medieval performance? Because it comes from within, not from the sky, nor from society. Medieval drama trumpeted with stomach gas the inner life that later playwrights would elaborate: the pauses of the psychological Russian playwright Chekhov, the lowered eyes of melodrama, and the great late nineteenth century heroine, Hedda Gabler, moving to the stove in a soul-chilling drawing room. What we think of in modern times as the strength of modern drama, a character inwardly struggling against social restraint—that expression of the personal-in-the-crowd is, in the time of the fifteenth century play *Everyman*, expressed as a fart and an occasional belch.

Cut off from rules of form, the impulse to create meaning rediscovers itself in bodily functions, just as symmetry in art is found by looking at the human body. Stored and waiting for the right time to reappear, the plays of ancient Greece and Rome stayed unread during the Middle Ages, or if read, as far as we know unperformed and unknown outside of the library. The medieval writing of plays was self-taught. Reading drama from the Middle Ages, we watch an art form finding itself. It's only later when the theater in Western Europe has grown enough to care about form that its creators look backwards to see what came before them as models for what might be done in the future.

Reading plays from the Middle Ages, we can deduce the medieval theater's assumptions from the lack of rules. The writers take for granted that members of the audience can move from place to place in their imaginations. The audience is expected to be pious and patient. The audience is expected to understand that the performers in a play though putting on roles retain their own identity, rather than somehow obtaining a soul other than their own, as in a ritual performed by shamans. We can also deduce from the available texts that the medieval audience liked rhythm and rhyme, especially rhyme with a certain roughness to it like pulp in orange juice. No one at the time seems to have had much use for suspense; they enjoyed stories with endings they already knew. The medieval audience's sense of history was ahistorical, and for that reason Jesus can be mentioned in *Abraham and Isaac*, a thousand years or so before Jesus is presumed to have been born. Just as the Trinity—Father, Son, and Holy Ghost—could be painted all on the same piece of wood, the stage could do the same, show three realities at once.

We know from the evidence of scribbling in the margins of manuscripts that medieval people had a robust sense of decoration and a love of ornamentation. Because contact with certain traditions had been lost, they had a freedom to create in drama (and in art) what remains exuberant and fresh.

Let's not sentimentalize, either. Their faith was a convenient way for those in power to keep people under social control without permitting them a means to change their social position. High and low, intolerance and ignorance were profound and enforced. Their plays appealed not to logic but to affirmation, a very different thing. The model of behavior presented was Christ as Lamb and the congregation of Christians as sheep with the Church and God as shepherd and, when necessary, benevolent butcher. When we read of Isaac's willingness to be killed, we can think of the Jonestown cult or last week's suicide bombers saying the same words.

We have only to listen to their music to understand that a function of their art was to smother, to overwhelm, to envelope, to lift spirits high, to leave the gross material world behind; their singing voices an accumulation of sameness where the individual is bent to praise God and obey orders.

If they could see with our eyes and hear with our ears, they'd probably complain that our senses are dulled. If they could peer into our hearts, they would be startled by our lack of spiritual life, as they understood the life of the spirit.

We study them not as cul-de-sacs of experience, but as a mode of being human, and a mode that will always rise, the same as a fart. Their way of thinking, we now know, repeats itself. They didn't know that. They thought they were exceptional, outside of history, that when their time ended, Time itself would end when their God returned.

The Age of Faith as a mode of living can be noticed in Western Europe six hundred years ago, but also now in America, in Islamic countries, in Communist China, and in parts of Israel. Living with faith is comforting, and wherever and whenever it exists a constellation forms of obedience, sacrifice, and a belief in a future paradise—here on earth or in the heavens—at the expense of this life now. The constellation of fixed social roles and spiritual control prompts interior liberation.

For all the self-inventions of medieval dramatists, there were some rules they accepted from the church that organized the world in which they lived. The sky was where God lived, the devil below, people in between, and these three in some continuum, often depicted by a ladder between Heaven and Earth and Hell. We know from the evidence of their architecture and the other art we call Gothic that their organization of space was vertical, high and low. This idea is built into the churches: the lifting up of the altar, the lifting up of the interior of the church, the songs sung in the church, the smoke from the incense that rises to heaven, the lifting up of their prayers in life, and, they believed, their souls at the moment of death.

Another thing we know about that time from the evidence we have available is that death was ever present, in a way the modernized world does not experience except in crises or catastrophe. It's estimated one third of the Western European population died of plague. The representation of death in sculpture, in woodcuts, and in carnival costumes is prevalent enough to be called a cult, but natural, too, considering death might overtake anyone at any time. They were at the mercy of the weather. Famine was a part of their lives.

Hunger made them enjoy feasting; the drabness of color in their lives made them appreciate red and purple, gold and silver. They had a sense of occasion. The dullness of their routine gave importance to Church festivals and fair days. They did not have a sense that they controlled what happened to them—this made faith that much more essential for survival.

Given the impermanence of life, the medieval mind found itself yearning for something beyond the physical. The twenty-first century's use of body parts in high art and popular art is an instinctive return to the physical as a necessity of human experience. In the Middle Ages, art, including plays, had a function to provide a glimpse of heaven. There are three forms of medieval dramatic literature we can identify and name. They are easy to remember and easy to confuse as the three M's: mystery, morality, and miracle plays.

Even before there was anything written down in medieval Europe that we would agree to call a play, there were the seeds of plays to come in the four lines now called the *Quem Quaeritis*. The Latin title, taken from the first two words of the first line, means "Who are you looking for?" The question was asked, though we are not sure by whom, to priests or altar boys impersonating the Three Marys: Mary the mother of Jesus, Mary Magdalene, and Mary the mother of Martha and Lazarus—the last Mary unimportant to be sure, out of the B-list of biblical characters. You can see how much the audience enjoyed threes.

The Three Marys stood in the aisle; remember these were men dressed as women. "Who are you looking for?" someone asked, repeating the words of the angel at Christ's tomb. "For Jesus," the three Marys said, chanted, or sang. The angel answered them, "He's not here, he's gone up to Heaven. Go and tell people." This was all in Latin, as was the Mass, but it was an addition to the Mass and was called a *trope*: not unlike a little jazz riff. One imagines that after their lines were spoken, the three Marys moved down the aisle enacting the spread of the gospel. A chorus of hallelujahs followed, though who said them is unknown— perhaps everyone in the church. As simple and crude as this was, we can trace from it the steps that will lead to Broadway in the use of dialogue, impersonation, symbolic actions such as walking down the aisle, and men or boys dressed in women's clothing.

The mystery plays are the first medieval texts we would agree to call dramatic literature. The word "mystery" probably relates to the old Latin word for trade or guild or occupation. The plays were paid for by trade unions—called in British English, guilds. Think of this sponsorship as early advertising: the baker's guild might pay for the play about the Last Supper, for example. The word might also be related to something else. In Latin, *mysterium* means *to do, to act,* which would put it in a line with more recent thinking about theater and performance. What the mysteries do is enact the stories from the Bible.

The late fifteenth century text of *Abraham and Isaac* found in the library of a manor house in Brome, England is definitively a mystery play. It's written in English, not Latin. The bare plot is found in Genesis. Abraham takes his son Isaac to a mountaintop so as to sacrifice him to God. One of the appeals of the story to the medieval Church was that Isaac's story could be related directly to the stories of Christ's sacrifice in the New Testament. The connection of all things, past and present, to the Gospel of Jesus is not accidental, either. As late as the King James Bible in 1611, this kind of understanding takes the Hebrew word for young woman and translates it as *virgin* in the Old Testament. The people who believe the Holy Spirit descended into the room where the translation was getting done believe these changes are revelations. You can think what you like. That's a mystery of another kind.

The miracle plays are the stories of the saints. Saints played an important part in the thinking of this time because they were the link between people and God. Saints stood on the ladder midway between heaven and earth. They offered hope because they walked among those on the earth and then, with God's blessing, climbed up to heaven, leaving behind their relics: their bones, their tongues.

Along with relics, the saints left behind their inspirational life stories. Miracle plays dramatize moments when the miracle of the saint is revealed. Performing a miracle play turns the audience into witnesses of miracles, in the role of Christ's disciples. Through an accident of fate, the earliest example of a medieval play we have is a miracle play, and odder still, we know the author: Hroswitha, although there's indication that her real name was Helena. We think she might have been born in 935 and died around 1002. Obviously educated and with some freedom of thought, she copied the form of the Roman playwright Terence, whose Latin is polished and sparkles with witty jokes. "Why,"

Hroswitha wrote "should the devil," by which she meant the pagan god who she assumed inspired Terence the way Christ inspired her, "have all the fun of writing plays?"

There are six plays written by Hroswitha. These are the first plays we know about from Western Europe, though they lead nowhere but back to the convent library until they were rediscovered and printed around 1500, around the time Columbus got to America.

The form of the miracle play is the same both then and in the later part of the Middle Ages when miracle plays were being written in languages other than Latin. The major moments of the plot: oppression, faith, miracle, and then God's triumph (though the saint might die). Sometimes soldiers, or an emperor, or an oppressor is convinced to join the Church, too. Clearly Hroswitha's play *Dulcitus* is a miracle play, though the saints it chronicles are called Agape, Chionia, and Irene (Love, Purity and Peace in Greek). Hroswitha wrote in clear and direct Latin. We can tell from the scripts themselves that they must have been funny, intentionally so, because there were no rules yet about maintaining genres, so the natural exuberance to include comedy with serious work was unchecked.

The third dramatic form we have from the Middle Ages is the morality play. Obviously, they have a moral: a lesson of how to live one's life. They're acted out parables or sermons with actors taking the part of personified ideas: Faith, Good Deeds, Family, Everyman. The play called *Everyman* is the most famous in English, though it might be a translation from the Dutch. Everyone forsakes Everyman: family, friends, wealth, beauty, everything but good deeds and knowledge. The story is an example of the medieval habit of using art to see the abstract rather than the specific. The character named Family is not anyone's mother or even third cousin, but simply the concept "Family." This is what's called an *allegory*. It's interesting to look at the root of that word, too. It's Greek, from the *agora*, the marketplace, itself derived from an earlier word that means *herd* and by extension *crowd*.

Allegory: what one says to the crowd or herd. Back we come to sheep. There is a kind of debate or argument that goes on between characters in morality plays. The dramatic event might culminate in Everyman getting good with God, but the way he gets there, the dramatic action of the play, is a comparison rather than a conflict or competition. In the 1530 edition by John Skot, when Worldly Goods abandons Everyman, other characters proclaim their superiority:

> **Strength**: Everyman, we will not from you go,
> Till ye have done this voyage long.

> **Discretion**: I, Discretion, will bide by you also.

> **Knowledge**: And though this pilgrimage be never so strong,
> I will never part you fro:

> Everyman, I will be as sure by thee
> As ever I did by Judas Maccabee.

But Strength and Discretion are not telling the truth, as Good-Deeds declares and demonstrates:

> **Good-Deeds**: All earthly things is but vanity:
> Beauty, Strength, and Discretion, do man forsake,
> Foolish friends and kinsmen, that fair spake,
> All fleeth save Good-Deeds, and that am I.

The point in all of these, miracle, mystery, morality, is the revelation of the sacred in human interaction, which is what all drama ultimately hopes to do. Written down, the plays become a formula for the public sharing of such an understanding. The Church wanted to share what was orthodox, which is often the use of theater for the people who finance it, maintain it, store it, and gather an audience to see it.

The moment of revelation in all of these plays is what's significant, raised up, dressed up, pointed to. The money note, to use a showbiz term, when the singer hits a part of the song they can sing so well the audience sits up straight, is the moment that the holy nature of the world is revealed. In the mysteries, it's when God appears, sometimes onstage. In the miracle plays, it's when the miracle appears that we in the audience become witnesses to. In the moralities, it's more subtle. It takes place in our minds, requiring us to put it together.

But that's only the official side of the story. To more fully understand medieval drama, we have to look beyond the pious formulae of orthodoxy and orthodox plays to the robust comic tradition and bend our attention to nonliterary traditions that enrich the medieval state of mind.

Chapter Two

COMMEDIA DELL'ARTE AND MOLIÈRE

Carlo Goldoni (1707–1793)
Niccolò Machiavelli (1469–1527)
Molière (Jean-Baptiste Poquelin) (1622–1673)

Beginning in the 1300s, what we now call the Renaissance rolled out in Western Europe. What is a renaissance or *The* Renaissance? The word means rebirth (*re*, meaning again; *naissance* from the same Latin word for birth as Nativity, the birth of Christ). What was being reborn? Had something died? The people who lived during this time had no name for what was happening. The French critic Jules Michelet coined the term *renaissance* in 1858; the Swiss critic Jakob Burkhardt further defined the epoch in 1860, two centuries after the Renaissance was over, as a time of rebirth in society, politics, philosophy, and the arts. Burkhardt's observations still hold our imagination. What was reborn or rediscovered in Europe was the idea that a person had value as an individual, not only as part of a group; that the world and the many things in it had value and interest in their variety, not their sameness; and that people, too, had value and interest in their variety, not their sameness. Curiosity drove people's lives—curiosity and the hope of improvement from the old way of life which was driven by obedience to authority and the fear of punishment for disobedience.

By the middle of the 1400s powerful Italian cities, Florence and Venice among them, thrived on trade with the world outside of Italy, outside of Europe, and outside of the assumptions which organized Italian thinking. New ideas and new stories brought on, inevitably, comparison and evaluation of familiar traditional thinking.

A relatively small sign of great change appeared in the paintings of the Renaissance: instead of a rich cloth or a wall behind the depictions of the saints or the Virgin Mary, as was the practice during the Middle Ages, the painter provided a window or a colonnade with a view into the distance onto a landscape. We see mountains, trees, and other people, and we get a sense that there's more to see. The painters are showing off facility by painting what's out the window, and they are doing it because it satisfies the people for whom they are painting. Curiosity of what was outside the window prompted voyages of discovery around Africa, routes to India, and then through the tropical islands of the East Indies to China. With the European discovery of the Americas in 1492, a very large window opened. If the direction of the Middle Ages was up—presumably to God—and the orientation of its thinking vertical, the direction of the Renaissance was outward—out into the world—and the orientation of its thinking horizontal.

Interest in the individual paralleled curiosity about the outside world, which set off a process of learning from the distant past. In Italy the ruins of the Roman Empire, gone for almost a thousand years, lay above ground. In the Age of Faith, ancient Rome's history was a cautionary tale: the fall of the Empire was, in the view of the Church, a punishment for pagan sin. Though the Church conducted its business and its liturgy in Latin, the literary texts of pre-Christian Rome, especially plays, were dismissed as the product of that sin and an impetus for sin. As curiosity about Ancient Rome changed, so did the study of Roman literature. These impulses shaped a new theater, different from the plays of the Middle Ages whose purpose was to ultimately lead people back to the Church.

Early in the 1500s, literary dramas called the *commedia erudita* (learned comedy) were written in Italian in imitation of

Classical Greek and Roman drama. In 1518 or so, Machiavelli, the theoretician of Italian Renaissance society, wrote *The Mandrake*, an amoral story of a young wife with an old fool for a husband. There are records of its performance at the Carnival of Florence in 1526. The situation, the character types, and the form of the play are taken from Roman comedies.

Characters are motivated by self-interest, and some characters succeed in their cunning goals, unlike plays presented by the Church that passed on as cautionary lessons the consequences of sin and the need for God. It's not a coincidence the first performance took place during Carnival—the holiday season celebrating licentiousness preceding the holy days of Easter celebrating submission.

Italian Renaissance theater had already begun without erudition—at market fairs in cities and in the countryside where people looking for novelties along with necessities ran into new goods, new fashions, and new distractions. There are no records of when and who, but we do know that entertainers—jugglers and musicians and groups of performers—could be found in the middle of the market, or off to the side. There was sometimes a group of people on a platform—so they could be seen—wearing brightly colored costumes and masks, speaking lines in the local language, and sometimes in different local dialects or accents. The appeal is horizontal, reaching out into the crowd that gathers around to watch.

The masked performers needed to catch the eyes and ears of passersby—and the performances needed to be interesting enough to hold attention. The audience at fairs was very different than the audience assembled to see plays sponsored by the Church during the Middle Ages. To begin with, people weren't usually at the fair to see a play—and whatever audiences that stopped to look and listen were subject to distractions.

The words spoken by the performers were made up on the spot in front of the audience. Audiences knew this, and so the performance had an immediate, daring quality that included the danger of falling flat, as with jugglers and acrobats. This was called *improvvisare* which means in Italian what's unforeseen or therefore not prepared. The theater that resulted was called the *commedia dell'arte*. *Arte* means skill, in the sense of artful. The *commedia del eruditi* came from writers who studied and were inspired by what they could learn by reading. The commedia dell'arte depended on the skill of the performers, inspired by the immediate circumstances of performance. Improvisors quickly eclipsed the written drama; nowadays when we say commedia, we mean only the theater they devised.

Commedia actors did not start from scratch each time they performed, and they didn't improvise on their own; instead, they worked as a team from the same stories. There were certainly repeated popular elements: mistaken identity, servants trying to outwit their masters, greedy husbands and cheating wives, and often young lovers outwitting their parents, especially their fathers.

These stories appealed to the audience as gossip. The same instinct that gets us to talk about our neighbors and spy on them (or at least notice someone coming home in the morning dressed in the clothes they wore the night before) is the instinct that prompts us to tell the story to someone else. That makes for a theater very different from the theater paid for by the Church.

We have records by 1545 of such performing ensembles in Italy, and we know that in 1568 a theater company was founded in Milan called the Gelosi, usually translated as "The Jealous Ones," but more properly "The Zealous Ones." The word gelosi is related to the Greek and Latin for zeal: zelosus, from *zelus*, from the Ancient Greek ζῆλος. The Gelosi motto *Virtù, fama ed honor ne fèr gelosi* means "We are zealous for virtue, fame, and honor." The Zealous Ones toured France and Spain where they inspired local variations of commedia dell'arte.

Onstage in the commedia dell'arte there were recognizable types: the angry old father, the hopeful young girl, the swaggering soldier, the scheming servant. It seems ironic that in an age that celebrated individuals there would be types onstage. Consider, though, the need to catch attention and the need to appeal to strangers at a fair. To be successful, the improvising actors needed to put something onstage that most people could identify immediately, or at least something onstage understandable enough to be intriguing and simple enough to be understood at once. Actors playing stock characters wore masks or distinctive makeup and bold costumes, so the audience would recognize at first glance who was who and, knowing who was who, would expect certain things from them.

Traditionally, commedia masks were made of leather, sometimes of papier-mâché. For some roles actors powdered themselves, so their faces resembled masks. Costumes for the commedia were designed to identify what role an actor was playing with colors and shapes associated with specific roles. Real clothing was a basis for exaggerated styling. For example, patchwork rags sewn together by poor people who couldn't afford new cloth or new clothing inspired the diamond pattern we call harlequin. For the audience first seeing them worn by the character named Harlequin, those diamonds meant Harlequin was poor.

Along with Harlequin a dozen major commedia characters reappear in play after play, sometimes under different names. We speak of the characters from the commedia in the present tense because they live again whenever they're enacted. Learning the specifics of these stock roles is like learning the basic ingredients of a cuisine. The costumes and masks are part of the specifics of a role.

Arlecchino is Harlequin's original Italian name. He wears a black half-mask with tiny eyeholes and arched eyebrows with a wrinkled forehead. Topping off his patchwork costume, he sports a hat with a little feather or rabbit tail, so that something about him wags as he chases after servant girls. Sometimes he carries a bat—to hit people with! He's famously from Bergamo, a town in the northwest of Italy with two sections, a rich neighborhood on the higher part of a mountain and Arlecchino's poor neighborhood lower down on the mountain.

Pantalone is the lusty old man of the commedia, immediately recognizable by his red leggings, Turkish slippers, and black cape. His mask has a big, hooked nose with a scraggly mustache and a white pointed beard that wiggles when he speaks. He's a stingy merchant from Venice, the great port city of canals on the northeast coast of Italy.

Il Dottore, the doctor, is a windy Doctor of Philosophy. If B.S. means what it means, then Il Dottore's Ph.D. means piled higher and deeper. Il Dottore is from Bologna, a city with a famous university. The doctor dresses all in black in a sort of smock like a graduation gown. His mask, sometimes flesh-colored, sometimes black, covers his forehead and nose.

Il Capitano is an ancient archetype, the bragging cowardly soldier. In the Italian commedia of the Renaissance, when Spain ruled over Naples and Sicily, Il Capitano was Spanish with a big mustache to twirl. To go along with his mustache, he has a big nose, a loud voice, a big plumed hat, a big sword, and a uniform in bright colors.

Pulcinella is a humpback servant with a nose to match his hump and big mouth. He often wears an all-white costume with a tapered cylindrical hat. Like Arlecchino, Pulcinella is from the poor part of Bergamo and lives in Naples. He's a rough man who rebels against authority; he enjoys life in his own coarse way. In England, where his name was shortened to the puppet character Punch, he outwits the devil.

Brighella is an intriguer—a gossip, a spy—known for his olive-colored mask, thick lips, licentious eyes, scruffy beard, and mustache. He's also from Bergamo, like Harlequin and Pulcinella. He prowls like a cat. He plays the guitar and dances well. He has a little dagger, which he uses. He can be a soldier in a green uniform with full trousers. Sometimes he wears a valet's uniform with snazzy yellow shoes.

Zanni, yes, as in zany, is a servant looking out for his own interests. He wears a mask with a nose like a mosquito beak. Zanni is a diminutive for Giovanni, or John. Poor John is hungry, desperate, and clever. He wears a loose blouse and full trousers so he may more easily perform acrobatics.

The Innamorati are lovers played without masks, the better to show off their beautiful faces to the audience and to each other. The innamorati are dressed, traditionally, in the latest fashion rather than a recognizable costume. At the time the innamorati first appeared, they didn't necessarily have anything distinct about them except that they were in love—and that's always ridiculous. They usually spoke elegant Italian—as if they were from Florence, the center of the Italian Renaissance—or they had an accent from Florence's Tuscany region. Although the performers of the young lovers wore no masks, their makeup resembled a mask—and enabled performers to play these young characters into old age.

Pedrolino or Pierrot is a simpleminded, honest, young servant. He is the youngest son, and he is shy. He wears baggy hand-me-down clothes. He wears a white jacket with a neck ruff and large buttons down the front, loose trousers, and sometimes a skull cap. Sometimes his sleeves are longer than his arms. An actor playing Pierrot plays without a mask, his face whitened with powder. Pierrot is forever in love with Columbina.

However, Columbina is Harlequin's girlfriend, which leaves Pierrot perpetually sad. Her name means little dove. When she argues with Harlequin, and she does, she gives as good as she gets, but still, she's sensitive and her feelings can easily be hurt. She wears the same kind of patchwork as Harlequin. She sometimes wears a little mask that covers her eyes; sometimes her face is powdered.

The other women's roles of the commedia include Isabella, the daughter of the house, decked out in fashionable clothes. She is named for a daughter of the Gelosi who died young. La Servetta, her chatterbox servant is identified to the audience by the apron she wears.

Commedia characters collided in familiar plots, especially the popular story of innamorati kept apart by their parents or older guardians until, to the audience's delight, the lovers pass beyond the obstacles of walls or suspicious fathers. Notice the action is horizontal, the lovers don't rise up, they unite. Notice, too, the tragic version, Shakespeare's *Romeo and Juliet* from the 1590s, in which the innamorati unite in death.

Often commedia plots dramatized life from the servant's point of view, sharing the difficulty fulfilling the wishes of a capricious master or mistress. The exposure of hypocrisy often drives a commedia plot. Those who pose become jokes when, for instance, the braggart Capitano is revealed to be a liar and a coward or the seemingly wise Dottore turns fool.

Actors played their roles for years, specializing in boasts for braggarts or tears for a young lover. Actors also prepared *lazzi*, physical routines, songs, and dances. The lazzi were things like head slaps or tricks with balls or practiced face reactions. The actor who specialized in braggarts knew how to wave his sword and drop it; the actress who could cry on cue knew how to wring out a handkerchief and blow her nose.

Most of what we know about commedia comes from illustrations and prints of the actors. These are like the shadows of sculpture. We infer what the movement or pauses might have been, and we learn for ourselves what commedia actors do. To fulfill the improvised scenarios of the commedia, we continue to improvise using the stories and the archetypes.

Within less than a hundred years after the commedia troupes appear in history, their stock characters and scenarios inspired a new kind of theater: texts written down which have become, in their own way, classics. In France, the characters and situations of the commedia were taken up in scripted comedies written by Molière, the stage name of Jean-Baptiste Poquelin, baptized January 15, 1622. His plays are considered among the greatest ever written. They are in French what

Shakespeare's comedies are in English: enduring standards of excellence.

Italian performing artists arrived in France in 1533, well before the tours of the Gelosi, when Catherine de' Medici from Florence, Italy married Henri II the King of France. Catherine was fourteen, and she brought several things with her from Italy to keep herself amused, including musicians and dancers. The French court provided a different audience than an Italian Renaissance fair. Courts were dominated by a king, or a duke, who now replaced the Church or passersby as patron. The spatial organization of performance shifted, still horizontal, but focused to the patron. Performances took place in a frame with the audience on one side, not surrounding the performance as in a fair. The most important person sat center in the audience. This change is also overt in the orientation of social dance, as rural circle dances in which everybody faces in were replaced by the minuet, which performs facing front, so a dancer can be seen by the patron of the dance for whom the minuet is performed. Who you are is now understood by who you hang out with, how close you are to them, and most important, who sees you with them.

Molière understood this firsthand. His father made furniture for the court; Molière had his first real success when he performed for the King. When the King's cross-dressing brother became his patron, Molière's social status changed and so did the fortunes of Molière's company of actors. Molière was careful always, when he was critical, not to criticize the King.

Molière wrote plays—not improvisations—but his setup was the same as a commedia troupe. He and the other actors played typed roles: the rascal servants, thwarted young lovers, fathers trying to stop them, and wise-cracking maids (often played by Molière's wife) who tried to help them.

At first, Molière's plays took the recognizable character types of the commedia—the jealous older husband, a younger wife— and translated them to then contemporary France. The formulae of direct address, dialogue, rhetorical rants, and prepared physical comedy were taken directly from the commedia. Molière wrote in prose and in rhyming verse. His plays included dance, songs, and occasions for lazzi.

Molière and his company spent fifteen years touring the French provinces. As the playwright's expertise at devising plays developed, the ensemble developed their performance skills, inspiring the playwright who wrote for them. When at last the troupe had a base in Paris, they shared a theater with the ensemble led by Tiborio Fiorilli, the creator of the commedia's Scaramouche, a sort of sly servant. Scaramouche is a pugnacious little fighter, a skirmisher, like a terrier. It's believed that contact with Fiorilli refined Molière's acting. Certainly, there's homage to Scaramouche in Molière's creations Sganarelle and Scapin. Fiorilli's work is known, however, only through oral tradition. We have no scripts, so we don't really know what he said, though we have illustrations of Fiorilli as Scaramouche dressed in all black with a guitar and a beret.

Molière worked with his own company writing stock characters with specific actors in mind to play them. The plot complications based on mistaken identity, thwarted lovers who eventually reunite, and angry married couples who eventually reconcile were also recognizable to the audience from the commedia.

Some of the stories in Molière's plays derived from medieval woodcuts, court gossip, Roman comedies, or from his own life. Molière's plays mix tone: a single play can move from farce to comedy to serious drama. Their enduring value onstage and off relies on just this multiplicity of meanings, yet even so, the plays written by Molière can be seen to have a pattern: a composition of characters, like a palette of colors by which we recognize an artist, like Cézanne's green and umber, or Tiepolo's pink. We do not know if Molière intended such a pattern, or considered his technique philosophically, or whether he was pragmatically writing for the members of his company who played certain parts and for whom he obviously wrote roles to display specific talents. The central character, always a man (for Molière wrote the leading roles for himself), is someone with an obsession: an *idée fixe* (ee-day FEEKS). The titles often establish the obsession that fires the drama: the Miser and the Would-be Gentleman are the centers of the plays named after them, *The Miser* and *The Would-be Gentleman*. The wife of the man with the idée fixe is often the victim of his caprice, as in *Tartuffe*; sometimes she opportunistically takes advantage of it and him. Molière sometimes included a role called the *raisonneur*, someone who provided the voice of reason, invariably ignored by man with the idée fixe.

There are, with few variations, young lovers, male and female, and one of them is usually the central character's daughter. The lovers, as in the Italian commedia, misunderstand each other and are brought together, often forcibly, by some third character, usually the smart-talking maid.

Servants who talk back and manipulate those they serve are a type that goes back to the Greek and Roman comedies. Molière had read these plays and, as he had with his commedia models, translated the rascal servants into recognizably, then contemporary, French characters. Another theatrical convention from ancient Greek drama called the *deus ex machina*, when a god would descend from Heaven and solve all the problems of the plot, was, perhaps ironically, given to the King's messengers to enact in plays written by Molière.

The behavior of individual characters in a play by Molière is best understood within the composition of society, just as the significance of any individual dancer in a court dance of the period is understood within the larger pattern of the group.

As Molière's writing matured, life as performance and identity as a pose are set up onstage, reflecting the reality of life at court. The distinction between country life and court life is presented as one of manners and style. There is the implication that all people, high and low—stripped of pretense—value the same things. This is embodied in the physical performance in Molière's day and in our own when the audience, high and low, laughs at the same things.

Creating roles such as the hypocritically religious Tartuffe in *Tartuffe, or The Impostor* and the society cynic Alceste in *The Misanthrope*, Molière built complex and contradictory psychologies, well beyond the types of the commedia or the obsessions of the early farces. The social role of these complex characters is outside the main society. As outsiders they may comment, manipulate, and operate beyond the rules that bring order to other people's lives.

The role of Célimène, Alceste's beloved in *The Misanthrope*, is Molière's most enigmatic and subtle—a woman tempted to leave society but does not. Molière's Sganarelle, also an outsider, has a similar enigmatic subtlety. The name *Sganarelle* is from an Italian word meaning *open your eyes*. He's a sly valet, a gentleman's servant. The type is descended from the commedia's scoundrel Brighella. Sganarelle appears in a number of Molière's plays.

In England the commedia characters transformed into puppets such as the Punch (short for Punchinella) of Punch and Judy. The violence of the commedia, which was matched by live performance styles, could really be unleashed by puppets smacking each other. In Spain there were scripted commedia plays and in Italy, too. The eighteenth-century Italian playwright Goldoni, who wrote plays using commedia characters, doubled the trouble of a commedia plot in his 1746 comedy *The Servant of Two Masters*, which features the hard-pressed Truffaldino, a variation on Arlecchino. In Goldoni's earliest versions of *The Servant of Two Masters*, a good deal of the text was improvised. By 1753 *The Servant of Two Masters* was totally scripted. Goldoni, when writer's block overtook him, admitted to asking himself, "What would Molière do?"

On February 17, 1673, Molière was onstage playing a hypochondriac, a man who believes he's sick, but isn't. Molière himself was so sick he couldn't finish the performance of *The Hypochondriac* (in French, *Le malade imaginaire*). He was taken home and died a few days later. He was fifty-one. Actors were considered disreputable, and Molière's play *Tartuffe* about religious fraud had offended the French Catholic Church, so Molière was buried at midnight in secret.

Molière never prepared his manuscripts for publication, never proofed corrections. The texts were first printed in 1682, more than ten years after he died. The first editions of Molière's plays included pictures of central events, which pass on information not available in the text. The image from the play *Tartuffe or The Impostor* of the husband hiding under the table spying on his wife as she's seduced by his pious-seeming friend is as familiar an image to French theatergoers as Hamlet and his skull is to the English. The traditions of the original performances have also been maintained, for better or worse, by the company Molière founded, still in existence and now called La Comédie-Française.

Tiborio Fiorilli outlived Molière. Still performing at eighty-one, Fiorilli was noted even in advanced age to be able to kick another actor in the face—a memorable lazzi. If Fiorilli said anything on the occasion of Molière's death those words, like any other words Fiorilli said or wrote, have gone unrecorded.

It is possible the commedia dell'arte derives from ancient Greek and Roman literature, and some of the glories of the commedia can be learned by reading the plays written by Molière. The physical forms of the commedia can be deduced from paintings, porcelains, woodcuts, and posters. The essence of the commedia, though—the relationship to the audience, the need for ensemble work, the combination of prepared and improvised work onstage that mixes dance, songs, dialog, and direct address—these cannot really ever be passed down. We must rediscover them for ourselves, so they live again, in the renaissances of our rehearsals and performances.

Chapter Three

SHAKESPEARE— TO BEGIN

David Garrick (1717–1779)
William Shakespeare (1564–1616)

The thirty-seven plays that William Shakespeare wrote have had six centuries to build relationships between actors, directors, critics, and readers. Let's begin with the relationship of actor to audience, which is renewed each time the plays are performed. Acknowledging that Shakespeare's original audience helped shape what his plays needed to do (and could do) helps to understand what the plays might do in performance with any audience now and in the future.

When Shakespeare came to London sometime in the 1580s, the people who first saw his plays did so in a city that considered itself, with reason, as the center of the world. Shakespeare was in his twenties. Elizabeth, the Queen of England, was in the middle of her forty-four-year reign. The Elizabethan era, named after the Queen, even during its own time was understood to be among the most glorious in any history.

England grew wealthy throughout the reign of Elizabeth thanks to trade with the outside world. Port cities grew in importance, and enterprising people came from the English countryside to live in the cities, especially London, in search of opportunity. A rich merchant class grew, made safe by a powerful central government, and protected by a powerful navy.

In the city of London, the aristocracy, merchants, and townspeople were crowded together, eager for diversion. Theatergoing was at its height of popularity. Not until fans flocked to cinemas in the 1930s did Londoners go to theaters so often as they did in Elizabethan England. The London theaters of Shakespeare's time welcomed anyone who could buy a ticket, with places set aside to accommodate poor people and places set aside for middle-class tradesmen, rich merchants, and the aristocracy and, it seems, a secluded place could be set aside in the audience for visiting royalty. Though plays in English were unpublished at the time, English-language plays in performance led the country's search for self-identity. Just as English ships explored the oceans and the "new" continents, the performances of plays in English at this time explored what it meant to be a human being.

The audience educated according to the standards of the day could be counted on to know Classical mythology, current poetry, and court politics. There was also a portion of Shakespeare's audience who were illiterate but educated according to the standards of any city: quick to find meaning—and interest—in their neighbor's doings.

To keep the attention of his diverse audience, Shakespeare alternated telling the story of a play and acting out the story of the play in scenes. Scenes were sometimes interrupted by a character who stopped the action to tell the audience what was about to happen—and stopped the action after it resumed to tell the audience what *was* happening. Often, when the action concluded, someone told the audience what *had* happened. Those who needed a guide got one. The relationship of the guide to the audience was dynamic. The audience could turn against a narrator; the narrator could turn against those watching.

The tradition of seeing plays performed in English dated back a few centuries, to the medieval plays based on Bible stories or saint's tales, plays in which storytelling mixed with enactment. The devil who turns and curses the audience was a tradition— and Shakespeare's hunchbacked Richard III carried that tradition forward to Shakespeare's audience. The hesitant Everyman, who explains the difficulties of his path in life to judgmental listeners, was also a stage tradition—and the actor playing Shakespeare's Richard II, not to mention the actor playing Hamlet, followed in that tradition. Even the illiterate part of Shakespeare's audience could be counted on to take their role in such relationships when listening to performers onstage. Changes in the point of view towards the action were made part of the drama. Characters lie to each other during enactment and confide the truth to the audience during direct address.

At first, Shakespeare's plays were performed in buildings open to the sky, which meant performances were held during the day with natural lighting, which meant the actors could see their audience. In the theater called the Globe, the configuration of the seats was rounded so the audience could see itself. The reactions of the audience were an unavoidable part of the show. Rather than pretend to ignore the reactions in the audience (as would happen in the coming centuries), Shakespeare's plays included such reactions as part of the dramatic events.

Actors who addressed the audience directly—an audience they could see—reacted to the audience as if the public was another character in the play. Shakespeare took advantage of this theatrically, especially in the genre he perfected, the Histories.

Shakespeare's Histories, of course, dramatize British history. There are ten of these plays titled after kings of England. The audience, all of it, could be counted on to know their history—and to know the reputations of each king. It might not be what is historically true, but it is what the audience knew. Shakespeare played with what they knew, not so much changing opinions, as amplifying those opinions by theatricalizing how such reputations were acquired through gossip, propaganda, trustworthy eyewitnesses, and slanderers.

Often in the history plays, Shakespeare casts the audience as the fickle British public, whose changing loyalties are the subject of the text as written and the essence of the play in performance. Fifteen years after his first history plays, Shakespeare had Octavian in *Antony and Cleopatra* call the Roman crowd (and by inference the watching—British—audience):

> This common body,
> Like to a vagabond flag upon the stream,
> Goes to and back, lackeying the varying tide.
> To rot itself with motion.
> (*Act I, scene 4*)

The reactions of that common body are the pulse of a performance for the text of *Henry VI part 2*, probably the first of the Shakespeare's Histories to be performed, probably in 1591. The action of *Henry VI part 2* is set around 1450 and as the title makes clear, during the reign of Henry VI (1421–1471). Discussions of when the play was written and the study of the sources for its story have distracted from recognizing that, in performance, the dramatic action of the play depends on the changes in the audience's understanding and reactions to what happens on the stage.

In scene after scene of *Henry VI, part 2*, beginning with the opening scene, the audience is led to an initial enthusiasm for what they will come to despise as the scene progresses. Throughout the play, characters who repel the audience gain sympathy (the Duchess of Gloucester, for example, whose ambitions for her husband turns monstrous and then pathetic). Characters at whom the audience at first laughs with in solidarity grow gross and terrifying to those watching. The rebel Jack Cade, for example, is funny enough when he claims that wine will run through the streets of London and not so funny after he demonstrates how the two heads he's ordered cut off can be made to kiss each other.

The moral ambiguity of the audience's reactions parallels the moral ambiguity of the onstage characters and historical events. Though Shakespeare's history plays descend in form from medieval theater, the history plays presume a doubtful somewhat cynical and rowdy audience rather than an audience united by faith in God and obedience to the Church. The educated part of Shakespeare's audience knew what a tragedy or comedy was meant to be, according to the examples set by university performances in Latin or Greek of ancient classical plays, or original plays written in the language of the classics in the sixteenth century, following ancient ideas of form and decorum. The Histories thwarted educated expectations, too.

The challenge for Shakespeare, always, was to unite the disparate audience into a reactive partner to what's onstage. This began with the pulse of what was spoken. The lines written in iambic pentameter, ten beats to the line, established a rhythm that was heard and, more importantly, felt by whoever listens. Ultimately listeners collectively breathe together and collectively hold their breath.

Picture the place of the performance: on the ground in front of the raised wooden stage poorer people, called the groundlings, stand. The higher classes sit in raised galleries ringed around the stage for better sightlines, clearer acoustics and, we're told, to avoid the smell of the groundlings. On the stage platform, there was a minimum of props and scenery—though there were some effects that went back to the medieval theater, notably trap doors. An upper gallery at the back of the stage could be used as a balcony. No matter where someone sat to watch the play, they saw the stage action framed by the audience's reactions. Live music—trumpets, drums, and squealing oboes—sounded alarms, announced entrances, and sometimes accompanied the appearance of ghosts. Costuming was minimal, enough to indicate who was who, based on the color and type of fabric.

What created the illusion of the play—opening the theater to the "otherworld" that all theater strives to attain—was the power of the spoken word; the power of enchantment over an audience that an actor can create with words: that the sun is rising, that an army is running away, that a mind is cracking, or a heart breaking.

Henry VI part 2 follows its king to the inevitability of civil war in England. *Henry VI part 3*, written soon after the first two parts, follows the king to the Battle of Tewkesbury, fought on May 4, 1471, when the forces of the House of York overcame Henry VI's House of Lancaster. In the second act of *Henry VI, part 3*, the King sees the battle at a distance. The actor is sitting on a stool, standing in for a hill, watching. He has a long speech. The length is necessary for the speech to function dramatically.

The speaking of these words casts a spell: a numbing rhythm of the passing days, months, and years shared by the speaker and the listeners. The audience might have compassion, might react in disgust, but in any case, they will be reacting to something they experience collectively.

As Henry waits, the audience knows how the battle will end, as in Greek tragedy in which the fate of the characters acts as a design against which the behavior of the characters (and their self-awareness) plays out. Henry lost the battle, that's known. How he faced this loss is what's of interest.

[*Alarum. Enter King Henry alone.*]
Hen.
This battell fares like to the mornings Warre,
When dying clouds contend, with growing light,
What time the Shepheard blowing of his nailes,
Can neither call it perfect day, nor night.
Now swayes it this way, like a Mighty Sea,
Forc'd by the Tide, to combat with the Winde:
Now swayes it that way, like the selfe-same Sea,
Forc'd to retyre by furie of the Winde.
Sometime, the Flood preuailes; and than the Winde:
Now, one the better: then, another best;
Both tugging to be Victors, brest to brest:
Yet neither Conqueror, nor Conquered.
So is the equall poise of this fell Warre.
Heere on this Mole-hill will I sit me downe,

To whom God will, there be the Victorie:
For *Margaret* my Queene, and *Clifford* too
Haue chid me from the Battell: Swearing both,
They prosper best of all when I am thence.
Would I were dead, if Gods good will were so;
For what is in this world, but Greefe and Woe.
Oh God! me thinkes it were a happy life,
To be no better then a homely Swaine,
To sit vpon a hill, as I do now,
To carue out Dialls queintly, point by point,
Thereby to see the Minutes how they runne:
How many makes the Houre full compleate,
How many Houres brings about the Day,
How many Dayes will finish vp the Yeare,
How many Yeares, a Mortall man may liue.
When this is knowne, then to diuide the Times:
So many Houres, must I tend my Flocke;
So many Houres, must I take my Rest:
So many Houres, must I Contemplate:
So many Houres, must I Sport my selfe:
So many Dayes, my Ewes haue bene with yong:
So many weekes, ere the poore Fooles will Eane:
So many yeares, ere I shall sheere the Fleece:
So Minutes, Houres, Dayes, Monthes, and Yeares,
Past ouer to the end they were created,
Would bring white haires, vnto a Quiet graue.
Ah! what a life were this? How sweet? how louely?

The Histories, unlike tragedies, are continued in the minds of the audience, which undercuts the finality of a conclusion. At the end of seven of Shakespeare's ten Histories, a victor proclaims the end of war and the beginning of peace. The audience knows the peace will not last: the resolution of war into peace is temporary. The theatricality of a hollow triumph was incomprehensible to later eras who tried to make the endings of Shakespeare's Histories emotionally convincing conclusions by tricking them out with musical numbers, dances, and processions. There is even a theory to support these shenanigans, that the Histories abandon words to achieve a glory in stagecraft. Nope. The onstage character's well-meant desire for peace and the smug belief in success is meant to be undercut by the life experience in the audience. It's a technique that Shakespeare would use for *Hamlet*, *Macbeth*, and the plays he set in ancient Rome. When Fortinbras announces peace has come to Denmark after the death of Hamlet, the audience knows it has not. When Macduff announces peace has come to Scotland after the death of Macbeth, the audience knows it has not. When Octavian proclaims Rome is at peace after the deaths of Antony and Cleopatra, the known history of the Roman Empire that Octavian founded makes his speech ironic and laughable. War has gone on, continues to go on, just as political bickering goes on. Again and again, the response of the audience completes the theatrical experience of the play, which is meant to be unsettling, especially to an audience living in a time of precarious—probably temporary—peace and prosperity.

By putting the action of the plays two hundred years earlier than the time he was writing for, Shakespeare kept out of trouble with the Queen, yet even so, some of these dramatic warring families were her direct ancestors. For safety's sake, the Histories flattered Elizabeth: her grandfather Henry VII is presented by Shakespeare as the culmination of English history, and he is diplomatically kept offstage. After Elizabeth died, Shakespeare brought the family saga up to her father, Henry VIII, the title character of a play in which the playwright had the daring to include Elizabeth's notorious mother, Anne Boleyn. The play named after Henry VIII even more daringly depicted Elizabeth's father's first wife, the very Catholic (and Spanish) Catherine of Aragon as a sympathetic figure, whose divorce prompted the break with the Church's authority over England.

In 1603 Elizabeth I died. As she had planned, after her death her nephew, the Scottish King James VI ruled as the English

King James I. James became the patron of Shakespeare's company, and the name of the troupe changed from the Chamberlain's Men to the King's Men. By the winter of 1609, the King's Men were performing at Blackfriars, a theater with a roof. They continued to perform at the Globe in the summer. Blackfriars tickets were pricey, which meant the audience was more elite, less inclusive. Blackfriars offered more technical possibilities than the Globe did, including the use of artificial lighting. The audience's growing appetite for spectacle was egged on by the popularity of masques, shows with dance, music, and recitation of verse rather than plotted plays.

Twenty-five years after Shakespeare died his works were no longer performed in England nor were any other plays. By 1642 religious bigots overthrew King Charles I, the son of James I, and seized control over the country. In the same year, an act of Parliament closed the theaters as places of perversion and moral evil. The chain of actors passing on their craft to future generations was broken. The traditions of the audience's role during a performance were also disrupted. In 1660 when the English monarchy was restored, London theaters reopened, and Shakespeare's plays returned to the stage. The beauty of Shakespeare's poetry was undeniable, the humanity of his characters recognizable and moving, but fashions had changed, as did England's estimation of itself.

The pleasure Shakespeare and his diverse audience shared in the disorientation of moving in a play from coarse humor to elegant verse met with incomprehension among educated English aristocrats eager to prove themselves as sophisticated as the elite in France, where tragedies were being written in imitation of classical Greek and Roman models. An inconclusive conclusion demonstrated a lack of craft.

In keeping with "good taste," Shakespeare's plays were mutilated by English editors and theater artists to conform to classical decorum by removing coarse language, "immoral" situations, and mixed genres. These mutilations held the stage for centuries, in some cases, up until the twentieth century.

Shakespeare's first editor, Nicholas Rowe, who took up where the Folio left off, wrote in his introduction of 1709:

> If one undertook to examine the greatest part of these by those Rules which are establish'd by Aristotle, and taken from the Model of the Grecian Stage, it would be no very hard Task to find a great many Faults: But as Shakespear liv'd under a kind of mere Light of Nature, and had never been made acquainted with the Regularity of those written Precepts, so it would be hard to judge him by a Law he knew nothing of. We are to consider him as a Man that liv'd in a State of almost universal License and Ignorance: There was no establish'd Judge, but every one took the liberty to Write according to the Dictates of his own Fancy.

A connection to the rules of the classical Ancient Greece and Rome was not simply aesthetic. As the French and English competed for world dominance, each wanted to demonstrate itself as the legitimate heir of the Roman Empire. England claimed to be in an Augustan Age, the name taken from Augustus the founding emperor of Imperial Rome.

Beginning in the early 1740s, the English actor and manager David Garrick urged anyone who would listen that Shakespeare was exceptional among English playwrights, an example of British genius, who given a little scrubbing and judicious emendation, rivaled any genius out of Greece or Rome or France. At around the same time, the education of the British Empire, and the necessity that children growing up in Australia, North America, India, and Africa should inherit a shared British culture, meant passages glorifying England from Shakespeare's Histories were included in schoolbooks, memorized, and honored. Patriotic passages plucked for recitation in no way passed on the ambivalent irony of the plays in performance.

The cultural prestige of Shakespeare as a sign of empire was such that Germany and Russia boasted of their own great traditions of performing Shakespeare's plays. At the beginning of the

First World War, Germans spoke of "Unser Shakespeare"—"Our Shakespeare," claiming, with no irony, that Shakespeare "belonged" more to Germany than England—and Russians claimed the same, and do so still.

The resonance of Shakespeare's words in cultures, languages, and times other than his own can be tracked to the circumstances of the play's first performances when they were spoken with the intention of affecting a diverse audience living as best it could in a volatile world. For better or worse, Shakespeare's work has been evaluated by differing sets of rules—from Ancient Greece to today's identity politics—but the plays defy being ruled. They can and have been praised and derided as signs of empire, the symptoms of rising modern economics, observations of human nature, cultural artifacts, national symbols, glorious poetry, and jokes gone stale over time, or jokes forever funny. Film adaptations and a robust international stage presence continue in this century, Shakespeare's sixth.

The speech from *Henry VI, part 3* in which Henry watches his army lose is no demonstration of British power, nor a proud moment in English history. The figures of speech Shakespeare gives to Henry are simple: watching the battle is like watching the sea or the weather—the observer has no control over the outcome. The King's wish to renounce power and go shepherding can be related to Ancient Greek pastoral traditions. The renunciation of political power in favor of living in the country is an ancient Chinese dream, too, the subject of a lot of Chinese poetry around 800 AD.

Without any cultural apparatus though, the repetition of Henry's words when spoken out loud creates what it describes, the lapping of time, the succession of days into numbing repetition. Notice the punctuation:

Ah! what a life were this? How sweet? how louely?

A question, not a resolution, inviting the listening or reading audience's response—is this so? Is it not so? —for over five hundred years. That's where power of the plays begin, and why the plays remain powerful, that invitation to respond.

Chapter Four

EURIPIDES— FOREVER MODERN

Aeschylus (ca. 525–ca. 456 BC)
Aristophanes (ca. 460–ca. 380 BC)
Euripides (ca. 480–ca. 406 BC)
Sophocles (ca. 497–ca. 406 BC)

T he culture we call ancient Greece lasted a relatively short time, about two hundred years, beginning about 2,500 years ago, so long ago the years are dated backwards from what is commonly agreed on as the birth of Jesus. The years before Christ are labeled BC, now sometimes BCE, which stands for "before the common era," so Euripides was born in 480 BC, yet he died at the age of seventy-four in 406 BC, a year that's less in number.

That puts Euripides in the middle of the two hundred years, roughly 530 BC to 330 BC, that we call Classical Greece. Because we can read the written language of ancient Greece, the history and literature of that time and place is known to us, including its plays—but remember, always, that what is recorded and passed down is due to power and accident. Yet even the efforts of the strongest political power to save its glories, traditions, and accumulated wisdom can be undone by fires, floods, and wars. Dissident voices—in particular the dissenting voices of slaves or women—were not written down by slaves or women in ancient Greece.

A tradition of what we would now call performances was deliberately kept out of history, neither written down nor talked about openly. The people who took part in such performances swore oaths not to tell what they did, how they did it, or what was meant by doing it. To the participants, these were religious ceremonies, called mysteries, very different from the mysteries of medieval theater. For two thousand years the Greek mysteries were secret religious rites performed to honor the gods, in particular the goddess of fertility. Honoring the goddess was, in its way, a form of dissent.

In theory and in public, the Greeks worshiped twelve gods who were said to live on the heights of Mount Olympus, led by a father-god, Zeus, who mirrored the lives of Greek men by balancing a jealous wife, Hera, with many affairs and outside of his marriage children. In Greek myths, Zeus commanded the universe with two of his brothers: Poseidon, who ruled the sea, and Hades, who ruled the world of the dead. The extended family of Olympians included Aphrodite, the goddess of love; Apollo, the god of light and truth; and Ares the god of war. We understand by this what holiness the Greeks placed on love, on war, and on truth. This male-dominated religion is said to have arrived in Greece from the north, replacing, in public, the ancient worship of a mother-goddess of fertility, Demeter, whose celebrations continued in secret.

The most important of the goddess celebrations were the Eleusinian mysteries, named for Eleusis, a town north and west of Athens where worshipers gathered after an eleven-mile procession out from the city to the secret shrine. Indirectly (because playwrights made fun of the celebrations) we can tell a ritual took place that involved all the participants who were brought in some way into the presence of the goddess. We know the name given to a part of the ritual, *dromena,* which involved saying words. What words were spoken we don't know, but we can deduce a story was told, whose effect was to take those who listened to the words into a visceral experience of another world, the ambition of all spoken theater.

Greek *drama* (different from *dromena*) is rooted in another religious tradition, the setting aside of a space, as we would for an altar, for public performance. In Greek history, drama grew out of the worship of Dionysus, who was the god of wine (and hence inebriation) and also the god of theater. Dionysus, like the mother goddess, Demeter, is separate from the other Olympians: he is a god come late to Greece according to legends from the East.

In Athens, the rituals in honor of Dionysus were held in a four-day festival called the Dionysia, also known as the Bacchanalia, because Bacchus was another name for the same god. The Dionysia was celebrated every year around the end of March and beginning of April—the end of winter—and the ceremonies included choruses of priests singing and dancing in praise of Dionysus. Greek plays evolved out of these songs and dances. The origins underlie the finished form: in classical Greek plays, spoken words were written in rhythmic verse, not prose; the parts enacted by performers alternated with dances and songs performed by choruses.

According to a Greek legend, which is perhaps true, theater as we understand it began in Athens when an actor named Thespis stepped out of the chorus and spoke as a soloist. Think of it as the transformation from The Supremes to Diana Ross and the Supremes. Thespis is also credited with inventing costumes for actors, presumably to further set himself apart from the chorus who were dressed in the robes worn by the priests.

All of those onstage, Thespis and the chorus, wore full masks covering their faces. Why? To begin with, for practical reasons. The performances took place in large outdoor amphitheaters where facial expression would have been lost to view. As many as 14,000 people could sit in rings carved into the side of a hill to watch what was happening onstage. We also think the masks included the equivalent of megaphones inside the mouths to amplify the sound of the voice. Maybe. The curve of the theaters made for marvelous acoustics, said to be capable of carrying intimate speech to every seat in the house. The masks were made of linen and cork, and none have survived, though we know what they looked like from stone copies.

Aeschylus, who is the first of the great Greek writers, was also responsible, according to history, for the invention of the cothurni (the plural for cothurnus). These were platform boots, laced on, with thick cork soles that lifted up the major performers so that they could be better seen. Solo actors towered above the chorus, who were not on such high platform shoes, which made it easier for the chorus to dance. The proportions of a mask, larger than a face, on top of elongated torsos padded under robes, embodied the larger-than-life performers' relationship with the audience. The soloists and the chorus members did not mirror those who watched and listened; the performers were representatives in a democracy to which those who watched and listened belonged.

In the same open kinds of space where the plays were performed in Athens, the same audience—men, free men—not women, not slaves—gathered to debate and discuss what would happen in the city and what the city would do. Someone stood up and spoke to the assembled group in order to persuade them what was good, what was wrong, what was right, and what actions should be taken as a result of these considerations. When votes were taken and counted, the majority ruled. This was, in Western history, the first democracy, government by the people—demos, means people. The Greek audience, then, was accustomed to listen and weigh what was being told to them. This is different from religious participation which relies on faith and obedience, not evaluation—and the difference between dromena and drama is, at heart, that difference between witnessing a sacrament and attending a play.

There is a theory that defines theater as a way a society works out its ideas in public, its images of identity, and shared values: what it means to be a man, a woman, a ruler, to be ruled, what current events have to do with the past, what it means to live in the present. Popular films do this in our culture. The Greek theater is a good example of the theory in action—again with the understanding that only a portion of the population, free adult men, were taking part either as performer or audience. Women were not included; neither were slaves, who were estimated to have been a third of the population of Athens. Even so, this admittedly elitist art form is demonstrably universal. The Greek plays' consideration of what it means to be human is so close to the bone it inspires and moves us 2,500 years later. The greatest of the Greek tragedies ask challenging questions that all audiences at all times might ask. In or out of a theater these questions will be asked as long as there are people. What does it mean to suffer? What does it mean to cause suffering? What does it mean to die? To live well?

Thirty-six full tragedies survive from classical Greece, thirty-six out of over a thousand classical Greek tragedies. The Greek tragedies we have intact are, by chance, and happily, from the three greatest Greek tragic writers: Aeschylus, Sophocles, and Euripides. Seven of the comedies by the great comic playwright Aristophanes also survive intact.

The great Greek playwrights were also directors and choreographers, known for their innovations in staging. Aeschylus added a second actor to the solo role, supposedly invented by Thespis, so the dialogue is spoken in his plays between characters, not just between chorus and a single actor. Sophocles added a third actor and enlarged the chorus from twelve to fifteen. From then on, that was all that was thought necessary in Greece to tell any story onstage: a chorus of fifteen and three actors who could play all the roles required by alternating masks. Sophocles added painted scenery. We do not know what was painted, but we know images appeared on three-sided columns called periaktoi, that could revolve in order to change the stage picture.

Euripides, who was the last of the three great Greek writers of tragedies, died in the same year as Sophocles. Euripides did not change the number of actors or the size of the chorus but, working with these givens, he changed tragedy in its essence, challenging the status quo for all time, asking questions without giving answers. His writing, because it is forever restless, is forever modern.

Of the thirty-six Greek tragedies that survive, eighteen—half—were written by Euripides. Though not considered the best writer by Aristotle, who wrote the defining critique of Greek theater called the *Poetics* in 335 BC, Euripides was considered the most tragic.

Best? Most tragic? Why did Aristotle think to rank them?

Contest is at the heart of Greek culture. The people who gave us the Olympics awarded prizes for best play; the three great playwrights, whose lives and careers overlapped, competed against each other for prizes, which were handed out by juries. Plays entered into contests at the Dionysia (and other festivals) were written in groups of four: typically three tragedies and a farce. Playwrights were paired with patrons, private citizens who paid for productions the way horse owners vie for the prestige of backing a winner at the track. The status of Euripides while he was alive is made clearer when we tally up that Aeschylus won first prize for his plays 13 or 28 times (depending on what contests you count), Sophocles 20 times, Euripides only four or five times—and he wrote maybe 90 plays. A year after Euripides died, Aristophanes placed him, dead, in a comedy titled *The Frogs*, staging a contest between Aeschylus and Euripides in the underworld. In *The Frogs* the souls of the dead playwrights argue before Hades, the god of the dead, who compares lines from their plays and weighs who is the better writer. Sophocles, who died the same year as Euripides, is also in *The Frogs* but diplomatically removes himself from the contest. Hades conservatively awards the prize to Aeschylus for offering better advice to the city than Euripides.

In writing their plays, all three—Euripides, Aeschylus, and Sophocles—worked from the same source material: current events and the myths of the gods as written down or sung, especially the stories found in the long poems of Homer, the *Odyssey* and the *Iliad*, which tell the story of the Trojan War and its aftermath. Though the three playwrights wrote within the same conventions, they held very different views of the world, of the gods, of the nature of life. Within Euripides' lifetime, Greece changed rapidly. The most significant change was in the nature, purpose, and fallout from war.

A little background is helpful here. Greece was made up of city-states (as was Italy during the Renaissance). At the time of Aeschylus (525–456 BC), the Greek city-states united to fight off an attack from a much larger power, the Persian Empire. The Greek city-states fighting together against a common enemy won. This was celebrated and glorified, sometimes directly, sometimes by dramatizing the epic story of the Greek city-states uniting together during the Trojan War.

Within twenty years after the end of the Persian Wars, the city-states fought each other, divided into two sides led by Athens and Sparta, a city-state to the north of Athens run as a military oligarchy, not a democracy. The struggle between Athens and Sparta, which lasted for twenty-seven years, is called the Peloponnesian War—the part of southern Greece where both cities are located is called the Peloponnesus—during which Athens went from honorable democracy to amoral empire without compassion for those it caused to suffer.

We know a good deal about the Peloponnesian War because the Greek historian Thucydides wrote about its origins, triumphs, and disasters as they were happening, though Thucydides died before the war was over. Thucydides is important not just for recording facts but because of his attitude towards what he wrote. The Greek historian before him, Herodotus, had reported on the past as if it were a parade of fascinating events. Thucydides wrote for a reason: to show the causes of the war and to prevent such things from happening again.

Euripides, too, wrote in direct response to the ongoing Peloponnesian War and with a purpose. In his writing he shows that war is not glorious but debasing. Using the same metaphoric source material as Aeschylus and Sophocles, the Trojan War, Euripides depicted the victims of war while a war was going on—and had the nerve to show his plays to the people who waged and encouraged war.

In the *Trojan Women*, written in 415 BC, the sixteenth year
of the Peloponnesian War, children are killed for political reasons and women mourn the uselessness of warfare. The play was
presented within months of an atrocity committed by the Athenians in the city of Melos. For refusing to submit to the Athenian
forces, the men of Melos were butchered—all of them—and the
women and children sold into slavery. The action of Euripides'
play, supposedly set hundreds of years before Melos, begins with
an old woman on the beach—it is the queen mother of Troy,
Hecuba, who is now a slave. Her city is in ruins; the Greeks have
overwhelmed it. Her sons have been killed; her oldest son's wife
is to become a slave. Her grandson is murdered offstage, thrown
off a wall, so he doesn't grow up to avenge his father. The play
ends with Hecuba holding her grandson's dead body. The chorus
who laments with her is to be sold into slavery. It is impossible
that Athenians could have watched this and not thought of Melos.

In *Trojan Women* and many other plays, Euripides articulated
eloquently the experience of women and those who were otherwise voiceless in public. In this play and in his others, the reasons
for tragedy and pain are given as personal and circumstantial, not
inevitable, nor part of some larger plan. Jealousy and sexual desire
are motivators of action. Even the gods are depicted as petty: still
powerful, but their motives are as capricious as mortals.

The play titled *Hippolytus* (428 BC) begins with the goddess
of love, Aphrodite, addressing the audience directly. She is angry at the young hero Hippolytus for his chastity, jealous he's a
follower of another goddess, Artemis, and she, Aphrodite, will
undo him by having his stepmother Phaedra fall in love with
him. As Aphrodite says:

> For that there is, even in a great God's mind,
> That hungers for the praise of human kind
> (Gilbert Murray, trans.)

In *Iphigenia in Tauris*, another play set by Euripides during the Trojan War, the son of the Greek King Agamemnon, whose family had also come to ruin, has this to say:

> Dreams, lies, lies, dreams
> nothing but emptiness!
> Even the Gods,
> with all their names for wisdom,
> Have only dreams and lies
> and lose their course,
> Blinded, confused and ignorant as we.
> (Witter Bynner, trans.)

Compare that to the religious plays of the Middle Ages. The power of the gods is accepted by Euripides (and in all Greek drama), but it is not the compassionate power of the Christian God, nor the law-giving fatherly Zeus who punishes according to law, it is the power of irrational gods who punish for unknown reasons, something terrifying to consider. Sometimes in plays by Euripides the gods reward men in irrational ways. In performance, a mechanical device would lower an actor dressed as a god onto the stage, a device later called the *deus ex machina*, the god from the machine. After landing, or perhaps hovering above the playing area, the god would sort out the plot and bestow grace, in short, save the day before rising back to heaven. These are perhaps ambivalent and ironic "happy" endings, meant to provoke disbelief. The great classical Greek author of comedies, Aristophanes, complained it was an easy way to end a tragedy, something he, writing comedies, couldn't do without angering his audience.

Euripides shook up the form of classical tragedy from within. He freed the chorus from plot responsibilities, which meant the songs sung by the chorus amplified the meaning of the action thematically, rather than gave commentary on the plot. The relationship between parts of his plays could be, deliberately, less logical, and more image-driven. Euripides wrote using a vocabulary less grand than other Greek playwrights, more like daily speech, though his lines are still in verse and adhere to the rules of poetry. Perhaps what Aristotle meant by Euripides being the most tragic of playwrights, if not the best, is that Euripides offered no consolation to his audience. In his own time, Euripides was the butt of jokes in other people's plays. In *The Thesmophoriazusae*, a comedy written by Aristophanes, Euripides appears in drag (along with his father-in-law) so as to crash an all-women's festival. The two men, and we in the audience, listen in as the ladies of the Thesmophoriazusae (it's the name of the festival as well as the name of play) denounce Euripides' revelation of women's secret desires. Watching characters like Phaedra onstage, the ladies claim, have made husbands suspicious of their wives, so much so it's become difficult to meet secret lovers. In another play by Aristophanes, someone goes to Euripides' house to borrow a costume but is not interested at all in whatever Euripides is writing or has to say.

Rumor has it Euripides was a recluse, shut up in his library, avoiding people, but Edith Hamilton, the American popularizer of Classical Greek culture, suspected Euripides stayed aloof not out of dislike for people but because, on the evidence of his plays, he was too vulnerable to them, too empathetic to other people's pain. Euripides understood people, but that is not the same thing as liking them.

He eventually moved from Athens to Macedonia, to the north and west of Greece, where Phillip the Great, the King of the Macedonians, was collecting power and the signs of prestige—great playwrights and philosophers—even as Athens was falling apart in war. In Macedonia, Euripides wrote *The Bacchae*, his masterpiece, named for Bacchus, that is to say, Dionysus and his followers.

In *The Bacchae*, as in the play *Hippolytus*, a god undoes a man, but here the god is Dionysus, the god of theater himself in his role as god of intoxication. The king's refusal to worship the god of ecstasy is a proud affirmation of logic, rule, and law—all of which led the Athenians in the audience to war and destruction, just as they would do in other times and places for the next 2,500 years and up until today. The metaphor for losing one's mind through obstinacy is lurid: the king's mother tears off the head of her own son and carries it around, thinking it's a wild animal she has killed in the wilderness. This action, like all violent actions in Greek drama, takes place offstage. The chorus is personified as women maddened to ecstasy by worshiping Dionysus. Soberly at the end of the play, the actors contemplate how the god has played them. There is a direct relationship in *The Bacchae* to the mysteries and power of the dromena and the limitations of the rational drama. Reason and logic, the glory of the Greeks, had limits. Euripides lived to see them, though he did not live long enough to see Athens lose the war, nor did he live long enough to see *The Bacchae* performed. It was presented the year after Euripides died, perhaps finished by his nephew (who was perhaps his son) also called Euripides. Posthumously it earned Euripides his last first prize.

In *The Bacchae*, after Dionysus hands out punishments, he goes back up in the machine to heaven and the chorus sings:

> The gods can do anything.
> They can frustrate whatever seems certain,
> and make what no one wants
> —all at once—come true!
> (Robert Bagg, trans.)

Chapter Five

AESCHYLUS— WRITING IN AN AGE OF CERTAINTY

Aeschylus (ca. 525–ca. 456 BC)
Euripides (ca. 480–ca. 406 BC)

Aeschylus wrote during an age of certainty—very different from the time of Euripides. Greece was on the rise, continuously, without public setbacks. Born 525 or 524 BC in Eleusis (yes, he was an initiate in the Eleusinian Mysteries), he died in Sicily around 456 BC. While he was a teenager, the city of Athens became a democracy, a defining event in Western history, by revolting against rule by a family of tyrants. The greatest event in his adult life was the war against Persia in which the united Greek city-states defeated the much larger Persian Empire. Knowledge of—or personal experience fighting in—famous battles, on land and on sea, including the Battle of Marathon in which Aeschylus fought, united his audience, and it was this the Athenians were certain about: united together, the Greeks had won.

The Persians, a play written by Aeschylus in 472 BC, within eight years of the real events it depicts, shows the outcome of war from within the Persian court, where the Persian king's mother is given news of the Greek victory at sea off of Salamis. Other plays by Aeschylus were set during the time of the Trojan War with a parallel made between the glories of the Trojan War and then contemporary Greece. As the Greek princes came together

to fight for Helen of Troy, so too the Greek city states came together against the common enemy of the Persians.

In all cases—Trojan War, current events, or Greek myths—
the audience knew the outcome of the story. This provides a
design for the action onstage: whatever happens in the play is
understood within the pattern of its conclusion, which is Fate.
The theme, always, is that there is a pattern to life unknown to
humans as they live, a pattern that unrolls over time and a design
understood at the point of death.

For Aeschylus, tragic fate is understood as ennobling. Facing death is part of what it means to live. His writing is positive,
not critical—again, very different from Euripides, and though
the writing of Aeschylus was in some ways monumental, the
language formal and grand, he was, after all, credited with adding a second actor, and therefore expanding the possibility of
displaying relationships between people—the medium of all
theater.

Aeschylus commanded strong metaphors, verbally and in
stage pictures. Action is not usually depicted onstage in Greek
theater, it is described, so the point of view of the story, how it is
told, and what effect it has on the listener (including the listening audience) are what make for the drama. So consider how
effective it is, when dramatizing a great naval battle, to do it from
the point of view of the enemy's mother receiving the news of
her son's defeat. This immediate theatricality is, in part, what
brings life to his plays in performance, even centuries after we
have stopped caring or knowing about the time or issues that
moved him. The value of his work is evident not only in an understanding of people but also in an understanding of theater.
A murderer scornful of the chorus—and the audience—boasts
of killing. That's a great setup for any speech, good enough for
Shakespeare throughout *Richard III*. Aeschylus is said to have
staged his plays himself, training the chorus to sing and dance,
designing the costumes and supervising the scenery. Perhaps—
we cannot know for sure—he played the leading roles, too.

Seven of his plays survive. It's estimated he wrote ninety—we know he won thirteen first prizes, though he competed for fifteen years before his first victory. After that first victory, he was very popular. His career in the theater lasted over forty years; he wrote a new play almost every other year.

Especially important among the surviving texts by Aeschylus are the three plays of the *Oresteia*, the only intact trilogy we have by any Greek playwright. The title means that this is the story of Orestes—the son of Agamemnon, who led the Greek forces to victory in the Trojan War.

The action of the *Oresteia* begins with an old man on a roof, crouched, as he says, like a dog, watching for a signal light to announce the war is over. The pattern of light and darkness, and the pattern of man as animal, will continue throughout all three plays. Agamemnon arrives home in triumph, but he is killed by his wife, Clytemnestra, who has been planning for years to revenge Agamemnon's sacrifice of their daughter Iphigenia. Agamemnon had his daughter killed on an altar, so he would win his war. The audience understands that Agamemnon's triumphant return home is shadowed by the murder that awaits him. Clytemnestra lays out a great robe for the victorious general to trample on as he enters the palace, a public demonstration of his power and pride. With the same robe she snares him when he takes a bath, then whacks him with an ax, three times. The bath and the whacks, characteristically, take place offstage. We hear Agamemnon cry out until the great doors open. It is possible that a moving platform slid out with Clytemnestra standing over the body of her husband. Defying the chorus and, of course, the audience, she tells us, without remorse, of her husband's murder and now, the dogs, as Clytemnestra tells us, will lick the great general's blood.

In the second play, which has a dull title, *The Libation Bearers*, the children of Clytemnestra, named Orestes and Electra, kill their mother to avenge their father. The brother and sister have been brought up separately from each other, and not knowing who they are to one another as adults, they meet carrying libations to pour at the tomb of their father. The scene that Aeschylus wrote for the pair to recognize their relationship is famously awkward. A lock of hair, a matching footprint, and clothing Electra made for her long, lost brother years before reveal to Electra that Orestes is not lost but standing next to her. The scene was so well known that Euripides, in his version of the story, titled *Electra*, makes fun of it. Euripides' Electra asks mockingly why should their hair match and why, as an adult, should Orestes still be carrying children's clothing? In the version by Aeschylus, Orestes and Electra enter the palace disguised so Orestes may kill their mother. She dies cursing her son, declaring that the Furies will avenge her by haunting Orestes as long as he lives.

The third play of the Oresteia, *The Eumenides*, has as its motif the conversion of the Furies to mercy. The title means the merciful goddesses. Orestes takes refuge in Athens, trying to escape the Furies who track him by the smell of his mother's blood, still staining him as evidence of his guilt. The city's goddess, Athena, convenes a jury of Athenians—remember this is performed in front of Athenians and the public's representatives are actors onstage, mirroring a real-life jury. Athena is judge, the god Apollo argues as lawyer for Orestes, and the Furies argue for Clytemnestra's revenge. The citizens jury is tied, which means Orestes is acquitted. Athena announces that mercy and forgiveness prevail. This was true for juries in Athens: a tie meant innocence. Again, the motifs of light and darkness and blood play out in words and images. The play ends in a procession led by Athena, which celebrates the procession in Athenian history from the ancient law of revenge to the classical Greek ideals of justice, reason, and mercy. A tragedy that ends happily is a different idea than we have of the genre.

One of the difficulties we have appreciating Aeschylus in English is jumping the hurdle of a translation. The Greek words are comparatively bare compared to the great embellishments of English writing—the models English translators emulated in past centuries to evoke greatness were Shakespeare's plays and the King James Bible, both ornate and rich. The languages of the Bible, including English versions, make their effect through repetition, something Classical Greek writing does not do. Classical Greek writing is stark, and Aeschylus especially so. Early translators, among the most famous is Gilbert Murray, explicitly said they had added to the original in order to give a sense of weight and dignity.

The off-putting Thee and Thou and ritual language of the King James Bible have also been added to the mix in order to indicate religiosity, but they do not function in that way anymore. On the page they distract our thoughts to references from the Bible—spoken in performance they are an obstacle to following what is happening onstage. A translation from Aeschylus cannot be taken word for word from the Greek, either. For purposes of performance, the lines must be speakable, not clumsy. The sounds of the words aloud, the rhythms of speech, too, must all build the stage effect if the scene is to be effective theater. The use of rhyme is so chained to English poetry that it was used for years to translate Greek drama, even though the Greek authors didn't use rhyme, but instead worked with subtly changing rhythms, themselves a challenge to translate into English verse.

Gilbert Murray, translating *Agamemnon* in 1920 into rhyming couplets, starts the play:

> This waste of year-long vigil I have prayed
> God for some respite, watching elbow-stayed,
> As sleuthhounds watch, above the Atreidae's hall,
> Till well I know yon midnight festival
> Of swarming stars, and them that lonely go,
> Bearers to man of summer and of snow,
> Great lords and shining, throned in heavenly fire.

This is effective, in its way, though the word-order is difficult and perplexing when heard (what are the "them?" and "that lonely go?") and takes us a while—too long—to figure out. "Yon" is now ridiculous.

The contemporary poet Anne Carson has her own version of the beginning, which is clear enough:

> WATCHMAN: Gods! Free me from this grind!
> It's one long year I'm lying here watching waiting watching
> waiting—propped on the roof of Atreus, chin on my paws like a
>   dog.
> I've peered at the congregation of the nightly stars—bright pow-
>   erful
> creatures blazing in air,
> the ones that bring summer, the ones that bring winter, the ones
>   that die
> out, the ones that rise up—and I watch I watch I watch for this
>   sign of a
> torch, a beacon light sending from Troy the news that she is
>   captured.

"Free me from this grind" is so colloquial as to announce the translator's intent to grab the audience's ears with familiar words but translating the lines into colloquial language loses the strangeness of Aeschylus—and even in his own time his word choices were considered strange. For one thing, Aeschylus coined new words, the way Shakespeare did. In the surviving plays and fragments written by Aeschylus that we know of so far, there are almost a thousand newly formed words. In *Agamemnon*, the watchman is arm-rested, nightly-rested, Clytemnestra is man-minded, birds are sky-voyagers, and an eagle is a winged hound (helping Zeus to hunt). Some of the phrases used by Aeschylus strike the mind and linger: a wingless voice is what Aeschylus called intuition—a thought that flies into one's head; violent warriors are said to breathe Ares, meaning they inhale the breath of the god of war. In describing the death of her husband, Clytemnestra says his blood ran in a rapid slaughter-tide.

In *The Persians*, boats are "sea-wandering linen winged chariots for sailors."

Like Shakespeare, Aeschylus put together startling images from incongruities: the chorus in Agamemnon has "no hope to wind off anything profitable from the burning flames of their mind," and they tell Electra to "drill this tale through her ear with the mind's silent tread." Sometimes the phrases are curious and obscure: a traveler's boots are covered with "thirsty dust, the brother of mud," and the "art of dying brass (a new color)" is something impossible to do. The chorus leader admits "I heard what was said like a racer straying off the course," that is, without understanding what he was listening to.

In particular, Aeschylus gave inanimate objects life: swords have hearts, the sea waves laugh, a ship's prow "fixes its eyes on the waters in front, paying good heed to the voice of the rudder." As A.E. Haigh wrote about the first scene of *Agamemnon*, the signal fire "is conceived as some mighty spirit, exulting in its strength and swiftness; it 'vaults over the back of the sea with joy'; it 'hands its message' to the heights of Macistus; it 'leaps across' the plain of the Asopus River, and 'urges on' the watchmen; its 'mighty beard of fire' streams across the Saronic Gulf as it rushes along from peak to peak until finally it 'swoops down' upon the palace of Atreidae."

The writer's exuberance is such that he piled adjectives onto adjectives in long chains, exhilarating to listen to—and it is this that needs to be remembered, the impact he had on his audience was fresh—the language may have been exalted and out of the ordinary speech, but it was like the oratory of Gospel preachers and Gospel music in its direct appeal to the emotions and the mind.

In the English Renaissance, Aeschylus was not as well-known as Euripides. Access was through Latin translations of the Greek, though Ben Jonson refers to him as thundering Aeschylus in the introduction to the First Folio of Shakespeare. The first English version of *Agamemnon* was published in 1773—Robert Potter used blank verse in imitation of Shakespeare's iambic pentameter. That's not so far-fetched. The dialogue in Greek tragedies is usually written in iambs, though three, not five to a line. Iambic trimeter is too abrupt to be used for long stretches of English, though Emily Dickinson's poetry demonstrates it can have power:

> The only news I know
> Is bulletins all day
> From Immortality.
> The only shows I see,
> Tomorrow and Today,
> Perchance Eternity.
> The only One I meet
> Is God, —the only street,
> Existence; this traversed
> If other news there be,
> Or admirabler show—
> I'll tell it you.

Notice the drama of Dickinson's break in the pattern. The dash after "Is God" stops the flow of the verse. The comma has the reader breathe, the dash that follows the breath enrolls the reader into a confrontation with the word and concept of God. Greek tragic verse also used such pauses.

From 1820 to 1920 there were many translations of Greek plays, and the plays of Aeschylus, more obscure than others, became a special challenge for translators and poets. *Prometheus Bound*, with its romantic themes—defiance of authority, sacrifice of self for a cause—appealed first and was translated first, spawning imitations from Shelley and Byron who fought for English words to articulate the wish of nineteenth century Greeks to be free of Turkish rule.

Reviewing a production of Euripide's *Medea* in 1920, the American poet T.S. Eliot attacked the approach of traditional translators, naming Gilbert Murray and his couplets as the problem with the production: "Professor Murray has simply interposed between Euripides and ourselves a barrier more impenetrable than the Greek language." Eliot suggests the modern poet H.D. (known by her initials) would be better as translator but makes the point that modern poets have not attacked the great challenge of translating *Agamemnon*.

The translations most often read now in America, versions which date to the late 1950s and early '60s, include hexameters: Shakespeare's iambs, but in lines of twelve, not ten, which is in theory two sets of six iambs.

Richmond Lattimore, translating the beginning of *Agamemnon* in 1953:

> I ask the gods some respite from the weariness
> of this watchtime measured by years I lie awake
> elbowed upon the Atreidae's roof dogwise to mark
> the grand processionals of all the stars of night
> burdened with winter and again with heat for men,
> dynasties in their shining blazoned on the air,
> these stars, upon their wane and when the rest arise.

Robert Fagles, working the same passage in 1966:

> Dear gods, set me free from all the pain,
> the long watch I keep, one whole year awake…
> propped on my arms, crouched on the roofs of Atreus
> like a dog.
> I know the stars by heart,
> the armies of the night, and there in the lead
> the ones that bring us snow or the crops of summer,
> bring us all we have—
> our great blazing kings of the sky,
> I know them when they rise and when they fall…

As a contrast, look at the romantic nineteenth century poet, Robert Browning:

The gods I ask deliverance from these labours,
Watch of a year's length whereby, slumbering through it
On the Atreidai's roofs on elbow,—dog-like—
I know of nightly star-groups the assemblage,
And those that bring to men winter and summer
Bright dynasts, as they pride them in the aether
—Stars, when they wither, and the uprisings of them.

It would be impossible for a listening audience to make sense of this.

The English poet, Ted Hughes, known for the violence of his verse, had an *Oresteia* published posthumously in 1999. This is not so much a strict translation as an attempt at finding stage-worthy potent English:

You Gods in Heaven, —
You have watched me here on this tower
All night. Every night for twelve months.
Thirteen moons
tethered on the roof of this palace
like a *dog*.
It is time to release me.
I've stared long enough into this darkness
For what never emerges.
I'm tired of the constellations
That glittering parade of lofty rulers
Night after night *a* little bit earlier
Withholding the thing I wait for—
Slow as torture.
And the moon, coming and going—
Wearisome...like watching the sea
Front a deathbed.

What matters, is that Hughes, a violent modern poet, was attracted to material from twenty-five hundred years before.

And as Anne Carson points out in the introduction to her translation, the British painter Francis Bacon was also attracted to Aeschylus. "The Furies often visit me" Bacon said in an interview. "Reading translations of Aeschylus…opens up the valves of sensation for me." Bacon's 1981 lithograph *Triptych inspired by Orestia of Aeschylus* is writhing flesh, identifiable as flesh but twisted, contorted, with identifiable bruises and blood. Bacon wrote describing the work: "I could not paint Agamemnon, Clytemnestra, or Cassandra as that would have been merely another type of historical painting…Therefore, I tried to create an image of the effect it produced inside of me."

Every age appropriates these plays with their strong imagery and heritage. Once Japanese poetry began to influence modern English poetry, audiences and readers were less patient with sonorous poetry and more ready to pay attention to simpler words that ring in the mind.

In any translation, and even in the original Greek, staging these plays by Aeschylus presents unusual challenges. Immediate questions: do they work psychologically, without masks, without raised shoes? Must there be music playing during the choruses? Should there be dance? Do the values of the text change when we stage these plays with barefaced actors speaking intimately in small spaces, rather than masked performers wearing platform shoes in large stadiums? The play's compelling imagery, verbal and theatrical, has fired the imaginations of audiences and performers for thousands of years. Euripides may be closer to us and more familiar, but the strangeness of Aeschylus—his words that open a window onto another world—will always be enticing.

Chapter Six

SOPHOCLES AND ARISTOTLE— DEFINING TRAGEDY

Aeschylus (ca. 525–ca. 456 BC)
Aristotle (384–322 BC)
Euripides (ca. 480–ca. 406 BC)
Sigmund Freud (1856–1939)
Sophocles (ca. 497–ca. 406 BC)
Friedrich Wilhelm Nietzsche (1844–1900)

Sophocles is centered between the other two great Greek tragedy writers. He was born almost thirty years after Aeschylus, around 497 BC, and died in the same year as Euripides in the winter of 406 BC. The stories about Sophocles as a man stress his personal grace: he danced at sixteen at the Athenian celebrations in honor of the victory at Salamis. True or not, it is an image for his verse: balanced, graceful, human.

His arrival on the professional scene was momentous: he won first prize over Aeschylus. His career was long and publicly successful. He won twenty first prizes, compared to thirteen for Aeschylus and four for Euripides. He never received less than second prize in any contest he entered. He is credited with adding the third actor, that is to say, for complicating and bringing depth to human relationships. As Aeschylus is credited with inventing costumes, perhaps a metaphor for the vividness of his characters, Sophocles is given credit for inventing painted scenery, perhaps a metaphor for his ability to set a scene.

Like Aeschylus, we have seven plays by Sophocles that survive—out of over one hundred twenty we know he wrote. He has his own version of *Electra*, and, like the *Oresteia* of Aeschylus, three plays based on the story of a family: *Antigone*, *Oedipus Rex*, and *Oedipus at Colonus*. These three plays were not intended to make up a trilogy, as the plays of the *Oresteia*; they're from three other trilogies written over thirty-six years.

Sophocles led a long life, ninety years, from the victory over the Persians to the fall of Athens in the Peloponnesian War. He took part in the civil life of Athens as a treasurer, as a commissioner for financial reform, and even as a general (though not a very successful one). He was an Athenian to the end, unlike Aeschylus who moved to Sicily (the gossip says out of jealousy over Sophocles' success) or Euripides who ended up at the court of Macedonia.

In 335 BC, seventy years after Sophocles died, seventy years after Athens had fallen to Sparta, the center of Greek culture moved to the Macedonian court of King Philip. There, the philosopher scientist Aristotle, tutor to the prince who would grow up to be Alexander the Great, wrote the *Poetics*—an analysis of Greek tragedy. For Aristotle, who considered tragedy the height of Greek writing, Sophocles wrote tragedies at the height of excellence. According to Aristotle, Sophocles' play *Oedipus Rex* was the best constructed of all plays, and the values of Greek drama were further demonstrated by Aristotle in their particulars with many examples taken from other plays written by Sophocles. For Aristotle those values include a moral quality inherent in what is best.

Though Aristotle wrote more than three generations after the last of the three great Greek playwrights, his connection to the heyday of Athens is direct. He was the student of Plato, who was the student of Socrates, and it was Socrates who lived among the great Athenian playwrights as their colleague and friend. Socrates began the method of teasing out, through questions and answers, a logical chain of identifying causes and effects as a means to understand what was real. Plato, using logic which he learned from Socrates, proposed a philosophy of eternal forms in a further effort to understand what is real. What is ultimately real, Plato taught, was not anything physical, but the essence of anything physical. The idea of a table was more real and outlasted any single table made of wood or even stone. Just so, in this way of philosophizing, a person's essence endures forever: a man or woman's body is a perishable vessel for his or her essential soul.

Aristotle, expanding on Plato, examined the natural world in order to identify and know its essence better, observing details as a means to derive systematic information about what he observed. He wrote about animals, plants, clouds, political systems, anatomy, and astronomy using this method of observation and assessment. In the *Poetics* he did the same for plays, in particular tragedies: he observed and assessed them, he read the texts of the great Greek plays, and presumably he watched them performed in a theater. He passed on what he observed and in order to do so, came up with terminology to describe what he was noticing. As he had with plants and clouds and bees, he drew conclusions. What he set out as observations of tragedies were not meant to become rules to follow, any more than his notes about cloud formations—as in his other investigations, his observations were reported as a way for others to explore further.

In studying Sophocles or any other Greek play, what Aristotle thought important is well worth thinking about, though it's not always necessary to align our modern perspective with the ancient point of view of the *Poetics*. Aristotle's pronouncements of excellence have been setting off discussions about theater in Europe for two thousand years. Disagreeing with the *Poetics* has sometimes been as productive as following its rules.

Oedipus Rex, of all Greek plays, is considered by Aristotle to be the greatest of the great tragedies. The story is told backwards in time and has been said to be the first murder mystery—in the sense of detective story not the mysteries of Eleusis or the mysteries of the medieval theater. A story precedes the play, a story the audience would have known. King Oedipus, whose name means lame foot, was brought up by shepherds, whom he believed were his parents. Tall, brave, naturally noble (whatever that means to you), he was adopted by the childless King of Corinth and became the heir to the throne. He ran away from Corinth when an oracle prophesied he would kill his father and marry his mother. In a hurry to escape the city and avoid what was foretold, he met an arrogant unyielding man at a crossroads, got into an argument, and killed the man without knowing who he was. Years later, Oedipus arrived in the city of Thebes and married its Queen, Jocasta, by whom he has two daughters. All of this happens before the action of the play, which begins with Oedipus asking the Gods for help in ending a plague in his country.

What he learns is that the plague will end when he discovers who killed King Laius, Jocasta's husband. As more information arrives, Oedipus learns he himself is the killer of Laius. And more, Oedipus learns Laius was his father. Witnesses reveal that when Laius was told the newborn prince would grow up to kill his father and marry his mother, he ordered the infant left in the wilderness to die. The infant's ankles were pinned together, so he couldn't crawl away—and that is why Oedipus is lame. His mother, Jocasta, out of pity, had him taken away and brought up by shepherds rather than die; now she knows what has happened after he survived. She is her grown son's wife. In horror at this, she hangs herself. Oedipus, at the sight of her dead hanging body, gouges out his own eyes—as usual in Greek drama these horrors happen offstage. As in the *Oresteia* when Clytemnestra is revealed, the doors of the palace in Thebes swing open to display Jocasta's body and Oedipus blinded, with blood streaming from his eyes, wandering out into the world. The former king has become a blind beggar.

Separate from the story of the play and from Aristotle's analysis, the story of Oedipus has become famous because the founder of psychology, Sigmund Freud, named an essential part of his theory of childhood development after the play. The Oedipus complex is the subconscious wish a male child has to kill his father and take his father's place in bed, but both of Sophocles' plays about Oedipus (there are two, remember) have no such subconscious motivations and no such organization as the Oedipus complex, since Oedipus obviously didn't know who he was killing or marrying. The whole point of the play is that the design of Fate was something Oedipus thought he was above, but which caught him the way Clytemnestra caught Agamemnon.

Aristotle identifies the willful disregard for Fate as *hubris*, or English pride. Hubris hits the stage when Aeschylus shows Agamemnon stepping on a glorious robe, and the hubris of the hero Hippolytus spurning the goddess of love sets off her revenge and the bull. It was hubris for Laius, the father of Oedipus, to think he could avoid the omen; it was hubris for Oedipus to think that he could run away from Fate. In *Oedipus Rex* the king who asks a question onstage (what is polluting the country?) gets an answer onstage (you who asked). The mechanism of cause and effect from hubris to tragedy—from impetus to consequence—plays out in front of the audience and is, according to Aristotle, superior to the action of a play in which the impetus is offstage or in the past, or a play in which the consequence is offstage or in the future.

Sophocles constructed *Oedipus Rex* so that the action of the entire play all happens in one location: the palace at Thebes. Oedipus comes onstage to ask a chorus of priests about the plague; everyone else comes to him. We do not see the field where the baby was left to die, and the play does not move to the crossroads where the old King was killed. We don't see the room where Jocasta hangs herself, nor do we watch Oedipus blind himself. We see onstage the consequences of these actions, and we hear about them in speeches delivered onstage by messengers. This, too, appealed to Aristotle, who deduced that unity in place was a virtue in writing plays.

All of the action of *Oedipus Rex* happens in one continuous time. As various messengers arrive, news accumulates, the plot advances, and the design of Fate for Oedipus unfolds. There is no next day, ten years later, fourteen years before, etc., there is only now, what is immediately happening in front of the audience. Aristotle thought this gave the play power.

Consistently, everything in the play is subordinate to the single story of Oedipus and his search for the truth. Even things we first think of as background—the hero's childhood, his name— become integral to the plot. All parts fit together, and the fitting together of the parts is both the theme of the play and its point: Fate is unknown, and when it is known, terrifying and painful.

Aristotle noted these unities of time, place, and action in the work of Aeschylus and Euripides too. In the *Poetics*, Aristotle identified other technical aspects of the plays he knew, and he devised words still used today to discuss all plays. Again, as with shellfish and birds, he was observing something, not handing down rules for what he observed—and essentially, what he was talking about was gone, the democratic society that the art form of tragedy grew up in was over when Aristotle wrote. Nothing Aristotle wrote inspired great writing in his own time. Not until the Roman Empire, 330 years later, would anyone else write significant tragedies.

Yet, the terms that Aristotle established are useful. Among them:

Stichomythia—the alternation of lines in dialogue, rather than speeches or narrative.

Mimesis—means imitation. Aristotle's famous definition of drama as the imitation of an action is significant because it establishes that what happens onstage isn't action itself (or real behavior or real people) it's imitation. It's a given for Aristotle that a play alternates between imitation and narration.

Catharsis—which we can translate as cleansing, is the purpose of tragedy, specifically to evoke fear (at Fate, which will ultimately catch even those watching the play) and pity (at what happens to those onstage in the play). To affect the audience in this way, cleansing the spectators, it is best, in the sense of moral good as well as aesthetics, that the audience be aware how the plot works out and best that they be moved by what happens to the characters.

Episode—is what happens between choral odes, that is to say an episode is an event that happens onstage, not as in life, but in performance, with a clear beginning, middle, and end. Episodes related by cause and effect are better in a play, according to Aristotle, than episodes that simply follow each other.

Peripeteia—is the reversal of fortune. The best plots, according to Aristotle, involve such a change: the rich turn poor, the powerful turn weak, those who seem content suffer.

Recognition—is when something onstage is understood that was previously hidden or unknown. Recognition may be joyous, as when Orestes and his sister recognize each other or recognition might be horrific, as in the *Bacchae*, when the mother realizes she's carrying the head of her son. Best, according to Aristotle, is when reversal and recognition happen at the same time as in *Oedipus*.

Pathos—is at the heart of tragedy, and the relationship of the audience to suffering. Properly, according to Aristotle, we understand that pain is the result of the hero's actions, his fate is to endure, ours to pity. That the spectators should identify emotionally with the hero is a given.

Aristotle's taste was to the generic, and all his life he lent thoughtful full support to the status quo. He spun theories about tragedy, drawn from what he thought best in what he observed. In the *Poetics* he claims characters who are related to each other, friends, or better yet relatives, make for the most tragic relationships, hence only a few families (where children kill their parents, for example) were really appropriate for tragedy. Actions that happen onstage need be spoken about, not ignored. Since characters were established by what they did and said, there could be no drama of indecision. Aristotle stated that scenery and costuming were the least important elements of the theater.

Tragic characters were, for moral purposes, necessarily serious, virtuous, and superior to the audience, not their equals. A prosperous famous character was best, from a good family (in which children killed their parents). The best characters were consistent and appropriate to their position (brave soldiers, dependably so, and if not brave then the reason made apparent to the audience). Propriety in character was essential; therefore, according to Aristotle, women should not be valorous or unscrupulously clever. As good portrait painters flatter their subject, so should writers depicting heroes, all of whom need be male. This nonsense is to be understood in the same way as his acceptance of slavery: it was a given in his world and he never thought to do more than understand it for what it was.

Aristotle emphasized that the plot (considered the most important aspect of a tragedy) should flow from cause to effect. What happened onstage should be logical. Aristotle may have thought so, but other people have thought otherwise. The necessity of reaching for something beyond a logical understanding of action as a way of imitating or even understanding the senseless deaths and ruined cities of the Peloponnesian War stirred Euripides to write plays in which a young woman offers her throat to be slit, announcing it to her mother, in a memorable translation by M.S. Merwin of Euripides' *Iphigenia in Aulis*:

> I give my life to Greece.
> Take me, kill me,
> and bring down Troy. That will be my monument
> for ages to come. That will be my wedding,

my children, the meaning of my life.
Mother, it is the Greeks
who must rule the barbarians,
not the barbarians the Greeks.
They are born to be slaves; we
to be free.

A few lines before Iphigenia has spoken rationally about living, not dying. What has changed her mind? Not logic. The mad spirit of the time that pursued the war has taken over her mind. Twenty-five centuries later, Bertolt Brecht, stirred by the vast scale of devastation after World War I, and the inability of Germany's classical tradition to confront, much less condemn, what had happened in the war, forcefully rejected Aristotle's authority to define tragedy. Brecht claimed to be following Shakespeare who, out of ignorance or defiance of the *Poetics*, wrote tragedies in which flawed men and women, not all of them nobles, go through the process of pain-filled self-revelation made up of irreconcilable opposing actions, not unlike Euripides' *Iphigenia*.

It was not entirely a good thing for Sophocles that Aristotle praised Sophocles so often. Sophocles' writing was more than the qualities Aristotle praised. Very quickly the understanding of what Sophocles actually contributed to drama passed into an oversimplified quality. As with other playwrights known for qualities—Chekhov, for example—it became difficult to appreciate Sophocles separately from what was said about him. Let's try, though. It helps to put him in the context of the other two great Greek writers.

If the subject of tragedy is suffering and its relationship to living, then Sophocles is noticeably the spirit of acceptance where Euripides is the spirit of criticism and Aeschylus of affirmation. We might agree the greatest play written by Sophocles is *Oedipus Rex*, greatest because of its ever-engaging construction and imagery. Even so, *Oedipus at Colonus*, written in 406 BC just before Sophocles died, and his tragedy of *Antigone*, written around 441

BC, show the spirit of Sophocles' work more clearly than *Oedipus Rex,* for all its excellence.

Antigone, in Greek myth, is the daughter of Oedipus, obviously a child of incest. The action of the play named after her is Antigone's insistence in burying her brother, Polyneices, after his death. The ruler of Thebes, Creon, has ordered that Polyneices' body be left for carrion—the greatest insult in that culture, a defilement Polyneices deserved according to the law. Antigone disobeys. Creon orders Antigone put to death. Defiant, she and other characters argue that there is a law, one more important than the civic law, the natural law, in this case of a sister burying a brother or of any person burying the dead. Creon's hubris in ignoring the rule of the gods is followed by (it's discussable whether it's punished or results in) the reversal of his status: all he loves is ruined or dead by the end of the play. Remarkably *Antigone* was written when Sophocles was a general leading an army, but the play is not propaganda for the state, rather for the obligation of the individual to be true to something other than the laws of the state. Antigone dies, but her life and death are an affirmation of what is right; she and the audience both recognize this by the play's conclusion.

Oedipus at Colonus, the last of the plays written by Sophocles, and the last in the sequence about the royal family of Thebes, starts after the action of *Oedipus Rex* and before the story of Antigone. *Oedipus at Colonus* begins with Antigone leading her blind father out onto the stage. Oedipus and Antigone have come to the town of Colonus—we believe it was Sophocles' birthplace—and arrive at a spot deep in the woods sacred to the Furies. There is little plot as we understand it. The action of the play is set up immediately: Oedipus has come here to die, and there are obstacles to his dying in the woods, many obstacles, one after another, which interrupt the action, but do not stop it. The unity of place is clear, the unity of action, for all the variations in obstacles, is clear. A messenger reports that Oedipus, dying, evaporated into a mist, his presence in the land now changed from curse to blessing. Even so painful a life as the life of Oedipus may end harmoniously, and in death every life, including the worst, acquires a design that may be contemplated as a balance of pain and curse. The most famous lines, spoken by the chorus, are translated well by the Irish poet William Butler Yeats:

> I celebrate the silent kiss that ends short life or long.
> Never to have lived is best, ancient writers say;
> Never to have drawn the breath of life, never to have looked into
> the eye of day;
> The second best's a gay goodnight and quickly turn away.

Oedipus at Colonus was produced in 601 BC, we believe by Sophocles' grandson. Sophocles had died by then; his last public activity was to lead a chorus in mourning Euripides.

Aristotle, examining the work of playwrights who flourished many years before the *Poetics* was written, spent a lot of time writing about Sophocles, some time on Euripides (who, despite what Aristotle wrote, was becoming more popular than Sophocles), and not so much on Aeschylus (who was a little out of date). In the manuscripts of Aristotle's writing that have survived, Aristotle did not comment on the tragedies being written in his own time. The court of Phillip was more intent on empire than theater. Phillip was followed as King by Aristotle's pupil, Alexander. What's called the Hellenistic Era began under Alexander. The term was invented in the nineteenth century by a German historian, to distinguish a culture, different from the culture of Classical Greece, that flourished in the Greek-speaking colonies established by force in Asia, Europe, and Africa. Alexander conquered Persia—and more. Alexander's armies conquered ancient Egypt and fought as far east as what is now Pakistan and Afghanistan where the Greek example changed the development of Buddhist art when the calm face of Apollo was adopted for the Buddha. Aristotle, by the way, moved back to Athens when Alexander became Great. The Empire of Alexander, three hundred years after he died, was itself taken over by the Empire of Rome, and the Romans aspired to extend the philosophy and theater of the Greeks by works of their own. More importantly they preserved the writings of the earlier culture, including the words of Aristotle.

When classical Greek plays were no longer performed in Europe or read, Arabic translations of the *Poetics* translated into Latin preserved knowledge of Greek tragedy for readers, if not for audiences. During the Renaissance, when Aristotle's writings were read again in Europe, his curiosity about the world was an inspiration to follow. What he recommended passed from personal preference to authority. Without any recommendations, though, the issues that Sophocles wrote about—for example, civic law versus natural law (in *Antigone*)—inspired later European thinkers to write about such issues in their own culture, especially in Germany.

Now, what we think about tragedy in our time is as much influenced by German philosophers as by Greek. The Italian city-states at the time of the Renaissance found an echo of their concerns in classical Greece, and, of course, in Imperial Rome. In the early nineteenth century, Germany, going through a process of amalgamating different parts of a country that, as in Italy and Greece, had the same spoken language in common, found models in Greek history and literature. The German art historian Johann Winckelmann can be considered to have created the modern idea of classical Greece, especially the emphasis on balance and harmony. The German philosopher Ernst Cassirer upheld that what nations had in common was language and literature—the Greek classics, including Homer and the classical Greek plays weren't products of Greek culture, they created Greek culture—that's what made Greeks Greek.

The early nineteenth century German philosopher Schopenhauer, who believed the world was Will—in the sense of the word as desire, the will to do something—had much to say about Antigone's willfulness and the play's arguments between natural law and imposed law. The later nineteenth century German philosopher Friedrich Nietzsche, who believed in will as destiny, wrote in *The Birth of Tragedy* that Greek tragedy was the essence of Greek culture because it was an art of rational thought and ecstasy, blending Apollonian calm with Dionysian abandon. These definitions frame our modern thinking about tragedy as much as Aristotle's.

None of these Germans wished to revive the forms of Greek tragedy, any more than they wanted to restore the worship of Greek gods. They were, it might be said, followers of Plato, interested in the essence and how it might inspire new forms, as a soul would bring life to a body. Freud, whether you consider him a scientist or philosopher, was also inspired by Greek tragedy, and in particular by the writings of Sophocles, as models for following self-understanding in a dark painful journey towards recognition, reversal, and, ultimately, harmony. Aside from appraisals by Aristotle, Nietzsche, and Freud, the value of Sophocles to us now can be made clearer by comparing him to his peers. Aeschylus is older, more primal, cruder, stranger; Euripides is younger, more recognizable, his work is easier to translate because the words imply petty motives we share. Sophocles is noble and ennobling, neither critique nor propaganda. That's what appealed to Aristotle: acceptance. Five times five hundred years of further experience in the West has brought us to appreciate the power of resistance—resistance against slavery and resistance to the subjugation of women, to begin with—but Sophocles, separately from anything Aristotle or anyone else has to say about his writing, offers outer grace in the words he wrote, and an inner grace in what those words pass on, hard to translate into any words or any life or any performance, but it's something worth attempting, worth failing at—and perhaps that's our culture's definition of tragedy and what it means to be a hero.

Chapter Seven

GREEK COMEDY

Aristophanes (ca. 460–ca. 380 BC)
Euripides (ca. 480–ca. 406 BC)
Herondas (also Herodas) (ca. 300–ca. 201 BC)
Menander (ca. 342–ca. 290 BC)
Theophrastus (ca. 372–ca. 287 BC)

L et's begin the conversation about Greek comedy in Hell. According to a Greek myth, there's a guy there named Sisyphus whose punishment for his sins in life is to roll a big round stone up a hill. It's difficult to do. The big round stone is very heavy; the hill is very steep. When Sisyphus gets to the top of the hill (or maybe it's a mountain), the stone somehow rolls back down to the bottom and then Sisyphus must begin rolling again. This happens every time, rock and roll and roll again. Sisyphus is endlessly tormented by the futility of his efforts, according to the most famous version of the story from an essay written by the twentieth century French philosopher Albert Camus.

If we conclude the story of Sisyphus where Camus does, it is, perhaps, pathetic in the sense of painful, or it is, perhaps, thought-provoking to consider as a model of human existence.

Let's not stop where Camus does; let's climb to the moment when Sisyphus, almost at the top of the mountain, smiles, hears a happy little blue bird singing, who then shits on him. Without thinking, Sisyphus brushes off the white wet bird crap, and the big round stone goes rolling down the hill; Sisyphus trudges after it, rolls it back up the mountain, is just about to get to the top when he trips on a banana peel, or over the laces on his sandals, or his hat with the sunshade slips over his eyes, or the sound of his own farts frighten him, or the happy little blue bird comes back and pecks him on the ass. And each time the stone rolls down the hill...

What makes any of this funny is that Sisyphus starts back over again, and then when again something stops him, still he goes on: an image of farce, not tragedy. A tragedy would end with Sisyphus on the top of the mountain staring (depending on who wrote the tragedy) down (Euripides), or up (Aeschylus), or out (Sophocles). For Sisyphus to be a tragedy, the story ends with life considered, not endlessly pursued.

This is the relationship of farce to tragedy. It's the same story, at a different point in the narrative. Farce celebrates that life goes on, too full of itself to stop for contemplation or to stop for anything else. In a farce you can hit Sisyphus with a frying pan, you can toss him off a cliff, you can flatten him like a pancake (as happens when the stone rolls back down over him) and still his life goes on.

In Classical Greece, farce and tragedy were on the same program. Greek tragedies were entered into contests in groups of three. To accompany those trilogies, the Greek authors of tragedy wrote a fourth shorter play, a farce called a satyr play.

According to Aristotle's rules of drama, drawn from Aristotle's evaluation the Classical Greek repertory, the leading roles in a tragedy should come from families the audience looks up to—princely families, nice families, families with a mythic history. Think of the family that Aeschylus and Euripides wrote about, a nice princely family in which a father kills his daughter, a wife kills her husband, and a son kills his mother. Satyrs are also from Greek mythology. A satyr is half man and from the waist down half goat. Aristotle suggested the leading roles of comic plays should be from families less nice than the audience, which is probably true if one side of the family are goats.

We only have one satyr play left to us in its entirety: *The Cyclops*. It was written by Euripides, though we know Sophocles and Aeschylus wrote satyr plays, too. Here's how *The Cyclops* is set up: Odysseus, famous for his cleverness, is sailing home from the Trojan War. He's stuck on an island where the giant Cyclops, famous for his one-eye in the middle of his forehead (that's what it means to be a Cyclops) has kept Odysseus and his crew captive. The Cyclops is planning to eat them when he can remember to find time. Odysseus outwits the Cyclops (which isn't hard to do) and pokes a stick in his one eye, blinding him. Chasing after the sound of Odysseus' voice, the big dumb giant races into a cave and bangs his head—again and again and again. As the play ends, Odysseus escapes, and the audience is meant to be laughing at the blind giant heard from the back of the stage banging around and saying rude things. The blinded Cyclops is not the only person who says rude things. There's a chorus of drunken rude satyrs who live on the island. The satyrs dance while swinging their rude things. They smack each other with them.

Though no one in the ancient world thought enough of the satyr plays to set down rules for them or to keep the text of more than one of them safe, we can deduce a few things from the one we do have and from the fragments of others. The satyr plays kept to the format of Greek tragedies: they were written in verse, in episodes with dialogue and stories, and the episodes alternating with songs and dances. The acting was broader and more physical than in the tragedies and the padding and masks more grotesque. The stories for the plays were taken from tales of the Trojan War and Greek myths—though not current events. The jokes were rude, the humor crude, and they added to the Greek motto "Nothing in excess" with an important coda, "Nothing in excess, including moderation."

They're comic, but they're not comedies, these satyr plays. The episodes are put together like burlesque shows or musical revues with jokes about sex, food, and drink. They are in a continuum with the roots of Greek theater, the goat song in praise of Dionysus the god of theater and intoxication.

Greek comedy, something different from the satyr plays, begins, in history, with Aristophanes. He wrote maybe forty plays, eleven survive. There were writers of Greek comedies before Aristophanes, but we have only fragments of what the others wrote. What we study, then, are the works of a master among playwrights, who included his own jokes, no less crude or rude than the jokes of the satyrs about sex, food, and wine pursued in excess or thwarted in the attempt at excess. Aristophanes also included choruses who swung their rude things. In his most famous play, *Lysistrata*, the swinging chorus is made up of old men, not satyrs, and the men are drunk Athenians too old to fight in the war between the Spartans and the Athenians.

That war was in its twentieth year when *Lysistrata* was first performed in Athens in 411 BC. Aristophanes places the Spartan enemies onstage. They speak with country bumpkin accents and swing their rude things desperately, as do the Athenian men onstage. What sets up this play set during an ongoing war is that the women on both sides have called for a sex strike until both armies end the war.

Lysistrata is the outspoken Athenian woman who came up with this stratagem for peace. She has enough success convincing women throughout Greece to go along with the sex strike that their husbands, eventually, give in. The ladies from outside of Athens are strapping, big-bosomed country girls. The Athenian women are sharp and citified. When a chorus of old women seize the treasury in Athens, so that money won't be squandered on war, creaky old men come with torches hoping to chase the ladies away with smoke. The crones pour water down onto the geezers. The battle of the sexes rages until the play ends with a drunken dance. Choruses of men and women join together, smitten with the sight of a naked woman whose name is Reconciliation. Reconciliation so captivates the warring Spartans and Athenians in *Lysistrata* that both sides agree to a truce just so they can stare at Reconciliation's beauty—a nice metaphor.

The eleven texts by Aristophanes that we have follow, somewhat, the format of the tragedies: episodes with dialogue and episodes performed between the songs and dances of the chorus.

There's an occasional messenger speech. Ten of the plays resemble *Lysistrata* enough that we consider those ten a genre, which we call Old Comedy. The difference between farce and comedy is not a sharp one, but there is a test. In a comedy a character may be in pain, real pain that provokes empathy. By the play's end that feeling shadows the happy conclusion. In a farce pain evokes laughter. If we are overly empathetic to the pain of the Cyclops, the performance stops being a farce.

Sometimes the action of an Old Comedy seems to end before the play does; the design of the performance is evidently carried forward by the dance and movement, as in *Lysistrata*. The comedies are written in verse, though unlike the tragedies, the speakers in Old Comedies could have accents or make funny grammatical mistakes or have speech impediments. The chorus in Aristophanes' comedies is personified, sometimes, as animals such as frogs or birds. Sometimes two choruses are involved in dramatic action: in *Lysistrata* choruses of old men and old women fight, throw dirty things at each other, get drunk together, and cavort.

As in *Lysistrata*, Old Comedies often place current events onstage. *The Clouds* is about a school of philosophy, supposedly led by Socrates, the philosopher/teacher who was coming into his own when the play was being written and staged for the first time. During a performance of *The Clouds*, Socrates stood up in the audience, so the spectators could see how much the mask resembled his famously ugly face. One of the complaints in *The Clouds* is from a father about his son attending the onstage school in which they don't teach enough respect for Aeschylus.

In *The Frogs*, Euripides is the butt of Aristophanes' jokes. Euripides hadn't been dead a year when Aristophanes entered him into a contest with Aeschylus in the underworld. It says something about the erudition of the audience Aristophanes wrote for that he could expect his listeners to laugh at jokes quoting famous tragedies. Euripides also appears in Aristophanes' *Thesmophoriazusae*, in drag, crashing a women's festival (the title of the play) where the women heap abuse on him and quote, disapprovingly, lines from Euripides' plays. In the same play, another playwright, Agathon, is shown at home wearing a woman's silk dress in order to get into the mood to write about women. Throughout the plays of the Old Comedy, women are ridiculed, yet for all the jokes about women, they speak thoughts that criticize and undermine the male domination of Greek society.

Other comedies by Aristophanes mock what Athenians boasted about as the glories of their city state. Aristophanes' *The Birds* makes fun of Athenian democracy as chattering nonsense; *The Wasps* ridicules the sting of the Athenian legal system. In *The Acharnians*, Aristophanes put actors onstage to play contemporary famous generals as cowards. All of this criticism of the law, the army, and democracy itself, happened onstage while Athens was losing the war. It's impossible to imagine the same thing in Shakespeare's England or Molière's France where it was given as a matter of survival that a play should overtly support the status quo and the powers-that-be. As with plays by Euripides, the plays of Aristophanes are forever challenging the status quo. In his time, they were performed with the authority figures who are being called into question sitting right there in the audience laughing along. Imagine the event like a "roast" in which politicians sit as figures of fun for a laughing audience. Kings and dictators don't like to do that. Aside from challenges to power, the plays challenge dignity with loud farts, swaying erections, drunken stupors, and laughter at pretensions of purity, honesty, and bravery.

The Peloponnesian War ended in 404 BC when Athens surrendered; Aristophanes lived eighteen years after that. His last play, *Plutus*, the god of wealth (who is blind), has nothing to say about politics. Scholars call this one play, Middle Comedy, and from this one example, we can deduce a genre more interested in social and family concerns than literary or political debates. A telling detail, towards the end of what passes for a plot in *Plutus*, Hermes, the messenger god, arrives complaining that no one is

worshiping the gods anymore, there are no more animals sacri-
ficed, and so in order to survive Hermes takes a job with a good
family.

What Aristophanes wrote survived for a number of reasons,
including luck. As the centuries rolled on, his work was used as
moral instruction, literary example, held out as example of femi-
nist politics, and held out as an example of amoral opportunism.
Lysistrata stays in the repertory because a war between the sexes
and a sex strike are as human today as they were 2,500 years ago.
It's been censored for 2,500 years for the same reasons. Certain
priggish Roman critics thought what Aristophanes wrote was a
stain on Greek literature.

The Peloponnesian War exhausted the Spartans who won
and Athenians who lost. Soon after the war ended, the King of
Macedonia, a kingdom to the north, easily conquered Greece,
including Athens. There was a short revolt in Athens against
Macedonian rule, which was quickly put down. Athenian society,
no longer free, went on under light rule from the Macedonians,
but with subtle changes in Greek culture. Comedy gave up on
politics, mythology, and literary ideas to focus instead on characters from ordinary life; the chorus sang and danced between
acts rather than interrupt the action. Actors still wore masks but
there are many more characters onstage than before. The ways
in which people lead their lives in tumultuous times was, as it
sometimes can be, more interesting to an audience than what
had made the times tumultuous.

Theophrastus, a favorite student of Aristotle, made a study
of characters separately from plays. These are thirty sketches of
unpleasant people, among them the man who laughs at his own
jokes, the gossiper, the flatterer, the cheapskate and, in *Characters,
an Ancient Take on Bad Behavior,* the delightful translation made
in 2018 by Pamela Mensch, we learn of the shameless man, "who
after shortchanging someone goes back to ask him for a loan."
Each of the thirty characters is laughable—and we do laugh, of-

ten recognizing bad behavior from the third century BC endures in our own era. There is the hopeful theory that we're missing the section where Theostratus wrote about admirable characters. Probably not. Some sketches include characteristic spoken phrases. The authoritarian, who believes in the rule of the elite rather than democracy says in Mensch's version: "Mob rule is no good thing; let there be one ruler" and "The common people are ungrateful, though they receive plenty of handouts and gifts."

Theophrastus, respected as a philosopher and scientist, was chosen to lead the Lyceum, the famous Athenian school of philosophy, after Aristotle was chased out of Athens for sympathy with the Macedonians. There is a lineage to follow: Socrates (who Aristophanes mocked in *The Clouds*) taught Plato who taught Aristotle who taught Theophrastus, whose favorite student was neither philosopher nor scientist, but Menander, the master of what was called New Comedy.

Menander wrote one hundred plays. One survives intact. It has a promising title—*The Grouch*, which might be one of the characters of Theophrastus. In Greek the title of the play is *Discolous*, and a grumpy man named Knemon lives near a popular shrine to the god Pan (the goat god). Knemon hates the crowds that gather. He's stingy, nasty, and deliberately mean. His wife left him. Do you need to be told he has a beautiful daughter? Do you need to be told a passing young man falls in love with her?

Menander's plays were admired greatly in their time and for hundreds of years after by the Latin playwrights who copied them proudly and claimed his writings as the origin of their own. Menander was ranked as the greatest writer of New Comedy. Reliable sources agree Menander's dialogue was elegant, realistic, and nuanced. We know from fragments of his other plays, most of them discovered in the twentieth century, that Menander depicted other stern fathers, young lovers, and sly slaves. We're told Menander's jokes were refined, his plots delightful, but unless more scripts are found (they might be, they might), we'll never know for ourselves.

Knowing what we know of commedia dell'arte plots and stock characters, we might guess that somehow, an oral tradition of performers rehearsing or keeping plots and characters in mind, even if lines couldn't be remembered, kept continuity from Knemon to the commedia's Pantalone and on to Molière's *Misanthrope* or Shakespeare's *Comedy of Errors*.

Certain forms of theater rise up on their own in different times and places. The Japanese theater, for example, combines raucous plays called kyōgen with the austere serious Noh dramas, much as the satyr plays were performed along with Greek tragedies—and certainly without knowing about them. Dramatizing current events in early twentieth century colonial Africa came about without knowledge of the classical Greek plays, *Lysistrata*, for example, doing the same. Acting out religious stories for people who can't read religious books is what priests have done in India, medieval Europe, and we strongly suspect in Ancient Egypt.

The art of storyteller who enacts scenes and impersonates characters can be found in many cultures: the African griots, the Japanese Rakugo artists, the Indian subcontinent's koothu performers, and the Greek *mimiamboi*, from the Greek word for solo performer, *mimos*.

The mimiamboi were spoken plays in which a single actor performed all the parts, miming invisible props and scenery. Maybe there was a chair and table onstage, or a stool, rarely more. Sometimes the mimos acted out all the characters in a scene. Sometimes the mimos played only one character and evoked other invisible characters by responding to unheard words or unseen behavior that could be inferred from the onstage performer's response; for example, the manager of a whorehouse who presents damaged goods as evidence in a lawsuit says, "Come here Myrtalê, come testify—Let the court see you. Don't be bashful now." We know from ancient records that a mimos performed without a mask; maybe shawls were moved over the head, or around the shoulders, or wrapped to make a skirt, to suggest different people. Stand-up comedians do this; certain performers have made careers of this: Lily Tomlin, Whoopie Goldberg, the great American monologist Ruth Draper, and her British follower Joyce Grenfell.

The liveliest mimiamboi were written by Herondas (sometimes Herodas) of Alexandria, in Alexandria, Egypt. We think they are from the third century BC. We know about earlier mimiamboi, written during the time of Socrates, but like the plays of Menander, the earlier texts are in fragments. Seven seemingly complete texts written by Herondas were discovered in 1890 on papyrus (which gives hope that some plays by Menander might yet surface). The subject matter was so scandalous to Victorian sensibilities that it took until 1922 for them to be translated out of the Greek. They were written in old-fashioned iambs, imitating older Greek poetry, and they are the conversations of common people in the city: a mother dragging a truant schoolboy to his teacher; the owner of a bordello appears in court to protest that one of his girls has run off. Two surviving texts by Herondas connect to make a continuing story. In the first, a woman learns where another woman bought her leather dildo and in the second there's a visit to the leather shop that's been recommended. The mimiamboi of Herondas are miniature comedy sketches, each are less than a hundred words, but they are polished and witty—the portraits are precise. There's a gray-haired procuress, Gyllis, who tries to talk Metrikhé, a respectable married woman, into fooling around with a young man who paid to have his proposal passed on.

> Metrikhé, poppet, give Aphrodite
> Half a chance, one lovely sweet naughty fling.
> We get old, all of us, quite soon enough.
> You stand to gain two ways: you'll be loved,
> And the boy is rich and generous.
> Look here, think what I am doing for you
> And I'm doing it because I love you.
> (Herondas, "The Mimes of Herondas," Davenport, trans.)

The offer is hotly declined, but the old lady is just fine since she's enjoyed the wine she was offered. Here's a nice detail: the fastidious Metrikhé, asks her servant to wipe the rim of the cup clean before serving old Gyllis. Is she showing off that she's not dirty? Drunkenness, lust, and disguise in all forms of Greek comedy are the flowers of the Greek theater's roots in the worship of Dionysus, who is the god of wine and theater, and also the god of ecstasy. The word is a combination of Greek words—ek, meaning out/stasis, meaning place—going out of place, leaving this world for another, sometimes in a trance, but not always in a trance. By laughing in the audience, the ancient Greeks invoked the presence of Dionysus; by laughing they left where they were to be in the presence of god. Like Sisyphus rolling that rock, the drive to make such jokes, despite setbacks, is unstoppable.

Chapter Eight

ROMAN THEATER

Plautus (ca. 254–184 BC)
Seneca (ca. 4 BC– AD 65)
Terence (Publius Terentius Afer) (185–159 BC)

Roman political power is and was dazzling. Rome began as a small town in the south of Italy, grew to rule a kingdom, then turned into the center of a republic ruled over by a senate, until ruled by an emperor, when the city became the center of an empire that included what would become England, France, Italy, Germany—and included what had been all the city states of Greece. Classical Athens at the time of Sophocles is estimated to have had sixty thousand freeborn citizens (that is to say, free-born males); Rome, as a city, is estimated to have had a population of 1.25 million. Rome as an empire, which included what are now Germany, North Africa, Spain, and Turkey, held a population of forty-five million at the lowest estimate.

The cultural prestige of Roman theater—plays written in Latin for audiences who spoke Latin—lay like a heavy weight for centuries in the scales of critics estimating the value of plays written in Elizabeth Tudor's England, Louis XIV's France, and the Italian city-states of the Renaissance. The value of Roman theater was conflated with the greatness of Roman political power.

Even after Germanic tribes disrupted Roman domination of the Western world in 476 AD (a date now known as the fall of the Empire), Roman culture held vast influence for at least another thousand years because Latin, the language of the Empire, was the language of the Church, an empire unto itself. When theater developed in Europe enough to model plays on the tragedies and comedies of classical theater, Renaissance playwrights and critics went first to the Romans, not to the Greeks, because Greek was not so commonly read or published or translated as Latin. The Latin plays were read, if not also seen onstage, because of their use of the Latin language was exemplary in style, if not as a moral example.

The most famous theatrical events in the Roman Empire, which is not to say theater, but theatrical, were mass spectacles performed in arenas, round ones, called circuses (from the word for circle). In distinguishing circus acts from drama, Aristotle's definition is very useful: drama is the imitation of an action, not the action itself. As much as mass spectacles resemble going to the theater to see a play—in particular a crowd watching, an area set off for performance—what was going on was action itself: knife fights, animal acts, people dying or pretending to die, and animals dying, not pretending. The colossal stone arena in Rome called, yes, the Coliseum could be flooded with water and ships could engage in naval battles, but this was all spectacle, not scripted, like a horse race, which the Romans also liked to watch.

Roman plays were performed during the time of the emperors, and there were some influential Roman plays written in the first decades of the Empire, but the greatest of Roman writers wrote for the stage at the time of the Republic, well before there was an emperor or an empire. Early Republican Rome was a cosmopolitan city where merchants, sailors, ambassadors, religions, and races gathered from all over the then known world. We know there were performances of plays—but they were not official state events as they had been in Greece, which meant they weren't paid for by the state. That meant playwrights were either rich or dependent on the favor of the diverse crowd, or, if lucky, a playwright might be supported by a wealthy patron.

Plays by three ancient Roman playwrights, Terence, Plautus, and Seneca are—though rarely performed these days in their entirety—still performed in part. The works of all three are still performed in essence, sometimes with an audience reaction at odds with what the author intended. During the Middle Ages in Europe, their plays weren't performed at all, at least in public.

How did the plays survive if they weren't performed? In Europe, the texts were stored out of sight of the public for hundreds of years in the libraries of monasteries and convents. Some monks and nuns read the plays, and we know the Saxon nun Hroswitha was inspired to write Christian plays by the example of what she found in her convent library. Sometimes the manuscripts of ancient plays were stored in order to be erased. The vellum they were written on was valuable, and when there was need, plays might be washed over so that a Christian text might be transcribed there instead.

In Islamic countries, scholars read Roman plays, and the texts were privately collected for personal enjoyment. However, we have no record of their performance anywhere—not in Europe or in the Islamic world—before the Renaissance. Fourteen hundred years after the last of the great Roman playwrights died, the vast majority of Roman (and Greek) plays were missing.

Though none of the plays written by Terence are missing, he is perhaps the greatest of ancient Roman playwrights lost to us, lost for the same reason as the ancient Greek writer of comedies, Menander—specificity. Terence wrote comedies, elegant city comedies, about people, not types. Nowadays, what interests us first about Terence are the specifics of his life. To begin with, he was African—the Empire was so vast it took in the northern coast of Africa, what we now call Libya, where Publius Terentius Afer was born a slave around 185 BC. He and perhaps his mother were bought and brought to Rome by a senator from whom the boy took the name Terentius. His owner was so impressed by the boy's intelligence that he was educated and freed. He didn't live very long, thirty-five years, and in that time, he wrote six plays, all of which survive. Terence wrote his first play, a very successful one, at age nineteen. The Roman theater scene was almost as competitive as the gladiator ring, and older playwrights attacked

Terence, hurling insinuations that, as a slave, he couldn't possibly have written the plays and must have been fronting for some aristocrat. Terence had the good sense to ignore this, as we will ignore anyone who hurls the same dirt about Shakespeare.

What Terence took time to respond to is significant. He was accused of straying from Greek sources. To this he pointed out he had been faithful to Menander, took his plots and characters and, in some cases, dialogue, directly from the Greek. If he wandered from a single source, it was to combine something else written by Menander—the combinations were called *contaminations*, by the way, with no negative connotations to the word contamination. For Roman theater a connection to the ancient Greek theater was a mark of distinction. The Romans, who bought and brought oranges from Spain, silks from India, and slaves from England, also brought and bought philosophy and theater from Greece. Empires in all cultures commonly claim the prestige of an older culture. The Chinese did it, going so far as to invent dynasties earlier than the historical ones. Often prestige has to do with borrowing a language, as when, at times in history, upper-class Russians spoke French, educated Japanese spoke Chinese, and educated people throughout Europe read Latin.

The prestige of the Macedonians led by Alexander the Great relied on the Macedonian inheritance of older Ancient Greece (Alexander slept, it was said, with a copy of Homer's *Iliad* under his pillow). Rome conquered Greece in 168 BC, but even before then, Republican Romans claimed they, not the Greeks, were the inheritors of Classical Greece. Terence defended the honor of his work by saying the sources for his plays were Greek, not original.

Terence was not just translating Greek plays. His changes to Menander's work were substantial. He cut the direct address, turned the characters into more realistic portraits, refined the plots, which are too complicated to remember or summarize coherently and therefore must be read or seen onstage to be appreciated. His language was beautiful—pure is the word often used to describe it. Like Menander, Terence's writings were so culturally specific as to remain untranslatable. He was one of those writers whose work sings out in its own language or culture but falls flat in other cultures and languages. When it was considered useful to know Latin, Terence's writings were held out to students as something to admire, including in early puritanical America, though the plots of the plays often involve less than puritanical characters. There are almost always a couple of young men fooling around with courtesans, to the dismay of their stern fathers, though plot complications with silly coincidences result in happy marriages. The direct descendant in English theater is Oscar Wilde's *The Importance of Being Earnest*—and it is no accident Wilde read Latin and Greek easily and for pleasure.

Terence had the luck to be writing new work at the time when the leading comic actor in Rome, Turpio, was looking for new material. Turpio—his full name was Lucius Ambivius Turpio—became Terence's producer and performed the leading roles. The prestige of the veteran actor/producer fueled the career and reputation of the young playwright. Show business was tough in ancient Rome. At the first production of *The Mother-in-Law* by Terence, in which Turpio identifies himself by name in the prologue, the audience broke up after hearing of a nearby, more entertaining, tightrope walker. The second production of *The Mother-in-Law* also failed when the audience left to watch gladiators.

The plays written by Terence are set in Greece, the way some of Shakespeare's plays are set in Greece and Italy, so the playwright is safe, avoiding offense to living Romans, by writing about people in another country. Terence stopped writing after he turned twenty-five. Ten years later, on a trip to Greece, he died. If he wrote nothing else worth remembering, remember he wrote this:

Homo sum, humani nihil a me alienum puto
(*I am a human being, I consider nothing that is human alien to me.*)

Roman history claims that in more or less the year Terence was born, 185 or 184 BC, the great comic writer Plautus passed away. Perhaps this is not literally so, but more of a metaphor that Terence replaced Plautus in ancient Rome as the writer of comedies worth emulating and studying. Yet the work of Plautus has survived in performance well past Terence's life and well past what Terence wrote, despite what the Romans might have thought worthy of greater esteem. Plautus is one of the greatest playwrights ever, a writer whose work has outlived the world for which it was intended. The theatrical situations Plautus devised are still in use in television and movies as well as onstage.

We don't know much about the life of Plautus, and that's fine. He supported himself. He wrote over fifty plays, maybe. We have twenty intact. He wrote wild comedies stuffed with rude language, many puns, and complicated plots explained to the audience at the beginning of the play. The plots are taken from the Greeks, the plays are set in Greece, but it was understood that Rome was implied. He wrote during the Punic Wars, a great war between Rome and Carthage, but you wouldn't know much about it from the plays. Often the plots rely on mistaken identities (with twins, sometimes). The wordplay—puns, riddles, slips of the tongue, and double entendres—is memorable and often difficult to translate. There are fart jokes in plays by Plautus. The names of the characters are funny and revealing: Philocomasium is "a girl who loves a party" and it's good that she does—she's a prostitute.

Plautus was writing for the Roman crowd, whereas Terence was writing for a cultivated circle of friends. What makes Plautus funny, then and now, is his explosive relationship to the ideals of his culture, a culture that was, we would say, high-minded and paternal. Romans idealized the family led by the wise father always looking after his flock, the kind supportive mother, the well-behaved son, the virginal daughter, and the loyal servant. These are all cultural types endlessly propagandized by the powers of the country, and as with orthodoxies of all sorts, just waiting to be exploded onstage with ridicule. In plays by Plautus (and all his followers since) the father is a letch, the mother is a big-nosed shrew, the daughter is dumb as a bag of hair, and if she's a virgin it's not by choice, the son is a ne'er do well, the faithful servant is a conniver, soldiers are braggarts, teachers are fools, and the only commonsense belongs to slaves—more on that later. This comedy is different than the humor of Aristophanes where the ridicule is personal. Aristophanes is making fun of Socrates and Euripides—not playwrights in general—and particular generals or politicians, not a fictional soldier. Plautus is making fun of types: windbag teachers and hen-pecked Roman husbands, types that endure beyond specifics: the plays and their characters are recognizable and enjoyable thousands of years later, if not word for word, then in situation, type, and plot.

The relationship of father to son is at the heart of the comedies written by Plautus. The root of such a relationship might derive from Menander, but it's a root that sprouted leaves and flowers for Plautus because the father/son relationship was the basis of relationships in Rome: the paternal concern for the citizens from the Senate, the paternal concern of Rome for its colonies, and the paternal concern of men over women. Father/son as subject matter is safely apolitical too—and as long as there are fathers and sons, it's something an audience can relate to.

Aristotle didn't have much to say about comedy in the *Poetics* (we can be grateful), but what he did say is that while characters in tragedies should be superior to the audience, the characters in comedies should be inferior. In Plautus, the audience's closest relationship is with the slave who often starts the play. He (never she) is our entrance into the play, he explains things to us, and even when he lies, we side with him. Slaves are punished in plays by Plautus, beaten onstage maybe, but with the essence of a farce that their life spirit will survive no matter what happens to them.

We have so many plays by Plautus to read because a monk who was supposed to be erasing the Latin text in order to transcribe a section from the Bible got lazy. Parchment, which is made from scraped animal skin, was expensive and lasted for a long time, so a common practice in monasteries was to erase the ink on old skins in order to write down something more valuable. There's a word for it: palimpsest, scraped again—often the original writing returns over time, rising up from under the newer text. Given a long manuscript of plays by Plautus, a clever monk (inspired by what he was reading, perhaps) thought to fool whoever was watching over him by erasing the front part thoroughly and the last part, too, but leaving the middle relatively unscrubbed, so we can read nine plays by Plautus and have the first two and the last three left to us in fragments.

How were plays by Plautus performed? During his lifetime and after, Roman theaters were privately owned temporary wooden stages, put up during the *ludi* (festivals), and taken down fast since the wooden stages were flammable. From the requirements of the plays, we know the fronts of three houses were shown onstage and an open area in front of them. Clearly the scene is set in a city. Scholars try to assign meanings to the left side and the right side, but these ideas, like Aristotle's about Greek tragedy, are written after the fact as observations rather than rules observed at the time of the original performances.

What we can tell from the text is that the closer relationship with the smaller audience (who stood or sat) meant a more intimate acting style. Terence's plays, with their wordplay, would seem to necessitate an even smaller, select audience who could hear every word spoken. We don't know for sure if the actors who performed plays by Plautus always used masks, perhaps they did, perhaps they didn't. It is not clear if Plautus wrote in verse or simply stressed rhythm—his plays are the earliest surviving Latin literature, and we have nothing to compare them to. He was sophisticated enough to use Greek words as well as words from Carthage; his audience was educated enough to understand the Greek and sophisticated enough to recognize the Punic language of Carthage, even if they didn't know the meaning of every word. The tone throughout is colloquial, more like everyday speech, and for that reason not so easily read or recommended to be read as examples of good Latin, which is what accounts for Terence's survival.

It's easier today to talk about Plautus in performance by referring to the ways his work survives onstage in plays by Molière and Shakespeare where the conventions of twins, braggart soldiers, and foolish fathers flourished. Studying comedy, especially the writing of someone like Plautus, without seeing the plays in performance is like studying a bicycle without ever seeing one being ridden, much less riding one yourself.

Though no one these days shares the living Latin language of 190 BC, there is a way in English to share something of the fun that Plautus offered his ancient audience. In 1962 two Americans, Larry Gelbart and Burt Shevelove, compiled several plays by Plautus to create the book for a musical comedy called *A Funny Thing Happened on the Way to the Forum*. Buffoonish humor, flashy showgirls, and the especially witty song lyrics by Stephen Sondheim bring the spirit of the plays written by Plautus to life onstage. The formulas of the Roman comedy fit the formulas of the musical comedy well: a virgin sings, "Lovely. All I am is lovely, lovely is the one thing I do"; a braggart soldier (named Miles Gloriosus after the play by Plautus) foils a young lovers' plans.

Pseudolos, a slave who longs to be free, is at the heart of *A Funny Thing Happened on the Way to the Forum*. In talking about the show, coauthor Burt Shevelove made the point that this plotline of longing for freedom was further emphasized than in the Latin plays, "In writing the book, we selected the characters from Plautus' plays and created a plot. The only thing extremely un-Roman was making a big thing out of the slave wanting to be free. Although slaves in Roman comedies wanted to be free, it was a very casual thing." When Whoopie Goldberg played the part on Broadway, it had the resonance of an African American wanting to be free.

Interestingly, the collaborators back-ended into a Plautus device: a prologue told by the slave. Jerome Robbins, who had turned down the offer to direct the show, came to see an out-of-town preview. He advised the creative team that the audience was confused by and didn't understand what they were about to see. Stephen Sondheim worked over a weekend to create an opening number, which includes these lines:

Nothing with kings, nothing with crowns;
Bring on the lovers, liars, and clowns!
Old situations, new complications,
Nothing portentous or polite;
Tragedy tomorrow! Comedy tonight!

And if you can memorize that and sing it you will have the basics of Plautus, who wrote his words to be performed.

Seneca is the third Roman playwright whose influence and importance extend well beyond ancient Rome. Unlike Terence or Plautus, Seneca wrote his plays to be read aloud, not to be performed. There is a whole genre of this called cabinet plays (cabinet meaning room), and the feeling for many years has been that they should stay in the cabinet.

Seneca—his full name was Lucius Annaeus Seneca—was born in what's now Cordoba in Spain, which was part of the Roman Empire, too. He came from a wealthy family. His father had been a famous orator in Rome, and his mother was unusually well-educated. He went to Rome as a child to study. After a time, he lived in Egypt, which was also part of the Empire. Seneca was famous even as a young man for his speaking ability. He was involved in politics and was in and out of favor until he was brought back to Rome in 49 AD to tutor Nero. In 65 AD when Nero was emperor, he ordered his former teacher to commit suicide.

Seneca was most famous as a philosopher, a Stoic, and he taught that one met pain with dignity. Supposedly he met death with dignity, but meeting death with dignity is not clearly reflected in his tragedies, and it is hard to define his plays as aspects of his philosophy, though that hasn't stopped people from trying. All the same stories told better onstage by the Greeks are rehashed by Seneca for stage readings, among the plays: *Medea*, *Phaedra* (from *Hippolytus)*, *Agamemnon*, and *Oedipus*. His tedious moralizing was quite popular with the powers in Rome and later with other would-be empires, so Seneca was studied, copied, and his influence as a playwright grew well beyond the merits of his plays.

We have a record of Seneca's *Oedipus* being performed in England in Latin by university students in Cambridge as early as the 1550s. The first translation into English of Seneca's plays was done in 1581 by Alexander Neville in *His Tenne Tragedies*. Neville was sixteen at the time. We now consider two of the ten translations outright fakes. Seneca's writings were known to English playwrights Shakespeare, Marlowe, and Ben Jonson among others, who were searching for models with which to write plays and borrowed techniques and the structure of five acts, among other things. The earlier English playwrights hadn't bothered with such study.

Neville's introduction to the 1581 *Oedipus* includes the unintentionally hilarious: "mark thou…what is meant by the whole course of the History: and frame thy lyfe free from such mischiefes." What this could mean is curious: don't kill your father unintentionally and marry your mother by mistake? And reading Seneca's play will convince you not to gouge out your eyes or hang yourself? Because otherwise you might? It's more likely this nonsense is a formula stuck in front of the plays as means to get them past the censor. For years the Church had been attacking theater, and it was precisely those badly behaved people in the Roman drama that they were thinking about. But here, in a tragedy from a Stoic philosopher, the theater could claim protection because what the plays were displaying was "educational," and Stoicism was pagan but passable because it was in some way Christ-like to suffer. Make no mistake, what the audience enjoyed (and the authors, too, including, Shakespeare) were Seneca's cut-out tongues, his ravished virgins, the heaps of bodies onstage, the gushing blood, the ghosts, the witches, the children baked in a pie and eaten, and the ripped open womb (Seneca's thoughtful addition to *Oedipus*).

What was copied from Seneca in the theater was the crudest part of his writing, the lurid part, and in that way the Roman circus acts entered the theater by a mistake. A good deal of Seneca's reputation is based on mistakes, beginning with the misconception that what he meant to be imagined by his listeners should be seen onstage. As our age confuses what's pathetic with what's tragic, the age of Elizabeth and James in England confused awe with awful.

Not always. There have been some attempts at bringing Seneca onstage with a modern sense of awe at the cruelty of the world. The British poet Ted Hughes, who excelled at visceral imagery in his own poetry, was drawn by the violence in Seneca's *Oedipus*. Hughes called his version "a raw dream." In 1969 the National Theater of England performed it. Hughes begins:

> fear came with me
> my shadow
> into this kingdom to this throne
> and it grew
> till now it surrounds me
> fear
> I stand in it
> like a blind man in darkness
> even now

This is more potent than Seneca. The gassy tone of Seneca's original Latin is better captured by this Edwardian version by Frank Justus Miller:

> When thou dreadest some great calamity, though thou thinkst
> it cannot befall, still do thou fear. I dread all things exceed-
> ingly, and I do not trust myself unto myself.

Now, even now the fates were aiming some blow at me; for what am I to think when this pestilence, so deadly to Cadmus' race, so widespread in its destruction, spares me along?

For what evil am I reserved? Midst the ruins of my city, midst funerals to be lamented with tears ever fresh, midst the slaughter of a nation, I stand unscathed—aye! Prisoner at Phoebus' bar. Couldst thou hope that to crimes like thine a wholesome kingdom would be granted? I have made heaven pestilent...

Reputations are manufactured, by chance and sometimes deliberately. There is a painting in Spain that's an interesting example of the manufacturing of Seneca's reputation. The painting itself is by the Flemish master Rubens, who was not only one of the greatest of European artists but also a diplomat to the Court of Spain. The picture hangs in the Prado in Madrid. Remember that Seneca was born in what's now Cordoba, Spain. He is honored, therefore as the beginning of Spanish literature; though since he wrote in Latin, it's another deliberate mistake.

What's depicted in Rubens painting is Seneca killing himself in the bath. There's someone taking down dictation as it happens. The painting is based on a sculpture said to be a classical Roman sculpture of the death of Seneca. What we know now (and Rubens himself had no way of knowing) is that the sculpture was nothing of the kind. It was a sculpture of an old man found with the legs broken off. To increase its value, whoever was selling the sculpture stuck the torso onto a sculptural basin, what might have been a birdbath, and turned it into *The Death of Seneca*. So Rubens' painting is the passing on of a fake.

Removed from the apparatus of their propaganda, Seneca's plays have something to say to us today because they are texts that resonate beyond their author's intention and their own culture's understanding. We can, with good reason, study Seneca's plays for what they are, not for what they aren't. They're artifacts, and they tell us something important about Roman culture because there were no other great playwrights from Rome besides Plautus, Terence, and Seneca, that we know of, even by reputation.

Yet, to quote Terence—*I am a human being, I consider nothing that is human alien to me*—the eight plays by Seneca, have even, in their off-putting tedious formality, something compelling, but not to tears.

If Plautus lives today in sitcoms, and he does, Seneca lives too. There is a universal human urge to watch violence and cruelty—at a distance. In ancient Rome the Coliseum provided real distance with the vast spaces of the arena. As Seneca intended, violence read aloud gains distance by taking place in the imagination. In the tradition of Elizabethan translator Alexander Neville passing off horror as moral education, today we slip horror into news, into crime shows, into violent newspaper headlines, and into slasher movies. In our time, the distance between violence and spectator is achieved by laughter.

The plays of Plautus, Terence, and Seneca, to put them in chronological order, are of a different quality than Aeschylus, Sophocles, Euripides, and Aristophanes. The Romans themselves understood this, but in the history of the theater, always, what survives—and how it survives, is as much accident as it is circumstance. In sitcoms, horror films, vaudeville, Shakespeare, Molière, and musical comedy, the theater of Rome not only survives—it thrives.

Chapter Nine

ASIAN CLASSICS AND RULES

Uemura Bunrakuken (1751–1810)
Chikamatsu (1653–1725)
Zeami (1363–1443)

I n 1490 there was no such a thing as a map of the world, but let's do what actors do and begin with an "as if." If in 1490 you looked at a map of the world showing where the largest concentrations of people were living, you would see there were several civilizations, in many places, who knew little or nothing about each other. In Italy, the Middle Ages were ending, and the Renaissance was beginning. In China, the Ming Dynasty (the tenth of eleven Chinese dynasties) was reviving Chinese learning after one hundred fifty years of Mongolian domination. In Mexico, the Aztecs controlled an empire from their capital city in the middle of a flowery lake. In Peru, the Incas held an empire together over a mountain range. In Africa, the inland Islamic Empire of Mali was three hundred fifty years old and weakening. In India the Mughal Empire was just beginning.

Each of these cultures had a history, each would have a future, and each survives in some way today. Each of them spoke a different language; each enjoyed its own literature and oral traditions. In each there was a cultural pattern: what was moral, what was important, what was beautiful—the Mona Lisa, a Ming vase, Timbuktu mud architecture, the Taj Mahal.

Discussing China and Italy and India—and Japan—we may speak of classical traditions that are continuous, that reassert themselves, that have known rules: a sonnet in Italy, a *wujue* quatrain in China. The classical tradition of Europe is not the same as in China, but in the arts, the *idea* of a classic is the same: an artist's spirit may fill resonant forms passed down from generation to generation. Passion restrained to form is a recipe for dynamic tension and inherent drama that is the same for a ballet dancer, a Chinese poet, and a Japanese actor.

There are many classic Asian theaters—in China, in India, in Japan—and each holds depths enough to invite lifetime exploration, and each, even today, inspires lifetime commitment from performers, teachers, audiences, and authors. We cannot hope to experience their essence, master their details, become familiar with their literature, or pick up their techniques in a week, in a month, or in a year.

Why study them at all in the West if we must be fast and risk being glib? For one thing, because the world is knit together more closely than in 1490, and our own Western European theater has been radically influenced by Asian theater, in forgotten and surprising ways. Studying Asian theater, we draw from a wellspring of our contemporary theater in the West.

Sometimes the physical beauty of Asian theater is compelling, even if we do not understand how it was achieved. Sometimes the level of craft is jaw-dropping even if we don't share the reasons for it. Sometimes the idea itself is alive, even when we cannot share the physical form or language of the original.

And though the classic theater forms of Asia are as varied as Asia, behind all of them we can trace a tradition from artifacts that are perhaps forty thousand years old—the tradition of the shaman.

The word shaman is from a 1692 description of a Siberian healer by Nicolaes Witsen, a Dutch explorer, who picked up and passed on the Siberian word. The Chinese claim it was first a Chinese word, there's a Sanskrit equivalent that some Indians claim, and Buddhists can trace it back to Pali, the sacred language of Northern India.

Witsen included an unforgettable illustration of a bearded man with antlers strapped to his head, beating a drum. In the engraving two dogs howl beside the shaman, whose legs are spread, and whose taloned feet resemble the devil's feet in medieval woodcuts. That's intentional. The Dutchman describes the shaman as the devil's priest who has the power to heal because he summons dark powers, inherently devilish powers according to Christian definitions. Unknown to Witsen, the figure in the engraving might be a woman with a beard. Shamans are often ambivalent in their sexual identity, bridging the spiritual world of men and women, just as they bridge the world of the living and the dead.

We find it useful nowadays to use the term shaman—less sensationally than to mean a devil's priest—for people who perform certain work in a tribe, in among many other places, Brazil, Australia, or Central Asia. The antlers are optional, the feet fiction, and that a shaman heals is possible, but what makes a shaman a shaman is their work as a messenger.

Shamans have an explicit job in a tribe, which is to travel to the otherworld, the world of spirits, including the spirits of the dead. Then shamans return to the tribe and report what they have witnessed. The words shamans use to tell their stories evoke the vision and experience for others in the tribe, allowing the listeners to visit the otherworld as they envision it for themselves.

Each aspect of this has its form and ritual. The journey to the otherworld is enacted symbolically. A shaman may climb a ladder, climb a tree, eat a mushroom, spin in a circle, or sniff gases that come out of the earth. These ceremonies are meant to achieve ecstasy (literally the removal of the soul from the body). The trip across to the other side is accompanied by a drumbeat, usually beaten by the shaman himself or herself. A trance is achieved as the body is suspended—the soul is free, in flight. Sometimes the spirit is thought to ride on the back of a goose, or on a reindeer that can gallop to heaven—which may be the explanation for the antlers in the engraving. Coming down the ladder or out of a trance, the shaman returns and relates the vision he or she has seen on the other side.

Questions from the tribe sometimes elicit a shaman's vision. Sometimes the vision is passed on in song or chanted rhythmically, sometimes (but rarely) the words are written down. The shaman's recitation, after the return to the tribe, is never private; it always has an audience, for its purpose is to communicate a vision, not just pass on words.

Shamans still perform in Buryatia (the Eastern side of Lake Baikal), in Mongolia, in Central Asia, in Northern Japan, and among Native American tribes. Shamans were also part of ancient Scandinavian, Celtic, and Germanic religions. We recognize shamanic rituals in Asian religious ceremonies, in Asian dance, and in Asian plays.

Though China boasts the oldest continuous historical culture in Asia, theater did not begin to develop a literary tradition in China until the period of the Mongolian invasion. There were, for sure, Chinese jugglers, acrobats, singers, musicians, and bards who told stories, but there is no evidence yet of any ancient Chinese troupes of actors who performed plays with a text. In Japan, the islands off the coast of China, Asian theater first developed an enduring literary form: the plays of the Noh drama.

The word Noh means the theater of skill. Noh is a theater of dance and music, as well as of the spoken word. Noh has a purpose, which is to create a communion of feeling between the audience and the performer: the feeling of yūgen (pronounced with a hard "G" as in yogurt). Yūgen is still beauty, still in the sense of motionless, calm, serene, at rest. As Aristotle laid out rules for Greek drama with catharsis as the aim of tragedy, a Japanese actor named Zeami (1363–1443) set out rules for Noh with yūgen as its goal. Aristotle wrote about Greek theater as a scientist would write, describing what he observed others had done and deriving rules from what he observed. Zeami wrote as a creative artist devising images to evoke and share what he knew to do. Yūgen, he wrote, is a white bird with a flower in its beak. Yūgen is "snow in a silver bowl."

Zeami was brought up as a child in the theater by his father, the actor/author Kan'ami (1333–84). At twelve Zeami caught the fancy of the eighteen-year-old shogun Ashikaga Yoshimitsu (shoguns, not emperors, ruled Japan at this time) who supported the boy's training. When he was eighteen, Zeami's father died. As Zeami matured, he wrote down what he had learned from his father and what he had discovered for himself about the goals of Noh performance and the method of Noh training. As Aristotle had defined Greek tragedy, Zeami defined the terms with which to discuss Noh. In addition, Zeami wrote the plays that are standards of excellence in the repertory of Noh dramas.

The texts Zeami wrote follow the form he received from his father who was himself following a form at least a hundred years old. The dates of the plays in the Noh repertory span seven centuries; plays considered classic Noh entered the repertory as late as the 1890s and new Noh plays are still being written. All of the texts are in verse. The performers recite a poetic language, not the vocabulary or rhythm of everyday speech. There are several types of plays with similar structures in which someone who is on a journey, meets someone, who, in a dream, is revealed to be a demon or ghost. Often the ghost or demon dances on a runway, stage right, that juts out into the audience. The ceremonies of the shaman are obvious: the drum, the runway as a horizontal ladder, and the report to the audience from the world of the dead.

The plays are short, three or as many as five make up a program with satiric plays, *kyōgen,* performed in between, not unlike the Greek programs of tragedies with a satyr play.

All characters in the Noh wear subtly asymmetrical masks, which cover the whole face and indicate, to those in the know, certain types or stock characters: old man, young man, young woman, old woman. All movement onstage is formalized, as in a ritual. Walks, in particular, are stylized rather than realistic. Sliding their feet along the floor gives the illusion the performers are gliding, as if floating in a dream. Actors, traditionally, were born into the trade of Noh and, like Zeami, learned their craft—including lines and onstage moves—from their elders. Traditionally, troupes did not include women. This is no longer so.

Live music—a traditional ensemble of three drums and flute—accompanies the performance. The stage is square, made of cypress wood, elevated slightly, and resonant, so when the actors stomp on it, the stage becomes another percussion instrument. The musicians play stage right, in sight of the audience. Sometimes there is a chorus that chants.

The wooden buildings traditionally built for Noh sat 300, but in modern times theaters grew larger. The only scenery in Noh plays is a back painting of three pine trees that is used for every performance of every play. The pine, a tree that's still green in the dead winter, has meaning for these plays in which ghosts dance and chant. The plays are always set in actual Japanese locations. Costumes, which are magnificently embroidered, establish season, place, and period. There are very few stage properties, but when present they are brought onto the stage by masked or veiled stagehands.

Performances are traditionally during the day, so there are no lighting effects.

The Noh requires knowledge to appreciate it; it is an art for connoisseurs. Yet the music, and in particular the rhythm of the three drums, unites those at a Noh performance, onstage and off, including newcomers. The eerie glide of the actors, the piercing austerity of the masks, the drone of the poetry are all compelling whether you share the culture of Noh or understand the language of the performance. Case in point: by the second half of the nineteenth century, when the Japanese concerned themselves with the prestige given to their culture in the outside world, the aristocrats who supported the Noh—and had been doing so for 500 years—were near to deciding they would end their patronage of this archaic art form. What place could Noh have in a modernizing Japan? Yet, in 1879 as an example of

the nation's artistic heritage, a powerful Japanese Minister offered a special Noh performance as a treat for an honored guest
from America: Ulysses S. Grant. Yes, the former general of the
Union troops during the Civil War. By 1879 he was a former
U.S. President on a goodwill tour. After the Noh performance,
he and his wife were visibly moved. When told this might be
the last of its kind, they insisted strongly that the tradition must
be maintained. It has been.

The classic form serves as a vehicle for new attempts in
search of yūgen. In the twentieth century, the Japanese visionary
author Yukio Mishima wrote "modern Noh plays" by translating traditional Noh practice and theory into twentieth century
circumstance, setting his modern Noh in a high-rise office building, a hospital, and a city park. The Irish poet William Butler
Yeats, trying to find a model for a Western poetic drama, also
wrote Noh-inspired plays. In America there is the twenty-first
century's Theatre Nohgaku's *Blue Moon Over Memphis* about the
death of Elvis Presley, and Nohgahku's majestic *Gettysburg*, an
English-language Noh play set during the American Civil War.

"There is an end to our life," wrote Zeami, "there is no end
to Noh."

Kabuki, chronologically the second of great Japanese theater
forms, began around 1600, several hundred years after the Noh.
It was performed for crowds in large theaters and still is. Kabuki
uses sensational effects in lighting, scenery, costumes. Scenery is
detailed and realistic and can have several levels. Staging Kabuki
often includes the use of trapdoors and elevators, so actors may
enter up out of the floor or disappear quickly by dropping suddenly out of sight. As in Noh, there is a runway called the hanamichi
(meaning the flower path) by which the actors can enter more
closely into the audience's awareness, like a film close-up. Traditionally, Noh is for the court; Kabuki is for farmers. Kabuki performances ran all day, so a meal was served. Kabuki audiences are
lively, talk back, and call out the names and schools of the actors.

The actors address the audience directly. The texts, at first, were not so much literary as they were vehicles for the actors to show off. The spoken Japanese is sometimes dated, but it does not contain the stiff formality of the Noh. Plays that imitate the language and forms of traditional Kabuki continue to be written, adjusting to the demands of the public. During Japan's war-mongering 1930s and '40s, there were propaganda-spewing Kabuki performances with tanks onstage and scenes inside submarines.

As in the Noh, a Kabuki performer is born into the trade and roles are passed down, including words and gestures. The actor's faces are painted so expressions may be seen at a distance and to establish types. Masks are not used in Kabuki.

A Kabuki actor's stage name is followed by a numeral, as a king's would be. Danjuro Ichikawa XII, for example, who took his title in 1985, is the descendant of Danjuro Ichikawa I (1660–1704). Names are passed on in a ceremony conducted onstage in front of an audience.

In performance, Kabuki poses are held so the audience may appreciate them—the pictures of cross-eyed Kabuki actors depict performers holding a pose at the climactic moment of a play. It's called a *mie* (meaning display), and sometimes the audience shouts out the name of the school that keeps the form of the *mie* intact over centuries. Dance is also part of the performance with different styles, rhythms, and speeds. There is always music played to accompany the scenes. The musicians sit behind a screen, sometimes in seats below the stage.

Splendid costumes are part of the tradition of the Kabuki, though not all plays require them. Rapid costume changes are very much part of the spectacle, such as the transformation of a woman into a bird or a beggar into a demon. Props and costume changes are accomplished with the help of onstage stagehands, though sometimes they cringe and crawl so that they are, practically speaking, unseen by the audience.

Again, women are not traditionally performers, and female impersonators, called *onnagatas*, have great reputations in the history of the Kabuki. There is a story here: Kabuki actually began with a woman, Okuni (1572–?), a dancer and attendant who put together a troupe of women who performed parodies of Buddhist prayers. This was too lewd to last for long and the government banned women from performing in 1629. Boys were banned in 1652. Since then, it's all men. Those who specialized in women's roles were often the most popular and respected of performers because they had given their lives to their art. Traditionally onnagata live as women offstage and on.

Unlike the Noh which took its stories from legend and religion, Kabuki took its stories from contemporary events, including sensational crimes and scandals. The great Kabuki playwright Chikamatsu (1653–1725) wrote a hundred plays, many of them for puppets. Chikamatsu's plots come from historical romance and also from current events, the bloodier the better. Double suicides in which lovers kill themselves, as in *Romeo and Juliet*, made a sensation. Chikamatsu wrote two plays with double suicides, which are among his most famous and popular. As in the theater of Western Europe during the Middle Ages, in order for the Japanese government to approve anything for performance the plays had to provide moral instruction: reward the good and punish the wicked.

For all the exuberance and abandon of the Kabuki—actors stamp, grunt, shout, cry out, run, fight with swords—to perform it requires restraining such passion enough to pour it into traditional forms of words and movements with precision, and so Kabuki may be considered classic. There are moments of serene beauty in Kabuki performance, especially in the work of the onnagata. During a fixed stance, where an actor, crossing his eyes, visibly vibrates with energy, the power of the shaman's trance is undeniable.

Bunraku is the great Japanese puppet tradition. Bunraku derives from the name of a troupe organized by Uemura Bunrakuken (1751–1810), though performances with dolls and storytellers date back centuries before then in both Japan and in China.

In legend, which resembles gossip, Bunraku began when a shogun's son ran off with an actor. To make sure that never happened again, all live performers were banned. Maybe. The puppets are two to four feet tall and manipulated in sight of the audience by teams of three. The performers are dressed in black and masked or veiled. Sometimes the head puppeteer's face is uncovered. Unlike the Kabuki or the Noh, the performers of the Bunraku choose their profession. The dedication to training is staggering: a person who operates the feet and the body studies ten years before being allowed to perform in public; a person who works the torso and left hand studies another ten years; a head puppeteer studies yet another ten years to work the head and right hand. By the way, the female puppets in the Bunraku traditionally have no feet; the puppeteer responsible for the feet is adept at manipulating the doll-sized kimonos.

The Bunraku puppets have detachable heads, so they can play many roles. The heads can have moving lips and eyebrows. The puppet's hair is very important. Human hair is fashioned into small wigs that identify a role's age, sex, and social class. The costumes are elaborate. The puppets, each with its team of three handlers, are capable of delicate and detailed behavior. Bunraku puppets can play musical instruments, climb ladders, and, more importantly, move audiences to tears performing serious literature written for puppets, not people.

The text is spoken by a storyteller, not by any of the puppeteers. The storyteller voices all the roles. In a play with more than one act, there can be a different storyteller for each act. There is a rotating platform stage left by which the storyteller enters, seated with musicians who are usually playing a three-stringed instrument called a samisen. The plays are like the plays from the Kabuki repertory; in fact, they are the Kabuki repertory since some plays were written first for puppets. Before a Bunraku performance begins, the chanter holds up the text and bows to it with a promise to be faithful.

In performance, Bunraku puppets seem to float. Many people are onstage, several teams of three for each puppet, to the side the narrator speaks, musicians play and yet the focus for the audience is on what the puppets do, not on any of the handlers or the narrator or the accompanists. All in a Bunraku ensemble share a vision that is passed on to the audience so that an object made of wood and metal and human hair seems to acquire a soul: the definition of magic, I'd say.

Chapter Ten

CHINA—THE PEAR GARDEN AND THE RED PEAR GARDEN

Chiang Ch'ing (Jiang Qing) (1914–1991)
Mei Lanfang (1894–1961)

T he Pear Garden, the first Chinese school for acting, was founded and funded in the Tang Dynasty (618–907 AD) by the Emperor Ming Huang. Since that time, actors in China, who typically begin training early in life, are traditionally called the Children of the Pear Garden. Despite the historic records of training, no theatrical text seems to have been thought significant enough to write down in ancient China, and none survives—except three slight plays from the Sung (960–1279 AD), the dynasty that followed the Tang. More polished plays were written and survive from the Mongolian Yuan Dynasty, perhaps because there was a Mongolian tradition of danced dramas or perhaps because drama was a relatively new form with which Yuan Dynasty writers might make their mark on Chinese literature.

The variety of Chinese theater over the centuries is overwhelming to imagine. It's claimed that three hundred different forms are still in practice today. As China changed over the centuries, so did its plays. The language, styles of presentation, and the reason for performance have all undergone a metamorphosis and continue to shape shift. Even so, we may draw generalizations about the Chinese traditional theater in the way that

Aristotle drew generalizations about the classical Greek theater, not so much rules that theater artists worked from, but what was commonly understood among audiences and artists and passed on for generations.

In the first decades of the twentieth century, Chinese theater had a wide impact on the West, often in subtle and unacknowledged ways. In Germany, the basis for Brecht's theory of modern acting can be traced directly to Chinese formal stage gestures and to the Chinese theater's mix of storytelling with enactment. The Chinese shadow puppet theater's migration to France began the vocabulary of movies. The great monologue artist Ruth Draper reinvented the ancient form of the Greek mimes, although knew nothing about them. She was inspired by a performance she saw on Broadway in 1912 of a Chinese-style play called *The Yellow Jacket*.

Asian drama has loose borders between dance, theater, and song. Let's agree to call Asian drama the performance arts of Asia that involve some kind of narrative. Let's further agree to call certain Asian theater traditions "opera" because they fall into the Western genre of impersonating a character while singing. In the West, the most famous Chinese theater is Beijing Opera (the word Beijing means "Northern Capital") which is performed in the Mandarin language. Cantonese Opera is, of course, performed in the Cantonese language of southern China. Beijing Opera is relatively new: it began in the 1790s, flourished in the 1850s, and reached a Silver Age in the 1920s. The roots of any Chinese opera, though, are much older than either Beijing or Cantonese Opera. The plots derived at first from the tales of ancient storytellers who recited or improvised long poems relaying historic events, poems with characters based on real people, including generals, emperors, courtesans, and Buddhist monks. There are plays based on romantic novels that date to at least the eighteenth century that feature the sorrows and pleasures of fictional romantic lovers as sentimental and troubled by their parents as in any other place and time. One genre of plays based on a classic Chinese novel *The Water Margin* features gangs of thieves, not unlike Robin Hood and his Merry Men. There is also a genre of animal plays based on the great Buddhist parable "Journey to the West" in which the Monkey King is the leading role.

Despite various genres and sources—novels, history, parables—written for the many languages spoken in China, Chinese audiences and artists share some common assumptions about what makes proper theater. Most importantly, whatever their origins in real life or fiction, characters onstage are stock figures dressed so that their type may be immediately recognized by the audience, as in the commedia dell'arte. The color of a costume (yellow for the emperor, for example) or the shape of a hat or a hand prop (a sword for a warrior) lets the audience know who has entered and what to expect from them. "Better ragged clothes, than the wrong costume" is a maxim of traditional Chinese acting. Masks are not used, though there is heavy mask-like makeup. Performances are accompanied at heightened moments by the steady beat of a drum punctuated by the clash of cymbals. The drumbeat is an overt connection to the shamanic rituals that underscore all Asian theater. The origins of Chinese theater in the enactments of a bard relaying history relates to a shaman's work, too, for a bard, telling stories and impersonating characters in them conjures the otherworld of the past, the world of the dead. In performance, traditional Chinese theater is an unreal otherworld set off by its conventions and types from the world of the audience. Understanding such a performance requires an audience initiated into the mysteries of its conventions. As in any other classic art, how the action is performed intrigues the audience; the plot is not very suspenseful since the conclusion of the action is already known.

The actors in traditional Chinese theater learn a vocabulary of symbolic movements. There are grand acrobatic techniques, martial arts moves for battles, gentle dances, as well as intimate psychological gestures. A cultured audience can be expected to be as familiar with the stage conventions as they are with the stories.

Stage conventions that an appreciative audience for Chinese opera would understand include:

- Walking in a circle symbolizes a journey.
- Circling the stage with a whip in hand is understood to mean an actor is riding a horse.
- When an actor holds an oar, a boat is implied.
- Four flags symbolize an army—sometimes these are part of a general's costume.
- A black flag flashed over the stage indicates a storm.
- A light blue flag indicates a breeze.

A single table and a chair are arranged by the stage manager, in sight of the audience, to indicate major scenic pieces: a mountain, a city wall, among other possible places. Sometimes the table is understood to indicate a bed. Sometimes there is a second chair.

In the Chinese opera traditional types of male roles include those who fight, those who study (or hand down the law), and those who make love. Female roles include faithful middle-aged women, women of any age who flirt, and women warriors. There are also male and female clown characters, the only characters who improvise. Elaborately painted characters, including generals and beautiful women, often have supernatural powers.

Chinese actors traditionally trained for seven years during childhood and then specialized in a particular type for the rest of their lives. As in the Japanese theater, there are men who specialize in playing women, though the Chinese actors do not live off-stage as women. Women perform in Chinese theater, and there are sometimes separate troupes of women. The earliest schools for acting in China, including the Pear Garden, were primarily for women.

In the eighteenth century, rich families maintained their own acting ensembles of servants or slaves (this was also true for a time in Russia), and these troupes would tour. Often scenes from operas would be performed rather than the entire text—for

Chinese theater connoisseurs already knew the whole play and could infer the whole from the part performed. In the eighteenth century the Chinese novel *Dream of Red Mansions* which depicts the splendor and decline of the Wang family, the grandmother of the Wangs has a passion for a theater. She assembles a troupe of young ladies to train, rehearse, and perform (at family birthdays), and chooses what they'll perform based on the auspicious title of the scene (usually having to do with longevity). When the Wang family falls on hard times, the acting troupe is dispersed, the girls sent to convents or given jobs as maids. As in Europe, independent Chinese acting troupes that toured held no reputable social status. To save money, independent troupes would practice in teahouses where, for a fee, they would allow people to watch rehearsals. In time these open rehearsals became popular and were essentially performances.

Training was strict: diction, acrobatics, memorization, singing, and dance were part of an actor's schooling. These continued into the twentieth century. As China changed from an empire to a republic and then a communist state, the opera changed, too, though it retained its conventions: stock characters, symbolic movements, symbolic costumes and props, and a limited vocabulary of scenic elements. All of these production elements in the service of song and dance combined with spoken dialogue.

One of the most influential performers in world theater was the great Chinese opera female impersonator, Mei Lanfang (1894–1961). His appearances in the West inspired and transformed modern acting. In 1932, at his first performance in Moscow, in front of the greatest Russian theater visionaries, Stanislavsky and Meyerhold, Mei Lanfang had the wit to perform out of makeup, wearing a tuxedo. Also in the audience were two visionary German directors, Bertolt Brecht and his teacher Erwin Piscator, both in exile from Berlin while Hitler was rising to power.

Bertolt Brecht, who would go on to establish a serious challenge to Aristotle's theoretical dominance of Western criticism, first used the famously Brechtian word *alienate* to describe acting after seeing Mei Lanfang. We think Brecht picked up the word from his Russian translator. The concept is to take something out of context—as Andy Warhol did when he silk-screened a soup-can label and framed the image, so it was art, no longer advertising. With alienation, what is customarily familiar is made strange, so what may have been overlooked is, when alienated, viewed with renewed interest and with new significance. What thrilled Brecht when he saw Mei Lanfang in Moscow was the Chinese actor's alienation of realistic behavior, something he (and Piscator and Meyerhold) recognized and studied in the texts of the Ancient Greek and Elizabethan theater but had never seen onstage in a performance. Watching Mei Lanfang, Brecht realized that because of the way in which the Chinese actor mixed narrative, singing, and realistic acting, the details of realistic acting were isolated from a realistic context—behavior was no longer reduced to a symptom of personality, but elevated onstage to achieve artistic, societal, and political meanings. To use Brecht's term, stage behavior was alienated, and this became Brecht's model for a modern theater.

> The Chinese artist's performance often strikes the Western actor as cold. That does not mean that the Chinese theatre rejects all representation of feeling. The performer portrays incidents of utmost passion, but without his delivery becoming heated. At those points where the character portrayed is deeply excited the performer takes a lock of hair between his lips and chews it. But this is like a ritual, there is nothing eruptive about it. (Brecht, "Alienation Effects in Chinese Acting," John Willett, trans.)

In the twentieth century, a revolution in China overthrew, in theory, the dynastic system that had organized Chinese life for three thousand years. After a brief period as a republic, a communist state was established in 1949 under the leadership of Mao Tse-tung, who was the chairman of the Chinese Communist

Party. As in Russia after its Communist Revolution forty years before, the Chinese Communists, intent on replacing a feudal society, borrowed the prestigious, often foreign, cultural forms that indicated modernity. Chinese plays, in the style of Western drama, copied from Chekhov and Ibsen, took the stage in China, as did classical ballet, copied from Russia's classical ballet. At the same time, as the Chinese Empire fell apart, in a great diaspora, Chinese merchants spread out into the world and Chinese immigrant communities, homesick and wanting to maintain their culture overseas, paid for touring productions of Cantonese Opera—since, for a time, the majority of overseas Chinese spoke Cantonese, not Mandarin.

It was recognized throughout communist Asia—in Russia and China, both—that theater was a way to establish modern, as well as European, models of behavior. In the 1920s troupes of actors toured the Soviet Union's Central Asian republics, challenging traditional authority by displaying modern ways of living and modern role models. It's said the first time a woman spoke back to a man in Central Asian Uzbekistan was onstage. As in Soviet Central Asia, the rulers of Communist China understood the power of the stage to reinforce changing behavior and identity in the interests of the state. There is a long history of this in China where the plays of the feudal Chinese empire, no matter what dynasty, served the same purpose as the religious plays of the feudal Middle Ages in Europe—to indoctrinate obedience to authority. The traditional Chinese theater upheld moral principles as they were defined around the year 500 BC by Confucius. In traditional Chinese theater, priests are respected figures and obedience to the social order is implicit. Onstage, as offstage, duty to family was taught and the virtue of obedience—son to father, soldier to general—culminated in obedience to the state in the form of the emperor.

Theater in China, because of its potential for popular appeal, was an obvious vehicle for the Communist rulers to display new ways of thinking and to educate the masses rather than entertain elite connoisseurs. In 1967, in an effort to undo two thousand years of habitual thinking, Mao set off what was called The Great Cultural Revolution, aligning all the arts with the aims of the Communist state. During the Cultural Revolution, displays of social change and model behavior turned violent. Great actors were humiliated in stadiums; costumes, masks, and scenery were burned in public. The traditional form of Chinese drama was still performed, though fundamentally altered, demonstrating again, that theater at all times and places serves those who pay for it.

Mao Tse-tung had a wife, his third, named Chiang Ch'ing. She had been a film and stage actress, with no great success. In 1964, at the age of fifty, she took over the reformation of the traditional Chinese opera. Traditional operas were banned, replaced by new texts written by Chiang Ch'ing with the help of committees. The traditional stories and moral instructions were turned upside down so that Buddhist priests, for example, previously honored, were revealed to be fools. The common man, not priests, provided wisdom onstage. In the new texts there were still stock characters instantly recognizable to the audience, but in keeping with communist theory, they were identified by their class background: peasant, soldier, factory worker, landlord, store owner, and priest. The morality of character types, good or bad, according to Confucius were now types identified as good or bad according to Mao Tse-tung's Marxist ideology. John Dietrich Mitchell, in his collection of the popular plays *The White Snake*, *The Wild Boar Forest*, and *Taking Tiger Mountain by Strategy* (the latter based on a real incident from the 1946 civil war establishing a communist state) has wittily called these plays, the specifics of their staging, and his anthology of texts, *The Red Pear Garden*.

Some conventions of the Red Pear Garden:

- Good characters pose heroically in the middle of the stage.
- Good characters are associated with the color red, the symbol of the Communist Party.

- Good characters are lit with pink spotlights.
- Bad characters pose grotesquely.
- Bad characters are lit with a blue spotlight, a color associated with evil in the traditional opera.
- Guns and rifles replace swords in the martial arts sequences.
- Chinese-style music is fortified with Western-style music (Chiang Ch'ing thought Western-style was more heroic).

Many stage conventions were kept from the traditional opera, heightened by leaps and military moves inspired by the vocabulary of Soviet Russian ballet. As was so traditionally, single scenes could be performed, and the rest of the opera inferred.

Chiang Ch'ing passed from power, yet the revolutionary operas have kept their appeal for different reasons than intended. To an aging generation who grew up listening to these operas onstage or on the radio, these are the songs of their youth. To such listeners the music is nostalgic—sentimental, not political. To the younger generation the songs are enjoyable as kitsch, and there is revolutionary karaoke in Red China now.

The movie, *Farewell My Concubine* (1993), directed by Chen Kaige, is an excellent introduction to the rigors and glories of the traditional Chinese theater and what happened to it in modern times. We follow two men for fifty-three years. Zhang Fengyi plays Xiaolou and Leslie Cheung plays Douzi. We meet them as boys who form a close bond in a Beijing opera school where the methods of instruction include heavy beatings. Over time the two earn favor with their teacher and with the eunuch who pays for the school and its performing ensemble. As young adults the students become stars and acting partners. Xiaolou (Fengyi) specializes in red-faced heroic generals, Douzi (Cheung) is acclaimed for playing beautiful women. They are valued so highly as Chinese cultural icons that, as trophies of war, they are ordered to perform for the Japanese who invade China in the 1930s. During the Cultural Revolution of the 1960s their artistry and their personal lives are declared counterrevolutionary. They are forced to put on their costumes and makeup and made to kneel in the streets to be humiliated by passersby eager to demonstrate revolutionary fervor. Throughout it all they are dedicated to their art. There is a scene where the young Douzi, who has run away from school, is so struck with wonder and admiration at an opera performance at a tea house that he knowingly returns to the pain of learning his craft. The older Douzi completes Fengyi's eyebrows when those who would mock them on the street roughly paint Fengyi's face like a clown's.

The Chinese authorities did not approve of the depiction of the Cultural Revolution in the film and thought even the hint of a love story between the men, though unrequited, offensive. Despite sold-out shows in Shanghai, the run of the film was shut down after two weeks. Foreign acclaim for the film and China's wish to host the 2008 Olympics, which was being considered at the time by the Olympic Committee, led to the ban being lifted. In China, the film is still only available with severe cuts.

In Hong Kong, where Great Britain forcibly established an island colony in 1842 off the coast of Southern China, Chinese opera escaped the reformations of Mao's wife. Even after the British relinquished their colony and "returned" Hong Kong to China in 1995, Hong Kong remains as a political entity separate from the mainland. Significantly, in Hong Kong, Cantonese is the language spoken by most people, rather than on the mainland where Mandarin is most common. Cantonese Opera, performed under British rule, continued unchanged by Marxist ideology and continues to flourish. The Hong Kong Academy of the Performing Arts, based on English conservatory training, offers a degree in Cantonese Opera, and theaters have been built as venues for performances. All of this is to preserve Hong Kong's cultural identity, separately from the mainland.

Wherever a Chinese language is spoken, there are other significant forms of traditional theater, among them the art of shadow puppets. Shadow puppets accompanied storytelling bards, and as in the Middle Ages in Europe, shadow puppet performances of Buddhist parables were a way to share a common culture with people who had not been taught to read or write. Shadow theater in China has a legendary origin: an emperor, distracted by mourning for his dead wife, returned to his duties after a clever prime minister cast her shadow upon a screen. Her silhouette convinced the emperor that his wife had come to life, enough for him to experience her presence. This reincarnation, a revelation of the other world of shadows, is said to have happened in about 100 BC during the Han dynasty. We can also choose to believe that Central Asian traveling entertainers brought shadow puppets to China, along with sword-swallowing, juggling, acrobatics, and fire-swallowing. Significantly, shadow puppets are not part of the Japanese or Korean traditions but can be seen in a highly developed form in Turkey and the parts of Western Asia settled by the Turkic-speaking tribes known to the ancient Chinese.

Seemingly one of the crudest of theater forms, shadow theater was to be the most influential. Shadow theater in the West, especially in France, began the vocabulary of film, a sequence of images created by projecting light onto a screen. French missionaries brought Chinese puppet plays to eighteenth century France with *ombres chinoises* (Chinese shadows) performances. The rawness of shadow puppets attracted artists in the 1890s, and in Paris—at the avant-garde Montmartre night club, *Le Chat Noir*—the painter Henri Rivière (1864–1951) presented shadow shows with a team of assistants, including elaborate color effects achieved with gaslight. The animation of these shadows led to "motion pictures" and to concepts in modern cinematography: the idea of framing, the sequence of frames, the movement from frame to frame, and the changes within a frame.

Traditional forms of Asian theater in China, in Japan, and in India, too, have been defined by the use of specific languages and the specifics of a cultural heritage shared by audiences and artists. By parallel routes, and despite differences in languages and cultural heritage, Western performances have arrived at their own versions of classical Asian theater techniques and concepts. The stage directions for Thornton Wilder's American 1938 classic, *Our Town*, are more than a little like the techniques of Chinese opera. Prompted by modern auteur directors' sincere desire to study and implement theater techniques that might reach to any audience, productions such as Ariane Mnouchkine's Kathakali *Oresteia*, or Lee Breuer's Bunraku adaptation of *Peter Pan*, are ways the classic theaters of Asia morph, grow, and endure. The Red Pear Garden is another way traditional Asian theater transformed to answer the demands of a time and place, a model for how all theaters, East or West, proceed if not progress.

NEOCLASSIC THEATER AND WHY THERE IS SUCH A THING

John Dryden (1631–1700)
Johann Wolfgang von Goethe (1749–1832)
Jean Racine (1639–1699)

Neoclassic is an adjective. Neo—as in new, or in this case, recent or revived. Classic? Means something timeless in its excellence? Sometimes. The idea of classical art is that form is to be inhabited, not invented. Forms that go back to Classical Greece and Rome are classic? Sure. China and India have different sets of forms that can also be called classic, and the principle is the same: the job of an artist requires working within the rules of form.

Within the European tradition, which extends to the Europeanized Americas, Neoclassic and the term Neoclassicism means looking to Greek and Latin models in literature, a revival of Greek and Latin forms in architecture and sculpture, adherence to what are supposed to be Greek and Latin rules in the theater, and inspiration in other arts—dance and music among them—based on what were (and sometimes still are) considered to be the ideals of classic Rome and Greece.

Neoclassicism is different than the Renaissance in Europe, which, for better or worse, was more intent upon following up on the seeking spirit of Greece and the conquering spirit of Rome. Neoclassicism has to do with following, not following up, and

obeying a set of rules with the belief that Classical Greek and
Roman culture held values that will endure for all time—harmony, balance, and restraint—and that such values were encased
in ageless forms from Greece and Rome, which derive from the
ruins and artifacts of those cultures, ancient forms artists at any
time might occupy.

Why? What's the attraction?

There will always be some who say that the qualities of harmony, balance, and restraint are timelessly human and timelessly
attractive. Those qualities are certainly an aspect, but not exclu-
sively the essence, of ancient Greece or Rome. A strong argument can be made that what later ages call Classical culture was a
dynamic process of confrontation rather than balance. It doesn't
matter. There's something else in Neoclassicism that's enticing,
and it's not aesthetic.

The attraction is to the signs of power. The forms themselves—white columns, Roman arches, for example—have cultural associations with power. That the forms are restrained is
also an association with power. When self-control is projected
(which is something entirely different from having self-control),
it's a sign of control over others. The reason that buildings in
Washington, D.C., or St. Petersburg, Russia, have Greek columns is that America styled itself in the eighteenth century as
the modern Athens and built public symbols to that ideal. The
Russians, eager to demonstrate their connection to the greatness of European civilization (and not the supposedly barbaric
Mongolians, who had ruled Russia for one hundred fifty years)
wanted to demonstrate their connection to the Roman Empire
and Greek ideals, too.

In France, Germany, and Great Britain there were similar
ambitions to realize an empire on the scale of the Romans, and
like the Romans, the French, the Germans, the English, and
the Russians founded the art of their empires—sculptures and
portraits with sandals and togas, for example—on earlier Greek
models. Plays, too.

Based on a collection of ideas put together after the fact, derived from ruins, or copied from what survived intact out of lasting materials like bronze and stone, a sense of Neoclassic "good taste" was established that could be recognized and shared internationally. Within the rules of Neoclassicism, creating or displaying marble white sculpture is what it means to be cultured. Reading Greek and Latin is what it means to be educated. Knowing who Julius Caesar was or Aristotle or Pericles is timelessly important. Knowing that Apollo was the god of reason and Dionysus the god of abandon (and theater) gave names to timeless (and therefore classic) oppositions. This system of order is not any more wrong or right than any other, but it has been used, deliberately, to devalue other languages, other materials, and other histories. It's worth noting that the ancient Greeks and Romans, who liked their sculptures painted in bright colors, would have understood immediately the differences between classic tastes and Neoclassic assumptions that kept statues white.

Neoclassic sculpture and architecture are ongoing forms. Neoclassic drama and acting thrived for about two hundred years—from 1650 or so until 1850. During that time the French excelled at Neoclassic literature and the early great French neoclassical playwrights such as Corneille and Racine became the standard of excellence in their country. Their plays followed the Aristotelian unities of time, place, and action: the action of the play happened in one place, over a twenty-four-hour period of continuous action. There was one plot, not several. There was decorum in language: no vulgar words, no dialects, no common speech, no grammatical mistakes. There was decorum in onstage behavior: bodies did not go horizontal unless they were wounded, dying, or dead. Nobility and grandeur were the aims in scenery, costuming, and everything else onstage, including posture. An actress' arms should not rise above her head, such a thing was unseemly. An actor's head could turn only so much, more would be grotesque. Tragedy could only be written about the aristocracy (because they had the most capacity to feel, right?). Comedy was better suited to lower class people (who were innately funny, right?). These rules were enforced. In France an academy licensed plays and those playwrights who didn't conform were considered pernicious to public morality and denied not only a license, but all-important social status and, therefore, access to funding. In Paris, French actors performed for an educated audience of aficionados.

The performances took place in theaters with proscenium arches: frames through which to look at artwork, not reality. The perspective of the performance was front and center where the king sat or where the most powerful person sat front and center as the king's emissary. The scenery was usually a painted flat background with an occasional practical staircase or doorway. Furniture was sometimes used for comedies: a table, for example, or chairs.

Serious plays were to be written in poetic verse, not prose. In France, Neoclassical playwrights spun lines in what are called *alexandrine*, twelve syllables, with stress on the last syllable of the first six and at the end of the line, and a stress on one more syllable in each half line. The English poet Alexander Pope (1688–1744) gave an example, contrasting the form with a typical English ten-syllable line:

> A needless alexandrine ends the song
> that like a wounded snake, drags its slow length along.
> (Pope, *Essay on Criticism*, p ii, l 156)

Audiences sensitive to the alexandrine, like audiences sensitive to Shakespeare's iambic pentameter, can sense obedience to as well as breaks from the rules. An example: in *Phèdre*, written by Jean Racine and first performed in 1677, a stepmother is in love with her stepson. In the scene where she confesses her love, she fails to complete her lines, three times in a row, which indicates to an aware audience that she is mad.

The story of Racine's Phèdre is taken from Euripides' play which takes its name from the stepson, Hippolytus. Racine's original title was *Phèdre et Hippolyte*. Racine also knew Seneca's play on the same subject. Racine would have read the version of the tale in Ovid's *Metamorphoses,* and he also would have known about the fragments of and ancient references to Euripides' first version of the story. Most neoclassic plots were taken from Roman and Greek sources, though the Bible was also a possible source if the story came from the Old Testament. Neoclassical plays could depict great moments in French history—if kept at a safe distance in time from current events. The Church weighed in on what was appropriate. After writing *Phèdre*, Racine was condemned for making a spectacle out of a woman's sexuality. Realizing he was out of favor, Racine retired to private life, waited till the heat died down, then wrote two plays with stories taken from the Bible and performed, for good measure, by convent schoolgirls. What the Church most objected to about *Phèdre* was just that which gives the play its power: the psychological tension between desire, shame, self-control, and loss of control that makes the role sympathetic and timelessly enigmatic rather than a monster to be condemned. The strict form of the play is an inseparable part of its emotional subject matter and heart. Constrained passion fuels the power of the text as it unfolds in performance until unrestrained passion overwhelms the role of Phèdre and the audience.

One of the distinctions of theater in France was that women appeared onstage and that great roles, such as Phèdre, were written for them. Given rules with which to measure, performances could be judged great, and there is a succession of such great performers that began with the teenage actress Rachel, of women (and men) who could enflame an audience with emotion. If the ultimate aim of the Greek theater was communion, this did happen in the best Neoclassic theater in France, and Neoclassic actresses more than a little resembled priestesses in their power and effect on those who were in their presence.

Here's a description of Rachel performing *Phèdre* in Russia:

> Rachel begins with full voice the tale of her criminal love. Soon the words, the couplets, as if driven by the thought, begin to run as incredible, barely audible speech. A whisper, which betrays her passion with a rapidity almost convulsive, becomes unbearable. Above it, from time to time, are uttered those contralto shrieks, which rend the soul…in mid-monologue. Phèdre, giving herself up totally to a single thought, loses self-consciousness and is almost beside herself. Her lips tremble, her eyes blaze with a maniacal fire, a gesture becomes insanely expressive, that ghastly whisper goes on the whole time, and the words run on, filled with agonizing truth. The paroxysm of passion increases even more, when, after Hippolyte's confusion in striving not to understand his stepmother. She exclaims, "Ah! cruel! to m'as trop entendue!", these verses must be heard from Rachel's lips in order to realize how much irony can be contained in them! And literally having drawn new strength into it. She bursts out in a thundering confession of her criminal passion in the face of heaven and earth until, filled to the brim with horror and self-revulsion, she seizes Hippolyte's sword and is borne off stage unconscious by her confidante. Only then does the parterre take a breath and rise as one man crying "Rachel!"
>
> Such is the scene.
> (Pavel Vaselivich Annenkov, *Theatre Research International*, Laurence Senelick, trans.)

Notice that Rachel was performing in Russia for an audience that understood French, the language of cultured people in Russia at that time. Racine's plays, and Corneille's, are so culturally specific and dependent on language that they do not often pass beyond the language in which they are written. That was fine for all concerned in nineteenth century Russia. The Russian audience was self-congratulatory about knowing French, glad to be there to see and be seen, and educated enough in classical literature to appreciate Neoclassic theater and the references to Phèdre's father King Minos and the Minotaur who was, according to the myth, Phèdre's stepbrother. It is an aspect of the performance's stature that such an audience was limited, and if it grew no larger that was fine—it was meant to be exclusive.

Dance was the theatrical form where Neoclassic ideas spread internationally and continues to be practiced internationally. Classical ballet means just that: dance positions and steps, based on the principles of classical sculpture, inhabited by performers, personified with the genius of interpretation understood by a dedicated audience. The marvel of its craft, as with the Japanese Kabuki, can be enjoyed even by those who don't have all the background necessary for full appreciation. Classical ballet usually involves a story line and characters. To dance the classical ballet repertory involves acting, and the art of the classical ballet developed as an aspect of high culture in Russia, France, England, Denmark, the United States, and the cultural colonies of Europe, including Cuba. The terms for the dance steps are, prestigiously, in French.

In England, Neoclassic theater was influential for about two hundred years and has affected critical thinking and education a bit longer. Invariably though, it dashes itself to pieces on the hard reality that the plays written by Shakespeare don't fit its rules nor do the master works of modern theater such as the plays of Ibsen, Brecht, and Chekov, among other writers. Adherence to classical rules is an idea that endures about good taste, though, and for a while this idea of good taste was so powerful as to prompt rewrites to Shakespeare and affect the ways in which his plays were performed and interpreted.

The Neoclassic plays in English, including turgid tragedies written by Ben Jonson and the esteemed English poet John Dryden, are curiosities of a certain taste and worth studying out of curiosity. *All for Love*, Dryden's 1677 version of the Cleopatra story, subtitled *The World Well Lost*, keeps the action of the play in the Temple of Isis in Alexandria and concentrates on the last hours of the lovers. Cleopatra is a temptress; the noble Antony gives in to her. There are long philosophical discussions, and events onstage parallel what was happening at England's then contemporary Court of James II. *All for Love* assumes an elite cultured audience (or an audience with aspirations to such an elite culture)—and the play relies on strong Neoclassic acting technique to achieve its effects. This could be relied on at the time because even though English Neoclassic writing, unlike the French plays, never amounted to much, Neoclassic ideals in England did create a great school of acting of its own with performers to rival the French.

Oddly, it's a brother and sister team who began the approach. Mrs. Sarah Siddons (1755–1831) and her brother John Philip Kemble (1757–1823) supposedly went to the British Museum to study and imitate classical sculpture. They stood and posed onstage like those sculptures, recited words accompanied by tasteful classical gestures, and were admired by audiences and critics for doing so. This kind of standing still and recitation is what made Rachel famous—acting in which the externals drive performance. The greatest of French Neoclassical actors François-Joseph Talma (1763–1826) laid down similar rules, announcing "One is an actor by virtue of being ahead of mankind in one insight: what is meant to have the effect of truth must not be true." Not until ideas of motivation were championed in Russia, did an approach to acting other than external display take the stage in Europe.

Application of Neoclassic rules to the rewriting plays during this period meant surgery for Shakespeare's mixed genres, scenes, and characters. In *Macbeth*, the bawdy Porter was cut—too low in tone, and so off-putting that the audience couldn't catch the relationship of the Porter's talk of equivocation to the major theme of the play. The fool in *Lear* had to go for the same reason—and a happy ending was added to that play so the good characters could be rewarded and the bad punished, which is something that does not happen in Shakespeare's original tragedy. The stated aim from serious theater critics and professionals was to rescue Shakespeare's poetic jewels from out of the dirt of his unruly plays. Not until the end of the nineteenth century was there much interest in Shakespeare's original staging practices or texts. Midway through the nineteenth century, a new paying audience in England—primarily factory workers—crowded large theaters, and not just in London, to watch melodrama and plays set in contemporary times for which the use of poses and gestures derived from Greek sculpture would have been ludicrous. Though new writing, acting, and staging developed, Neoclassic ideals continued to mutilate Shakespeare's work as a perverse sort of respect. The unities of Aristotle were used to dismiss other approaches to constructing a play. A countertrend, as there is always a countertrend, of romantic acting sprung up based on the Romantic idea that an artist's passion would create its own forms, not just inhabit received forms. In England, great Romantic actors, Edmund Kean, chief among them, did just that with electrifying, erratic performances. In France, Sarah Bernhardt, though she performed the Neoclassical repertory, was the exemplary Romantic performer.

In Germany, there was also a Neoclassic drama and a romantic countertrend. The prestige of the theater was such that the greatest German literary figure, Johann Wolfgang von Goethe (known simply as Goethe), wrote plays and directed them. As a thinker and artist, Goethe is associated with a movement in Germany known as Weimar classicism, named after the court of Weimar in southern Germany where Goethe lived, worked, and maintained an acting troupe. Goethe's novels changed Europe with their radically unclassical themes and story lines. His Neoclassical plays were in line with those from other parts of Europe. Although he wrote his version of the Iphigenia story—based on a play by Euripides—in prose, not verse, Goethe's Iphigenia remains an impossible ideal of womanhood, a talking statue rather than a person. Goethe, a complex artist, was also a part of the countertrend of Romantic writers who found inspiration in Shakespeare and German legends. This had its political aspects in the derivation of Germanic culture from pagan, German, and Norse sources rather than material borrowed or copied from Italy or Greece. Other Neoclassic German writers, Friedrich Schiller among them, held honored places in German literature and drama, but the countertrend against such rules was strong and would eventually provide the origins of Ibsen's "modern" theater.

In a similar way, Rachel's tours of Moscow spurred Russian actors to establish a more realistic—and more Russian approach—rather than follow the French. In other places, eager to acquire the prestige of belonging to an international order, Neoclassicism was considered, well, classy, as classy as speaking Chinese in medieval Japan.

The Neoclassicism of Germany, France, and England shared not only the rules of Aristotle, but an underlying belief, derived from Greek philosophy, in the chain of logic. Onstage action followed a pattern of cause and effect—someone did something and the consequences of what they did were responsible for the action of the play, a design of cause and effect the audience found pleasure in recognizing. In such tragedies, what is said onstage is meant to be intelligible to an audience. If the audience doesn't fully understand, at first, the implications of what is being said (in a prophecy, for example) all should be clear by the conclusion of the play. Whatever mystery there was should be resolved. Tragedies that didn't conform to this—that left the audience without a clear moral or without an emotional resolution—needed to be improved and were.

Ironically, in Greece itself there was no Neoclassic theater since Greece was under Turkish rule, and there was no Greek drama of any kind performed publicly. In Rome, visual artists were still under the influence of the Renaissance, and if the Italian theater was sometimes used as a model of good taste in France, the Italian themselves, not overly concerned with their ancient traditions, were developing a new form of opera, for which plays in verse were written to serve as librettos for musical scores rather than take stage by themselves.

In America the cultural associations of Neoclassical theater and the aspiration of America to be an imperial power of its own meant an emphasis on Aristotle's unities as an aspiration for educated playwrights. Eugene O'Neill emulated the form and specifics of Greek stories writing his own versions of *Hippolytus* and the *Oresteia* set in America. Even so, a countertrend in dance from the American choreographer Isadora Duncan returned Greek theater forms to their roots in the Dionysian rather than the Apollonian tradition. In Germany and France, schools, with a desire to pass on rules, taught Aristotle's *Poetics* for years, but a strong countertrend that began with the Romantics in the last decades of the eighteenth century swelled as the nineteenth century turned into the twentieth century. Momentum for a countertrend to the Romantics gathered as Ibsen wrote *Peer Gynt* and Brecht wrote *Baal* and Alfred Jarry concocted *Ubu Roi*. These theater artists were inspired by the ancient pagan world in their own way, putting forth outrageous antiheroes as avatars of abandon following Dionysus rather than neoclassical good taste and measures of excellence.

Chapter Twelve

SHAKESPEARE'S CLASSIC

John Dryden (1631–1700)
David Garrick (1717–1779)
William Shakespeare (1564–1616)

The history of the theater is a good example of the difference between progress and progression. Progress nowadays implies improvement; it didn't always, but it does now. A progression is a sequence, a procession in time going forward that doesn't necessarily become better or worse than what happened before. The history of the theater is just such a progression. There might be technological progress: lighting and sound equipment improves, master actors or designers develop skills and pass them on, great playwrights create and leave behind plays that change the expectations for the future of the theater—but as the history of the theater progresses what is considered good and better changes, too, and one generation's excellences are not always treasured by future generations.

As a model for how this has happened in the history of English-language theater, it's useful to look at the origins and stage history of the plays Shakespeare set in ancient Rome. Given the same stories to dramatize as the classical playwrights, what did Shakespeare do? And what happened to those plays after he'd written them?

The principal "Roman" plays written by Shakespeare are *Julius Caesar, Antony and Cleopatra*, and *Coriolanus*. Other plays by Shakespeare that touch on Classical Greece or Roman history are *Midsummer Night's Dream, Troilus and Cressida, Timon of Athens, Pericles, Cymbeline,* and the early, crudely exuberant, *Titus Andronicus.*

Let's be clear how little these plays were literally set in Rome: the actors did not wear togas and sandals; the characters talk about wearing nightcaps and doublets; there were no Roman columns or replicas of the Forum; famously, the town clock strikes in *Julius Caesar*; and in *Antony and Cleopatra* the Egyptian queen wants to play billiards, which weren't mentioned in history until fifteen hindred years after she died.

The stories of the plays set in Classical Rome were taken from Roman history. Shakespeare kept the characters' Roman names and, for the most part, their Roman reputations. The places where the scenes are said to occur kept their Roman names, too, and their relative places on a Roman map. Shakespeare's Roman geography is more or less accurate, unlike the seacoast of Shakespeare's Bohemia (Bohemia is, in reality, landlocked) that we hear about in Shakespeare's play *The Winter's Tale*, which no one objected to, because not enough people in early seventeenth century London knew enough to object. Renaissance learning in England meant that educated people did know Greek and Roman classics and some related geography. Though Shakespeare clearly received some such education, even in his own time his contemporary Ben Jonson claimed he had "little Latin and less Greek." We can deduce from the texts of certain plays that Shakespeare read the Roman historian Plutarch, if not in Latin, certainly in English translations. How do we know this? From the similarities of the source material to Shakespeare's verse. A famous example from *Antony and Cleopatra* allows us to compare Shakespeare's description of Cleopatra on the Nile with Sir Thomas North's 1579 translation of Plutarch's *The Lives of the Noble Greeks and Romans* (ca.46–127).

> She disdained to set forward otherwise, but to take her barge in
> the river of Cydnus, the poope whereof was of gold, the sailes

of purple, and the owers of silver, which kept stroke in rowing after the sounde of the musicke of flutes, howboyes, citherns, violls, and such other instruments as they played upon in the barge. And now for the person of her selfe: she was layed under a pavillion of cloth of gold of tissue, apparelled and attired like the goddesse Venus, commonly drawen in picture: and hard by her, on either hand of her, pretie faire boyes apparelled as painters doe set forth god Cupide, with litle fannes in their hands, with the which they fanned wind upon her. Her Ladies and gentlewomen also, the fairest of them were apparelled like the nymphes Nere-ides (which are the mermaides of the waters) and like the Graces, some stearing the helme, others tending the tackle and ropes of the barge, out of the which there came a wonderfull passing sweete savor of perfumes, that perfumed the wharfes side[…].

Shakespeare's version in verse, beginning at line 902 of the First Folio edition, from what we now call Act 2, scene 2:

The Barge she sat in, like a burnisht Throne
Burnt on the water: the Poope was beaten Gold,
Purple the Sailes: and so perfumed that
The Windes were Loue-sicke.
With them the Owers were Siluer,
Which to the tune of Flutes kept stroke, and made
The water which they beate, to follow faster;
As amorous of their strokes. For her owne person,
It beggerd all discription, she did lye
In her Pauillion, cloth of Gold, of Tissue,
O're-picturing that Venus, where we see
The fancie out-worke Nature. On each side her,
Stood pretty Dimpled Boyes, like smiling Cupids,
With diuers coulour'd Fannes whose winde did seeme,
To gloue the delicate cheekes which they did coole,
And what they vndid did.

…

Her Gentlewoman, like the Nereides,
So many Mer-maides tended her i'th' eyes,
And made their bends adornings. At the Helme,
A seeming Mer-maide steeres: The Silken Tackle,
Swell with the touches of those Flower-soft hands,
That yarely frame the office. From the Barge
A strange inuisible perfume hits the sense
Of the adiacent Wharfes.

There's a personal connection, too, with Shakespeare and the publisher of the English version of Plutarch. The publisher's name was Richard Field, and he also published Shakespeare's long poem *Venus and Adonis*. Field was from Stratford, and his father was close enough to Shakespeare's father that the older Shakespeare helped with the older Field's estate when he died.

Plutarch was a historian who wrote to give moral instruction which was typically Roman—the impulse could be translated into theater, of course, as a morality play would. There was also a connection between Rome and England in the minds of the English. At the time of King James, England was at the doorstep of becoming the British Empire. A few months after *Antony and Cleopatra* was first performed, James gave the authorization for the first English colony in America at Jamestown. As Great Britain grew into a world power, the United Kingdom, as it is now called, patterned itself on the Ancient Roman Empire. James I called himself the second Augustus, a historical character that appears (under an earlier name as Octavian) in *Antony and Cleopatra*.

A little earlier, during the reign of Elizabeth I, when *Julius Caesar* was written, Shakespeare was attracted to Roman history as source material not only because there were good stories to turn into plays, but because there were politically safe stories that could continue a major theme of his history plays: what it means to be a ruler (king, general, emperor, queen), and what it means to be a ruler in line with or against the popular crowd.

Shakespeare could continue major themes of what it meant to be human in his Roman settings, and there is continuity of those concerns in the plays no matter what the setting. *Julius Caesar* was written after *Henry V* and covers similar issues of heroism, daring, and personal responsibility for what happens to a nation. *Antony and Cleopatra* was written after *Macbeth* and expands the Scottish play's explorations of a good man doing what he knows to be wrong, as well as what it means to be a woman of strength and power matched to an indecisive powerful mate.

Following *Coriolanus* there was a run of plays written by Shakespeare from Greek and Roman sources available in English translation: *Timon of Athens, Pericles*, and *Cymbeline*. *Cymbeline* makes the connection directly, set while England was part of the Roman Empire, and so it seems safe to infer that around that time, 1605–1610, Shakespeare was looking at Greek and Roman writing, though maybe not reading it in the original languages. Earlier, *The Metamorphoses* by Ovid (43 BC–AD 17) in the 1567 translation by Arthur Golding had given him the stories used in *Midsummer Night's Dream*, set in Athens, and *Titus Andronicus,* and the Trojan War of *Troilus and Cressida*, which Shakespeare would also have known from Chaucer.

And what, along with Plutarch, Ovid, and the Trojan War and sensational biographies did Shakespeare know about classical theater? He knew who Aristotle was. He mentions him in *Troilus and Cressida*, impossibly so since Aristotle lived at least 400 years after the earliest dating of the Trojan War. But, had Shakespeare read the *Poetics*? Did he know about Aristotle's rules for theater and willfully break them? Perhaps he understood or felt intuitively that Aristotle's rules distilled the experience of an ancient culture but were not usefully applied to capture or represent the turbulent ambivalence of his own experience.

What we can tell from the texts of his Roman plays is that the scope of the Roman stories inspired Shakespeare's theatrical imagination and set it to soar in its own way. The audience is personified as a crowd, not a chorus, and as reflection of the audience, the portrait is mocking, not congratulatory as are portraits of the audience in Shakespeare's history plays. The heroes—and all the characters of any Shakespearean tragedy, including the tragedies set in Rome—are not meant as moral examples of good or bad. In Shakespeare's tragic plays men and women are tormented by the world and by themselves—and their struggles are found in action as well as internally. They are tormented by their thoughts as they are by the environment or fate. As with the history plays, the use of material in Shakespeare's plays based on Roman history in which the conclusion is known means there is interest in the way things are done. The audience already knows what will happen to the character. Fate hangs over the action of such plays as it does in any classical Greek drama.

There are also certain specifics of the Elizabethan and Jacobean understanding of Ancient Rome to consider. Suicide as a noble end to life is called the Roman Way by Cleopatra. Shakespeare assumes she—and her audience—knows suicide is associated with Seneca, the Roman playwright/philosopher. There are suicides in all of Shakespeare's Roman plays. There is also always violence, and the hot-blooded Italian was a type well known to British audiences. Specific to Roman playwrights, Shakespeare and his audience knew enough of Plautus and Seneca to laugh at their reputations when Polonius in *Hamlet* talks about acting: "Seneca cannot be too heavy, nor Plautus too light."

Shakespeare's theatrical technique is emphatically different from that of Greek and Roman drama, and it does not correspond to Aristotle. Whether from ignorance or defiance, plays by Shakespeare command the stage by breaking with the Aristotelian unities. Shakespeare's modulation of diversity is dazzling in its virtuosity. His technique reflects the complications of urban life, the intrigues of the Jacobean and Elizabethan court, and the Renaissance concern with the inner drama of a character rather than the formality of presentation of character in "classical" theater modes.

Instead of action confined to one location, one of Aristotle's three prescriptive unities for a good play, there is a cinematic use of space. In *Antony and Cleopatra* there are forty separate scenes—the most of any play by Shakespeare. The action flies from the deck of a boat to inside a monument overlooking the sea; the play hurries for short short scenes, from Egypt to Rome, to Athens, to Syria. The audience sees action from one part of the battlefield to another, as it did in Shakespeare's Histories, but in *Antony and Cleopatra* over much longer distances and with an implied clash of cultures of Egypt and Rome, or the Romans and the Volscians in *Coriolanus*. The quick alternating of these locations forms a rhythmic aspect in Shakespeare's drama.

Unity of action, as defined by Aristotle as a single overriding chain of cause and effect, is embodied onstage in a very different way than by Aristotle in Shakespeare's Roman plays. Several plots relate to a central theme, not a single action. We follow the consequences of action as it affects different people in different ways: how the death of Caesar does none of the conspirators good, how the love of Antony and Cleopatra affects history, and how the pride of Coriolanus affects his mother. The diversity of story lines gives the plays depth. In *Antony and Cleopatra*, for example, the various stories of politicking in Rome, Cleopatra and Antony's personal relationship, the political intrigues of Pompey pile up like music into a unified theme, which might be put simply as the relationship of desire and responsibility, but it is not that simple; it is complex.

Unity of time, another aspect of classical construction, is obviously not an aspect of Shakespeare's "classic" plays. The gaps in time Shakespeare insists on make for wonderful dramatic effects, and the plays would be poorer without them.

If we look at what Shakespeare did with his Roman material, we can see he continued the line of theatrical practice from the medieval theater of dramatizing narrative in a free-form way that kept the attention of a diverse audience. His responsibility was to that audience rather than an obligation to follow the cultural associations of his subject matter.

After he died, Shakespeare's approach was eclipsed by the fad for classic "good taste" which banished his text for *Antony and Cleopatra* from the British stage for hundreds of years. Hundreds. John Dryden's *All for Love* was performed a good deal more than *Antony and Cleopatra* until David Garrick's 1759 partial staging of Shakespeare's play. Even after Garrick, the theater audience needed to be weaned off Dryden for another hundred years with mixtures of Dryden and Shakespeare.

As the centuries progressed, the growing taste for realistic scenery led to cuts in scenes or rearranged scenes in Shakespeare's Roman plays, and there was pantomime instead of dialogue, the display of paintings rather than acted-out scenes. Funeral processions and dances took up stage time and that time was made up in production by mutilating the texts.

This has changed. The attempts at bringing good taste to the material—and especially attempts to bring it to classical rules—were undone in time by the survival of the material itself and the response it commanded and still commands from later generations of imaginative theater artists.

In this way, these plays survived past Neoclassicism. A strong appeal to audiences and actors, no matter what the theatrical approach, is the excellence of the central women's roles, Cleopatra—and Volumnia in *Coriolanus*—for example. These are not young girls or the monstrous queens of the history plays, but something much more complex, in line with Lady Macbeth and Gertrude from *Hamlet*. Even the smaller roles of Calpurnia or Portia, the wives of Caesar and of Brutus, are nuanced older women. Shakespeare knew who he was writing for: talented older boys or perhaps mature actors playing women's roles. Once actresses took their place on the English-speaking stage in 1660, it was only a matter of time before actresses would want to play Cleopatra or Volumnia. The ambiguities and contradictions of these characters make them eternally fascinating to interpreters and audiences. Shakespeare himself understood the appeal when he has his Cleopatra say:

> The quicke Comedians
> Extemporally will stage vs, and present
> Our Alexandrian Reuels: *Anthony*
> Shall be brought drunken forth, and I shall see
> Some squeaking *Cleopatra* Boy my greatnesse
> I'th' posture of a Whore.
>
> *Iras:* O the good Gods!
> *Cleo:* Nay that's certaine.
> (*Folio 3459*)

The great men's roles in the Roman plays were also an inducement to return the plays to the repertory. Again, hardly neoclassical heroes, these are psychologically mixed characters, which attracted Shakespeare to the Roman material in the first place; they are conflicted, contradictory, and rather than lessons, forever interesting as conundrums.

Shakespeare seems to have been willing to put to use anything he came across that might work theatrically, including what he could use from Roman and Greek theater practices. The ancient Greek device of the deus ex machina, when a god was lowered down by some device in order to conclude the action of the play, is quoted exactly in *Cymbeline* Act V Scene IV when "Jupiter descends in thunder and lightning, sitting upon an eagle: he throws a thunderbolt." And there is the same effect of the deus ex machina when Hymen, the Greek goddess of marriage, descends to solve the lover's confusions in *As You Like It*. In *Pericles*, "ancient" Gower comes as a chorus, and there is a character named Chorus in *Henry V*. The lurid parts in *Titus Andronicus* derive from the Roman playwright Seneca—but the presentation of them onstage also has roots in the medieval theater. Significantly, during and following his spate of plays from classical sources, Shakespeare's plays become wilder in their dispersions, the romances are still considered difficult in their range and mix of genres, story lines, and irreconcilable contradictions. Like Euripides' work, they seem to be forever problematic.

The British director, William Poel, began a movement at the end of the nineteenth century to return Shakespeare's plays to Elizabethan staging practices: a bare platform, minimal scenery, adherence to the text—though with women onstage in women's roles. This freed Shakespeare's plays from the framing of the proscenium arch, from realism and distracting spectacle and outdated ideas of decorum. The plays with Roman and Greek settings could be seen and heard now without the distractions of archaeological detail. As time goes on, the continuing relevance of Shakespeare's interrogations of gender construction, imperialism, the clash of desire and responsibility, the monstrosity of dictators, and the conflict of a woman who is powerful in a man's world, continue to inspire strong new productions and interpretations of Shakespeare's Roman plays.

Shakespeare's *Julius Caesar* has its own history. Unusually, it was not adapted or cut after the Restoration, but performed as Shakespeare wrote it. Yet, it's stage history, too, illustrates the progression in modes of theater. Throughout the eighteenth and nineteenth centuries the play's appeal as a star vehicle for actors was matched by its appeal to directors and designers as an opportunity for stage pictures: processions, crowd scenes, and battles. Scenes were performed in a different order than the original to make the scenic effects more easily achieved. In 1874 when the Duke of Saxe-Meiningen, who began the modern approach to directing, put together his *Julius Caesar*, it was the work with the crowd: the crowd's unity of purpose, even while maintaining the variety of individuals as individuals, that most impressed the audiences who saw the German ensemble perform on tour in Europe and in London in 1881. The Moscow Art Theatre's attempts to stage an archaeologically correct and psychologically real *Julius*

Caesar in 1903 (with Stanislavsky as Brutus) took two years of preparation for the cast, including trips to Italy, and was a famous flop, the intentions for realism undone by the nonrealistic text.

The panoramic capabilities of silent film inspired live extravaganzas of the Roman plays. In 1916 there was a one-night performance of *Julius Caesar* in the natural bowl of Beachwood Canyon outside of Los Angeles, featuring silent film stars Tyrone Power, Sr. and Douglas Fairbanks, Sr. Students from Hollywood and Fairfax High Schools played opposing armies for an audience of 40,000. An even larger version of the play was performed in 1926 at the Hollywood Bowl. The stage was the size of a city block with a central tower eighty feet tall. Three hundred gladiators fought together, three hundred girls danced as Caesar's slaves, three thousand soldiers fought.

Orson Welles staged *Julius Caesar* in New York in 1937 with direct references to the current self-styled dictator in Rome, Mussolini, and the then contemporary Italian invasion of Northern Africa. Welles cut the text to a hundred minutes, streamlining the plot to turn the play into something more pointedly political. In 2012 a production of *Julius* Caesar at the Guthrie Theater in Minneapolis in modern dress, and with video monitors of talking heads, had a right-wing cabal assassinate a lanky tall black man resembling then President Barack Obama. Five years later at the eighteen hundred seat amphitheater in New York's Central Park, Caesar was transparently depicted as Donald Trump with a Slovenian-accented Calpurnia very obviously intended as a portrait of his wife.

Three weeks into the run of the Trump-inspired *Julius Caesar,* a few days before the production closed, a woman ran onstage interrupting the performance to "stop the normalization of violence against the right." She was removed from the stage. Her collaborator recording a video of her protest was removed from the audience. According to a statement from the producers: "The show resumed with the lines 'Liberty! Freedom!' The audience rose to their feet to thank the actors, and we joyfully continued."

Within the context of the play those lines are ironic, their triumph undercut by the horror of Caesar's bleeding body. In an age of unambivalent political advocacy, right or left, irony is as unwanted as moral ambiguity was during the Age of Dryden. Through cheers or protests, productions of *Julius Caesar*, and Shakespeare's other Roman plays, proceed though not necessarily progress, for the purposes of new audiences and artists.

Chapter Thirteen

BAD BOYS BREAKING THE RULES

Bertolt Brecht (1898–1956)
Henrik Ibsen (1828–1906)
Alfred Jarry (1873–1907)

A study of the more than one hundred years of modern drama should begin with the laughter brought on by reading or watching Henrik Ibsen's *Peer Gynt*, Alfred Jarry's *Ubu Roi*, and Bertolt Brecht's *Baal*. Each of these three plays is named after a bad boy who takes the stage thumbing, if not picking, his nose at the rules of order, including the rules set out by the expectations of the audience.

The dogmas of good taste, the doctrines of good theater, and the drivel of useful morality are not just ignored but ridiculed in these three funny plays. Modern drama began with the relief of being freed from authority without the responsibility of setting up any other authority. Later playwrights developed modern drama by dramatizing the itch to break rules with plays shadowed by anxiety over what would happen in a world without rules.

Peer Gynt, written in Norwegian in 1868 by Henrik Ibsen, begins with young Peer lying to his mother. Peer's ability to lie convincingly is at the heart of his power in life, and Ibsen slyly hints that the ability to lie convincingly is what powers any play. Ibsen was thirty-nine when he wrote *Peer Gynt* while living on the Italian island of Ischia, off of Naples, freed from the expectations of the Norwegian theater establishment where he'd been grinding away for decades. At twenty-three he began six years of work at the Det norske Theater in the northern Norwegian city of Bergen, followed by seven more years as the artistic director of a theater in the capital city of Christiania (later called Oslo). Ibsen staged over 150 plays in provincial Bergen and Christiania. Most of these plays were sentimental melodramas, patriotic pageants, neoclassic tragedies, and silly French farces that his middle-class audiences enjoyed almost as much as they enjoyed showing off their new hats to each other in the lobby.

By 1864 Ibsen had enough. Thirty years after he left Norway, Ibsen described in a speech at a banquet how he and his family took the train south, rolling beneath a heavy curtain of clouds and diving into the Alps. From the mists of the train tunnel they escaped into sunshine, moving from darkness into light. All his writing from then on, he said, would be stamped by the beauty of that light, though not all his writing would be as beautiful. He resettled at first in Rome.

Peer Gynt was set down in Norwegian verse which captured and still releases the sparkle of the Italian sun. Ibsen wrote eleven other plays before *Peer*, six of them had been performed. Even so, *Peer Gynt* was published as a text to be read, not staged. On the title page it is called a dramatic poem. The form of the text matches its author's ambitions—and its central character's hankering—to obliterate the limits of convention.

The entire text of *Peer Gynt* is rarely staged—it takes eight hours to perform. As the action spills down from a farmhouse in the Norwegian mountains to the Hall of the Troll King under the mountains, Peer passes from a swaggering young buck to a sorry sinner. That's just the second act; in the next two acts the story flies over Europe to land on the Moroccan seacoast, treks to the Sahara Desert where Peer, now rich from slave trading, savors dancing girls and lingers under the nose of the Sphinx. By the fifth act a penniless Peer returns to Norway when his ship capsizes.

Troll costumes! Dancing girls! The Sphinx! A shipwreck! The budget! Ibsen did not expect what he had written could or would be staged, nor did he expect the play's blasphemies to pass by a censor. Rather than bend to enter the low front door of the theater, the playwright challenged the theater to tear down its walls to accommodate what he had written. Even as poetry *Peer Gynt* was controversial. Literary critics complained about its lack of decorum, to which Ibsen wrote in an 1867 letter to another Norwegian playwright, Bjørnstjerne Bjørnson, that *Peer Gynt* "is poetry; and if it isn't, it will become such. The conception of poetry in our country, in Norway, shall shape itself according to this book."

Ibsen conceived the poetry in *Peer Gynt* after Shakespeare's example. As in Shakespeare's plays, there are five acts, and *Peer Gynt's* action follows the seemingly familiar arc of a beginning, middle, and end. As in Shakespeare's *Antony and Cleopatra*, the story skips from continent to continent and dives inside the earth and the sea. As in Shakespeare's *A Midsummer Night's Dream*, characters from fairy tales and myths alternate with romantic heroines and insightful, realistic portraits of villagers. As in *Midsummer* and also in *Macbeth*, the verse changes form according to who is speaking: witches and warriors, trolls and village maidens have each their characteristic rhythms and rhyme schemes. As in Shakespeare's plays, *Peer Gynt* sparkles with an intermittent realism, and Ibsen's effervescent verse taps into the same strong force that invigorates Ibsen's later prose plays: the drive to free the soul from the chains of convention, including self-imposed conventions.

Such freedom is not without a shadow or consequences. Damnation is part of the design. In the fifth act, Peer Gynt, shuffling with age in the Norwegian wilderness, comes across the Button Molder, a fairy-tale character invented by Ibsen, who carries a strange, crooked contraption in which impure souls are melted down to be reused for better purposes. The Button Molder announces his plans to melt down Peer's soul unless Peer can show some integrity. This seems easy: Peer Gynt has been nothing but himself, purely himself, living purely for himself, and for no one nor nothing else. But what is that self? Who, purely, is Peer? In the course of Peer's life, he has had so many selves. The Troll King insists Peer is a troll, his mother would insist he is a very human son, others would claim with their good reasons he's an unscrupulous businessman, a lover, and a beggar. Who, really, is he after all the years?

Ibsen raises these questions and doesn't answer them. In a crucial scene within the fifth act, Peer peels an onion. The audience watches and listens as layer by layer Peer calls out his past identities—among them emperor, beggar, a Gold Rush panhandler—but Peer never arrives at the core of himself or the onion.

What makes *Peer Gynt* modern is just this urge to enthusiastically unpeel the onion knowing a core might never be reached. Though written before electrical power, before the telephone, before airplanes, before Mickey Mouse, before Cubism, before Jazz, the play is modern in the same way a play by the ancient Greek Euripides is modern because the author insists on the inability to sum up life logically or for a purpose. This unravels Western European conclusions about modernity in 1868, that life was logical, science was wonderful, and the whole world was improving thanks to technology and the domination of European culture.

In 1868, the globe was knit together more closely than ever before. Trains and steamships became more efficient, there were better canals (the Suez Canal opened in 1869), the colonization of Africa, India, and Australia—and the cultural ties maintained by former colonies in North and South America—made for an international culture outdoing the Roman Empire in its smug assumptions of superiority. China and Japan tried for centuries to resist European culture, but their borders were ignored, and their port cities were forced open. Ibsen's play written in verse, defied Western Europe's belief in progress, cast doubt on the received explanations of cause and effect, and unchained drama from melodrama.

On the island of Ischia, where he was finishing up *Peer Gynt*, Ibsen met someone on the beach and—obviously thinking of the

Button Molder—wondered aloud whether there could be an apparatus large enough to melt down something the size of a person. No, he and his chance acquaintance agreed: another obstacle
to ever staging the play. Over time, though, Ibsen rethought the
text of *Peer Gynt,* and the play was performed in 1876 in Christiania eight years after it was first published. Ibsen had shortened
it and, cleverly, invited the great Norwegian composer Edvard
Grieg to write incidental music for the show. Then and now, the
popularity of Grieg's music (his morning music is a cliché in
animated cartoons) directs attention back to Ibsen's play and its
images: the underground court of the Troll King, the death of
Peer's mother, the dance of an Egyptian girl in the North African
desert, the lullaby of his village sweetheart patiently waiting for
Peer to return home to Norway.

After he left Norway, Ibsen continued to apply the discipline
necessary to fulfill his Det norske Theater contract to write a new
play every year, though while he lived outside his home country,
he wrote a new play every *two* years. Ibsen's sensitivity to the
nuance and beauty of words for poetic drama like *Peer Gynt* was
applied to his realistic prose plays. He paid close attention to the
conversations he overheard in German hotel lobbies where he
jotted down what words were spoken in the morning, and what
words at night, and what words were spoken by men, and those
by women. The character of Peer might be unruly, but the play
named for him is polished. Crafty, in all senses of the word, it
goes down smoothly.

As the nineteenth century moved into the twentieth, the in-
creased mechanization of Western Europe and the smugness of
its convictions progressed to the horrors of the First World War,
provoking thinkers and artists, including playwrights, to urgent-
ly articulate a worldview neither smooth nor smug nor logical,
but defiantly illogical, rough, and raw.

In 1918, when Bertolt Brecht wrote his first play, he was
twenty. Born into a middle-class family in Augsburg, Germany,

Brecht was doing what he could in 1918 to avoid the World War, then in its fifth year. By taking a medical course at a college, he earned a deferment from the German army. Briefly he served in a venereal disease ward, but he was quickly discharged. To continue escaping the draft, Brecht next took up classes in dramatic literature at the University of Munich. After an argument with his teacher, Brecht began writing his own play, *Baal*, and began a life of creativity based on being disagreeable.

Baal, the name Brecht borrowed for his first play and first hero, is a false god reviled in the Old Testament, so detestable that the Hebrew prophets sometimes replaced the name with the word for shame. Brecht's Baal is a young poet without shame: a shameless liar, a shameless womanizer, and a shameless drunk. Like Peer Gynt, Baal spins arresting webs of words. Unlike Peer, we don't see Baal late in life sadder but wiser. Baal dies young, not so pretty, alone in the forest—a good example of the moral from a modern fable by the American cartoonist James Thurber:

> Where most of us end up there is no knowing, but the hell-bent get where they are going.

Within a decade of writing *Baal*, Brecht would organize his thinking, become a Communist, declare that rules of middle-class decorum were created to suppress lower-class dissent, and that the cardinal virtues of Patience and Obedience were taught to keep the strong in power and the weak in their place. Reading *Baal*, let's not assess the early work by its later evaluation; let's consider it for what it is in its own time: a smart-ass kid's hunch (which was correct) that the rules of decorum were there to keep him dumb in both senses of the word—quiet and stupid—so that fools and scoundrels could get away with their tricks. Brecht's first play is an obstinate refusal to follow the precept "if you don't have anything nice to say don't say anything at all."

Baal is very not nice. He steals his best friend's girlfriend, he gets her pregnant, he abandons her, and he takes money from his patrons and spends it on gin. He commits murder. Up to a point he resembles the line of Romantic antiheroes of German novels and plays, but he has no higher ideals than Peer Gynt's self-satisfaction. The play's aesthetic is jagged and rough, unlike the polished verse of *Peer Gynt*. Though Brecht reworked the text in 1926, along with some other early plays, it was never his intention to present Baal as noble. Baal is common and low, that's the point of his being and the origin of his poetry. The structure of the play is episodic: scenes and actions do not lead logically to the next scene or action; instead, they butt up against one another, challenging audiences to make connections, or better yet, take pleasure in noticing the contradictions of life.

Brecht waited five years for *Baal* to be performed, and when it was, knowledge of the play burnished his growing reputation in the German theater, culminating soon enough in the 1928 triumph of *The Threepenny Opera* in which the criminal Macheath sings and dances an elegant variation of the same type of outlaw.

The spirit to rebel is universal, and Brecht was lucky to be born at the right time and place for the rebellious spirit of a young man who came from a good middle-class family, but dressed and acted like a truck driver, to find his way to a career in the theater. In different times, such a smelly rebel would not have had access to stage productions or publication of his plays; he would have been jailed or executed or sent home to wash, learn better manners and buy better clothes. The disarray of Germany after World War I gave Brecht a chance. In England, where the censor still ruled, a performance of *Baal* would have been unthinkable.

A rebellious woman who wanted to write plays was not so encouraged and had no such opportunities as a man. The rebellion open to women was sexual, and openly sexual women in these modern plays written by men are signs within the culture of the same rebellion of the spirit. Ibsen's heroines Nora, from *A Doll House,* and Hedda Gabbler are more polished versions. Brecht's women are cruder.

In life, Brecht, treated women like utensils, yet collaborated with women on many of his greatest works, usually without giving them credit. Elisabeth Hauptmann may have written much of Brecht's *Threepenny Opera*, but the guiding intelligence of the collective was Brecht, who worked communally and with a creative ensemble. Outside of Brecht's orbit, with very few exceptions, the women who found success in the theater as writers did so by participating in the existing profession, rather than challenge the establishment outright. The few women who wrote for a theater that didn't yet exist, as did Ibsen, have yet to have their work fully accepted or staged. Though the urge to rebel crosses genders, early modern theater was, for sure, a boys' club.

And by boys, we mean boys. Alfred Jarry begat his masterpiece of a monster, *Ubu Roi*, at the age of fifteen by doodling mean caricatures of his fat physics teacher. If Ibsen's Peer is unscrupulous and Brecht's Baal is immoral, Jarry's Ubu is exuberantly unscrupulous and ferociously immoral, or rather amoral. Ubu is an insatiable maw of pleasure swilling down whatever he pleases without concern for consequences. Ubu becomes king by killing everyone else. Like Macbeth, Ubu is urged on by his ambitious wife. Ubu taxes as much as he can; he then runs away with the money. He ends up happy.

Memorably, the play *Ubu Roi* begins with the word *Merdre...* not quite the French word for excrement, but a crappy version of crap. On the opening night, December 1896, at Lugné-Poe's Théâtre de l'Œuvre in a low-class section of Paris, when the first word was spoken—by a puppet—the audience shouted and whistled for the next fifteen minutes. Though the puppet play resumed, throughout the performance the audience interrupted with whistles and catcalls. After that performance the run was cancelled. The play was next performed eight years later. The mischief Ubu began inspired more mischief—the surreal theater in France—opening doors to an unsettling alternate reality—the sur in *surréalisme* is the French suffix meaning "over" or "in addition to"—a reality in which farce could be as moving and incisive as a Greek tragedy.

At roughly the same time as *Ubu*, *Peer*, and *Baal* were being written in France, Germany, and Norway, artists in those same countries were reviving the medieval art of woodcuts. At the turn of the nineteenth century, an assortment of Germans took up the crudities of woodcut illustrations to depict the increasingly crude world around them. The French artist Paul Gauguin, moved to Tahiti in 1893 in search of primitive—meaning primary—sources for his paintings. Returned to Paris he glorified his Polynesian travelogue, *Noa Noa*, with deliberately rough and crude prints made from blocks of wood Gauguin purposefully needled and gouged.

The Norwegian painter Edvard Munch, who knew Ibsen and Ibsen's Swedish contemporary August Strindberg socially, seized upon the lack of refinement in woodcuts to refine his art. Munch, creating a woodcut titled *The Kiss*, began with realistic charcoal and pencil drawings taken from life, detailing a naked woman leaving a man's bed in the morning. In the first sketches, both lovers linger for a final embrace, and there's a bed, there's an end table, there are curtains, and there are geraniums in a window box. The large oil paintings that followed the sketches had all these details, too. When it came time for Munch to carve an image out of wood, the furniture was removed, and the scene in the woodcut is reduced to its essence: the two figures, man and woman, melting into each other. The hard-won smooth surface of oil-painting technique, considered in good taste, is undone by Munch's streaks of ink. The swirling woodgrain from the printer's block is undisguised, another repudiation of the smoothness of good taste in oil painting. Munch's vigorous woodcuts parallel what Jarry and Brecht were writing in their crude plays.

Such art and such plays changed tastes enough that writing that had been ignored or thought to be unfinished or crude was now appreciated and valued. The Bavarian Georg Büchner, who died in 1837 at the age of twenty-three, left behind three plays. The first, *Danton's Death*, written in 1835, wasn't staged until 1902. The play takes place during the French Revolution of

1789 when Georges Danton challenged the revolutionary leader Robespierre about the honesty of whoever claims to be superior to sin.

> You and your virtue, Robespierre! You've taken no money, you've run up no debts, you've slept with no women, you've always worn a decent coat and never got drunk. Robespierre, you are infuriatingly righteous. I would be ashamed to wander between heaven and earth for thirty years with such a priggish face, for the miserable pleasure of finding others less virtuous than myself. Is there no small, secret voice in you whispering just occasionally: 'You are a fraud'?
> (Victor Price, trans.)

Büchner's second play, *Leonce and Lena,* satirizes the ideals of the Romantic movement in Europe. The last, *Woyzeck,* is based on a real-life murder. At the time of Büchner's death, *Woyzeck* was left as a series of unordered and unfinished scenes. The first public performance of *Woyzeck* was in 1913. Audiences and critics had come to value what the play was, not criticize for what it wasn't.

The earliest modern playwrights found inspiration in sources outside of classical Greece and Rome. Ibsen spun plays out of Norwegian folktales and Viking sagas; Büchner dramatized real-life events in France and Germany. Jarry and Brecht found early inspiration in various sources including the Bible and Shakespeare. What other people found "wrong" about Shakespeare—the lack of unities, the mix of farce and tragedy in the same work—were just the aspects these writers found worth emulating.

There is a direct relationship between *Peer Gynt, Ubu Roi,* and *Baal* and medieval performances—storytelling combined with enactment and the medieval theater's broad characterizations, body humor, vulgar speech, and farcical ways to deliver memorable spiritual content. Isn't it interesting that the propaganda techniques from the Age of Faith were used by those who meant to mock faith in systems?

After the First World War, to think of modernity involved despair—often chalked up to the death of God. Pleasure in earliest Modern drama is the same as when Ibsen crossed the Alps and saw the sun coming out over Italy. The spirit that lives in these three plays is willfully irresponsible. The pleasures enjoyed by the title characters won't be diluted by consequences. If these plays uphold an aesthetic of sacrifice and willful damnation, that aesthetic is something pagan, not Christian. Most importantly, the spirits of Baal, Ubu, and Peer live to make you laugh. Laugh rudely.

Chapter Fourteen

INSIDE OUTSIDE

André Antoine (1858–1943)
David Belasco (1853–1931)
Anton Chekhov (1860–1904)
Henrik Ibsen (1828–1906)
Konstantin Stanislavsky (1863–1938)
August Strindberg (1849–1912)
Ivan Turgenev (1818–1883)

A udiences had to be trained to understand theater that pretends to be real. In what's called Realism in the theater, which is not the same thing as reality, the actors onstage in the light behave as if the people out in the dark aren't there—as if an invisible wall separates the audience from the stage. Unlike the commedia, or plays by Molière and Shakespeare, in which actors talk directly to the audience, Realism has actors pretend to talk as if overheard, unawares, though loudly enough to be heard because, again, realistic theater is not reality, but an illusion of reality. This is why the actors position themselves to be seen by the audience that they seemingly ignore. Along with the adjustments actors make to construct the illusion of reality for the audience, the illusion relies on the audience deducing, from what they see and hear, what is unseen and unheard: the minds and hearts of the play's characters.

In late nineteenth century Europe as realistic plays were written and increasingly performed, audiences honed their skills deducing thoughts and feelings from stage behavior and speech. There hadn't been so much of a necessity before when characters made announcements to the audience.

It is my lady! It is my love! O, that she knew she were!
(Shakespeare, *Romeo and Juliet*, Act II, scene 2)

What's weighing my eyebrows down?
Hu, how my forehead's throbbing—
a tightening red-hot ring— !
I cannot think who the devil
has bound it around my head!
(Ibsen, *Peer Gynt*, Act II, scene 4, William and Charles Archer, trans.)

I watch I watch I watch for this sign of a torch,
a beacon light sending from Troy the news that she is captured.
(Aeschylus, *Agamemnon*, Anne Carson, trans.)

The characters made no such declarations in Ibsen's *Hedda Gabler*, written in 1890. The play was incomprehensible to some critics who read it and audiences who saw it—and didn't like it. There didn't seem to be any action in the play, much less dramatic action. Ibsen had established plot and psychology with relationships between characters, not with announcements. With precise stage directions, Ibsen provided clues about psychology and dramatic action to readers and to actors who might perform the roles he had written.

[*She takes up an album, and places it on the table beside the sofa, in the further corner of which she seats herself. EILERT LOVBORG approaches, stops, and looks at her. Then he takes a chair and seats himself to her left.*]
(Ibsen, *Hedda Gabler*, Act 2, Edmund Gosse and William Archer, trans.)

This was meant to direct actors who were trained to perform mechanically: approach, stop, look, sit in the chair. It was written before there was a system for actors to base their performances on internal mechanisms: Hedda's need to explore, to protect, or to avoid. That Hedda gives room on her love seat for Eilert, that he looks at her and decides to sit someplace else, tells us something of what Eilert is thinking and something about their desires for each other. Ibsen's next stage directions for the scene—that Eilert's eyes go to Hedda's face as Hedda's eyes go to the album, not Eilert—are subtly ambivalent. She might be avoiding his glance in order to egg him on. She might be avoiding him because she's afraid. She might be avoiding him because her husband can see her and doesn't want to betray whatever it is she's feeling. These are all interpretations Ibsen gives as possible, but he doesn't have Hedda turn to the audience and declare: "Oh, it is my Eilert! Oh, it is my love, Would that he knew he were!"

What Hedda and Eilert do and say does not establish the dramatic action; what they do and say masks the action.

> HEDDA [*Opening the album.*]: Do you see this range of mountains, Mr. Lovborg?
> It's the Ortler group. Tesman has written the name underneath. Here it is: "The Ortler group near Meran."
> LOVBORG [*Who has never taken his eyes off her, says softly and slowly*]: Hedda—Gabler!

Ibsen does not specify Hedda's possible objectives—to fool her husband or to spur her lover on—when she looks at the album not Eilert. Nor does he specify what Eilert intends. That dash, when Eilert pauses between saying *Hedda* and *Gabler*, is as important dramatically as any word of the text to establish the relationship between Hedda and Eilert. Gabler is Hedda's maiden name, and it isn't clear why Eilert hesitates to call her by it. Ibsen directs where the actor's eyes go. For this small behavior of his eyes to make an impact within the flow of words requires audience members perceptive enough—and close enough—to notice what is happening and to infer from Hedda's averted head and Eilert's pursuing eyes that the action of the scene is a chase, though it takes places while both characters are seated.

The visionary Swede August Strindberg, who wrote at roughly the same time as Ibsen—and sometimes in response to Ibsen—considered intimate relations between audience and actors essential to performing his plays in which a contest of wills is the equivalent of bravura swordplay. Strindberg specified his ideas to focus the audience's attention by removing what he considered obstacles of artifice. In his 1899 preface to *Miss Julie*, a one-act play that follows a young countess infatuated, for a little while, with her father's servant, Strindberg suggests the spoken words and equally important silences assert their own power over the audience's emotions. For the language of a play to work effectively, a producer would need to abandon the then conventional practice of underscoring scenes with music. Strindberg suggests actors use very little makeup, allowing the audience to see an actor blush or wrinkle his forehead. Remove the footlights, let the audience see light from above as if outdoors, or maybe see sidelight as if from a window. Let the dialogue be roundabout, as in life, rather than witty or proclamatory. Let behavior onstage be observed and seem real, rather than be staged and seem stagey.

> I have no illusions about getting the actors to play for the public and not at it, although such a change would be highly desirable. (Strindberg, Preface to *Miss Julie*, Edwin Björkman, trans.)

In 1907 Strindberg created a theater with 150 seats called the Intima to showcase the plays that he was writing. By 1912, when he died, he had written more than sixty.

As Strindberg predicted, removing familiar artifice from production was difficult. There were those who doubted the effort would achieve anything worthwhile. Dismissing Ibsen's *Hedda Gabler* as dramatically inert, a distinguished Norwegian critic— that he was distinguished explains in part why Ibsen stayed away from Norway for twenty-seven years—wrote that the internal thoughts of characters were impossible to establish onstage; this is what novels could do, not plays.

Yes, this is what novels did and do—inspiring nineteenth century playwrights like Ibsen and Strindberg to imagine what the theater could do. In a novel a person can sit on a couch and daydream as the novelist describes for the reading public what the character is thinking—and in so doing set up a dramatic situation by contrasting inaction with desire. Shakespeare set up just such a dynamic opposition with the character of Hamlet.

"Now I am alone," Hamlet announces in *Hamlet's* second act, but the actor isn't alone; he is talking to the audience, revealing a private drama: he should kill his uncle but doesn't, he should speak out against murder but has not.

> I, A dull and muddy-mettled rascal, peak
> Like John-a-dreams, unpregnant of my cause,
> And can say nothing
> (*Hamlet,* Act 2, scene 2)

But he does say something, making public his anger, shame, resignation, and resolve.

In 1848, almost two hundred and forty years after *Hamlet* was written, a Russian novelist, Ivan Turgenev, wrote a five-act play called *A Month in the Country.* As in *Hamlet, A Month in the Country's* lovesick characters, when they are alone with the audience, declare their anger, shame, resignation, and resolve. The dramatic contrast of public face and inner turmoil is common to Turgenev's many short stories and half-dozen novels that portray men with big dreams who don't do anything. The *superfluous man,* as this type was called in nineteenth century Russia, was understood to be the spiritual descendent of Hamlet—in novels, though, not in plays. Turgenev wrote *A Month in the Country* assuming the play would be read like a novel. He never dreamed it would be performed because the dramatic action in the play relies on unspoken thoughts and desires not acted upon, as had the action in his novels. Readers, audience members, and performers weren't yet ready to appreciate unexplained motives and the drama of inaction. Like Büchner's *Woyzeck* and Ibsen's *Peer Gynt*, Turgenev's text waited years to find understanding interpreters.

The plot of *A Month in the Country* revolves around an elegant twenty-nine-year-old married woman, Natalya Petrovna, who falls in love with her son's twenty-one-year-old tutor. Then Natalya Petrovna learns that Vera, the teenage girl who is Natalya's ward, has fallen in love with the same young man. Turgenev's play also offers performers marvelous opportunities to enact shame, resignation, and resolve. Even so, when *A Month in the Country* was first staged in 1872, twenty-two years after it was written, the production failed. Turgenev was not surprised. Seven years later, Maria Gavrilovna Savina, a thirty-year-old actress, approached Turgenev for permission to stage a new production. It was her wish to play the sixteen-year-old ward, Vera. Turgenev warned the actress that it was impossible, not because she couldn't pass for a teenager, but because, in his opinion and based on its only performance, the play wasn't any good as a play. Savina insisted and she was charming. Turgenev was seventy and he gave in. When he came to Savina's premiere, Turgenev prepared for public disgrace. He sat at the performance hidden behind a curtain in a side box. Applause at the play's conclusion and calls for the author forced him out.

A Month in the Country still includes monologues where characters, as in *Hamlet*, say aloud what they are thinking. The married woman in love with the tutor also has a lover (it's complicated). His name is Rakitin. He sits on a bench to muse:

> Ah, how absurd a man is who has only one idea in his head, one object, one I have never deceived myself, I know very well how she loves me; but I hoped that with time that quiet feeling…I hoped? Have I the right to hope, dare I hope? I confess my position is pretty absurd…almost contemptible… [A pause.] What's

the use of talking like that?
(*A Month in the Country*, Act 2, Constance Garnett, trans.)

The actor in the role of Rakitin might be pretending to talk to himself, and this can be played that Rakitin talks to himself to screw up his courage or talks to himself to figure out how to stop doing what he's doing. It can also be played as a direct chat with the audience, but in any interpretation, it relies on the actor explaining himself. In a scene where the tutor asks Vera to help tie a tail to his kite, there are no such monologues or explanations. The audience is asked to watch and deduce what's going on by observing behavior, often very small and subtle. At Savina's 1872 revival of the play, the Russian audience was laughing and crying; they were prepared to react to the play, in part, by their experience with, of all things, what were then modern Russian paintings.

Oil painting in Russia followed a very different track than in Western Europe. In 1863 fourteen student artists at the St. Petersburg Academy of Art refused their final assignment to paint a mythological theme. They insisted what they had learned should depict what was going on in the country around them—a social revolution—and, in particular, they felt it necessary to portray living people of all social classes, not mythological figures. They wanted their paintings to engage a viewer in immediate emotions and real-life situations, not noble sentiments or legends. As a group, these Russian painters came to be called the Itinerants, not because they wandered the country in search of subject matter after they were thrown out of school for insubordination (though that sometimes did happen). The Itinerant touring exhibitions and the reproduction of Itinerant paintings in Russian newspapers trained the Russian public to look at painted poses and to pierce the surface of painted canvas to get to its psychology.

In Ilya Repin's *The Unexpected Return*, painted between 1884 and 1888, two women stand in a doorway. The older woman, a peasant, has her head wrapped in a scarf. She peeps in shadow from behind a young, aproned housemaid, whose face is a complex of worry and surprise. The housemaid is holding the door open for a gaunt bearded man in a long brown coat and dust-covered boots who has entered the room, towards those of us viewing the painting. He doesn't look at us. His burning eyes are turned to a gray-haired woman in black who has half-risen from a flowery armchair to stare back at him. We don't see her full face, just her profile; her posture tells us she is startled. To her right are two children, a wide-eyed little boy who looks up with a smile. A wheat-blonde girl stares at the man with what might be fear. In the corner is another young woman, perhaps a governess. This might be as much a scene in any play. As an audience would in a theater, the viewers of the painting are meant to deduce from what they see that the man is the father of the family (the deference of the maid to him is the clue), and his appearance is an unexpected surprise (the reaction of the children gives us that). In 1888 Russians would have recognized from the man's coat that he's come home from a term of forced labor in Siberia.

The wallpaper, the piano in the corner, the pictures on the wall, and the governess—if that's who she is—tell us something about the family's upper-class social status. The painter has reinforced his theme with color. The wallpaper is a delicate blue and white, in contrast to the brown coat of the returning prisoner. The color and composition, the furniture and the clothing are all in the service of the scene. In just these ways the words and scenery of realistic theater support the audience's understanding of the scene.

In Russia—where audiences were familiar with such psychological paintings as Repin's and such insightful novels as Turgenev's—an actor who called himself Konstantin Stanislavsky began a Russian revolution in theater, anticipated by Scandinavian playwrights such as Ibsen and Strindberg.

Stanislavsky is an alias. He was from a Russian family rich enough—they manufactured gold braid—to have their own private theater. From the time he was fifteen, he kept a notebook with ideas for acting, and even in his amateur days he experimented. He attended the prestigious Paris Conservatory and learned from some of the same teachers as Sarah Bernhardt. When he became a professional, worried that he would disgrace his family, he asked permission, which was granted, to take over a Polish actor's stage name. Instinct and training met inspiration when Stanislavsky watched Italians perform: Eleanora Duse, who specialized in Ibsen, and Tommaso Salvini, a virtuoso in the role of Othello. These actors performed in Italian, a language Stanislavsky did not know well.

Performances in a foreign language prompt audiences to a heightened awareness of behavior and speech separate from the meaning of words. In the history of the theater, breakthroughs often happen in such circumstances. Before Stanislavsky's fundamental changes to the art of acting, the art of directing plays changed for many people, including Stanislavsky—and Ibsen— after watching the ensemble work of the private theater run by the Duke of Saxe-Meiningen. Audiences far from Saxe-Meiningen in southeastern Germany, audiences who couldn't even speak German, were nevertheless mesmerized by the Saxe-Meiningen touring productions of Shakespeare's *Julius Caesar*. Each of the many actors who made up the crowd for the Saxe-Meiningen *Julius Caesar* seemed an individual, bent on an individual task. Their roles and personalities were revealed by the way the characters combined their efforts or thwarted each other. The actors' emotions are the result of their success or failure obtaining what they wanted.

Stanislavsky recognized that what Duse and Salvini were doing onstage was the result of the same sort of process as the crowd scenes in the Saxe-Meiningen *Julius Caesar*. Applying this insight over decades, he developed acting and directing techniques in which character may be revealed by the reactions of someone pursuing a task. Stanislavsky reorganized what an actor does. Rather than display or announce emotion, a Stanislavsky-trained actor may *experience* emotion in performance, not feign emotion, because emotion is a function of wanting something and what happens to thwart or abet the accomplishment of a task. Taking their cues from Stanislavsky, instead of reading scripts for outer action and emotional display, modern actors read plays to establish a structure of desire (called "objectives" in America) and obstacles. Modern audiences observe realistic behavior in performance and deduce emotional states from what they see and hear, rather than from what they're directly told.

Stanislavsky formed his own company, the Moscow Art Theatre (MXAT are the Russian initials, pronounced moo-hot) during a famously long lunch in June 1898 with the director Vladimir Nemirovich-Danchenko. They began talking at two in the afternoon and continued sharing ideas and sketching plans for their new company until eight o'clock the next morning. MXAT's first major success was the 1898 production of Anton Chekhov's play, *The Seagull*. As with *A Month in the Country*, the play had been disliked at its premiere in St. Petersburg the year before.

When the curtain rose on the Moscow *Seagull*, a bearish schoolteacher asked memorably, "Why do you always wear black?" "I am unhappy," a young woman in black replied. The schoolteacher rattled on, boring her. She took snuff, and the Moscow audience, who we may imagine leaning forward to catch the meaning, rather than leaning back to judge the play—understood the bear was in love with the provincial bohemian and she with someone else offstage. With his *Seagull*, Chekhov mastered the evocation of subtext to channel dramatic action; what is said, as in *Hedda Gabler*, masks rather than illustrates what is going on between characters. Like Ibsen, Chekhov quoted realistic behavior and dialogue while organizing the words and metaphors of the play as a poet would a poem. Chekhov wrote three more plays for the Moscow Art Theatre company and married one of the ensemble's leading actresses, Olga Knipper, for whom he wrote major roles.

Chekhov knew he was dying when he wrote his last play, *The Cherry Orchard*. It's his funniest comedy. In *The Cherry Orchard*, if Lopakhin marries Varya, he will save her life and her family's life, too. Her mother, Lubov Andreyevna, played by Olga Knipper in the original 1904 production, waits offstage after conniving for the two to be left alone together. The translation by Julian West, one of the earliest English versions of *The Cherry Orchard*, is faithful to the plain and simple language of the Russian original.

[*There is a restrained laugh behind the door, a whisper, then VARYA comes in.*]

VARYA. [*Looking at the luggage in silence*] I can't seem to find it…
LOPAKHIN. What are you looking for?
VARYA. I packed it myself and I don't remember. [Pause.]

What is dramatic here is what is not said. She's run out of courage.

LOPAKHIN: Where are you going to now, Varvara Mihailovna?
VARYA: I? To the Ragulins…I've got an agreement to go and look after their house…as housekeeper or something.
LOPAKHIN: Is that at Yashnevo? It's about fifty miles. [Pause] So life in this house is finished now…
VARYA: [*Looking at the luggage*]

The drama is that she looks away from him.

Where is it?…perhaps I've put it away in the trunk…Yes, there'll be no more life in this house…
LOPAKHIN: And I'm off to Kharkov at once…by this train. I've a lot of business on hand. I'm leaving Epikhodov here…I've taken him on.
VARYA: Well, well!
LOPAKHIN: Last year at this time the snow was already falling, if you remember, and now it's nice and sunny. Only it's rather

cold...There's three degrees of frost.
VARYA: I didn't look. [*Pause*] And our thermometer's broken...
[*Pause.*]

Varya is waiting for Lopakhin to propose, and he doesn't—that's the dramatic action, what he doesn't do. The pauses while they wait, and think, and worry are moving and funny. What makes it funnier is what they talk about to avoid talking: a broken thermometer.

VOICE AT THE DOOR: Ermolai Alexeyevitch!
LOPAKHIN [*As if he has long been waiting to be called*]: This minute. [*Exit quickly.*]

[Varya, *sitting on the floor, puts her face on a bundle of clothes and weeps gently. The door opens.* Lubov Andreyevna *enters carefully.*]

LUBOV. Well? [*Pause.*] We must go.

In that last pause there is everything: the mother's compassion, the daughter's distress, life has ended, life goes on.

An audience attuned to that pause is an audience transported like no other. Those gathered to watch—and listen—breathe with the actors, exulting and agonizing over what is said or done on-stage, an audience thrilled and worried as much as they would be at a dangerous trapeze act by what is left unsaid or unperformed on an ugly chair or a garden bench. Chekhov's words on the page are a formula for the emotional communion that Stanislavsky dreamed of offering his audience. Stanislavsky's acting technique could reliably deliver and teach what had before been credited to divine inspiration and genius. In an 1895 description of Eleanora Duse, George Bernard Shaw extolled the actress for "the drama in which emotion exists only to make thought live and move us." The audience at the Renaissance market fair knew to move back and watch the commedia; the audience for a realistic play learned to lean in with empathy. What actors should do, according to Stanislavsky, is provide the stimulus for that empathy.

There are other ways to coax an audience to enter the world of a play besides empathy. Some people believe all art, including the theater, has a moral imperative to improve the world. In this way of thinking, the theater should train the audience to sit in judgement of what is happening onstage and in judgement of the world outside the theater. In this way of thinking, actors might provide the stimulus for scrutiny, not empathy. This invitation for the audience to scrutinize the stage defines that genre called Naturalism, easily confused with Realism.

You can think of the relationship of Naturalism to Realism the way a grapefruit would seem to be the same as a grape—but isn't. "Naturalism in the Theatre," the subject and title of an 1881 essay by the French novelist Émile Zola, addresses the human impulse to detail outer forms for moral and political reasons specifically to focus on overlooked or deliberately ignored parts of society, especially those poor and outcast as if misery and squalor were somehow more real than splendor and happiness. In America, Naturalism evolved into kitchen sink realism. In Italy it set off opera composers like Puccini to flower in *veristi* operas set in slums. For a while Strindberg claimed to be writing Naturalistic plays. Some of Ibsen's plays were claimed as Naturalism—though Ibsen famously said, "Zola descends to the gutter to bathe in it while I descend there to cleanse it!"

What Zola had in mind was more impersonal: a play could be a photograph of the gutter. As a photograph was thought to do, a play could fix attention to a reality that was too fleeting to be noticed in life, or too confusing in its details, or so nasty someone encountering such unpleasantness would immediately look away. Fixed onstage, as in a photograph, the audience could study a slice of life in detail. The image of the slice was taken from what a scientist would study under a microscope. An aesthetic of realistic detail gained momentum separately from Zola's intentions.

In 1887 in France, André Antoine, a champion of Naturalism, founded the Théâtre Libre, which means the Theater of Freedom. Antoine's Théâtre Libre, like Strindberg's intimate Intima Theater, was a small private theater, free of the censor, free from the necessity of attracting large crowds, and free, as a result, to challenge the accepted melodramatic formulas of the day. The Théâtre Libre lasted for ten years, during which Antoine presented the first important productions of Ibsen's *Ghosts* and Strindberg's *Miss Julie*. Antoine made a sensation by having live chickens onstage for a play set on a country farm. It's easier to talk about scenery and chickens than to talk about the intangible relationship between audience and performers, actors and text. That doesn't mean it's more important. Still, the chickens got publicity and brought in an audience.

Spurred, in part by the development of photography and journalism, the physical depiction of reality onstage grew elaborate: live animals, environmental sound effects, the construction of "historically accurate" scenery—which the Duke of Saxe-Meiningen had advocated—and slavishly detailed reproductions onstage of what was then contemporary life. There was a corresponding interest in the realism of the scene in sound. There were so many bird chirps in MXAT productions that Chekhov complained in letters about Stanislavsky's effects, yet he knew and was grateful the company had discovered the way to bring life to his work.

In 1902 the Moscow Art Theatre staged Maxim Gorky's *The Lower Depths*, set in the lowest class of boardinghouse. Preparations for the ragged roles were intensive. The MXAT ensemble studied photographs of poor people taken by the playwright, who was also a journalist. Gorky, by the way, is his pen name, the Russian word for *bitter*. Gorky led the actors on tours of the slums and offered to introduce the actress Olga Knipper to a prostitute, the better to catch the details of the role she would play. Knipper passed.

In America, the fashion for realistic scenery was, well, less bitter, more tasty. Well-publicized realistic scenery was fabricated in 1912 by American producer David Belasco (whose nickname was the Bishop of Broadway) for a forgotten play called *The Governor's Lady* written by Alice Bradley. The production is remembered for a scene set in Childs Restaurant, a real diner in New York City. Belasco arranged to reproduce Childs Restaurant onstage. Performances were catered by Childs Restaurant, so the smells of cooking drifted into the audience. In this and other productions, as Antoine and Strindberg had done with their intimate theaters, Belasco paid attention to lighting, removing the footlights, adding lenses that could focus attention on the behavior and details of action and actors, as film cameras were soon to do.

Stanislavsky believed that realistic scenery, lighting, and sound effects stimulated the audience to believe in the truth of a performance. The most convincing aspect of production was the truth of the relationships between the actors, which led to the truth of an emotional relationship with an empathetic audience. When we say such audiences were moved, we mean the actors move their listeners to live, beyond the reality of the physical theater, in an imagined world. Just so in ancient rituals, storytelling shamans and their listeners took journeys together to the world of spirits.

At first, Stanislavsky and his company worked from play to play solving problems without a system, but with the consistent aim of making the character's inner life visible to the audience, in the way a novel might or the way a Russian painting might. The Stanislavsky System was first used by the whole ensemble— which thought it was odd—in a 1909 production of Turgenev's *A Month in the Country*. Olga Knipper played Natalya Petrovna. Stanislavsky, who directed, played her lover Rakitin. Throughout the first act Natalya Petrovna is upset about something; no one can tell why, not her husband, not Rakitin, not even the doctor who examines her with a stethoscope. Turgenev gives clues to what's up. Throughout the scene card players in the same room have been shouting "Hearts" and Natalya's young son has entered, like Cupid, with a bow and quiver. Alone with Belyaev, her son's tutor, Natalya's conversation meanders, but an audience sensitive to what is unspoken may enter the circle of her concentration—a technique Stanislavsky borrowed from yoga—and may enjoy the play as much as they would at a marketplace commedia.

NATALYA PETROVNA: …We are going to be friends, Alexey Nikolaitch, aren't we? I feel confidence in you; the way I've been chattering is a proof of it…

[*She holds out her hand for him to shake hands.* Belyaev *takes it irresolutely and after some hesitation, not knowing what to do with the hand, kisses it.* Natalya Petrovna *flushes and draws away her hand. At that moment* the doctor *comes in from the hall, stops short, then takes a step forward,* Natalya Petrovna *gets up quickly,* Belyaev *does the same.*]

NATALYA PETROVNA [*embarrassed*]: Oh, it's you, Doctor… here Alexey Nikolaitch and I have been…[*Pauses.*]

Chapter Fifteen

BEYOND ILLUSION

Adolphe Appia (1862–1928)
Edward Gordon Craig (1872–1966)
William Poel (1852–1934)

n Act 3, scene 2 of *Hamlet* the title character lectures a group of actors:

> The purpose of playing, whose end, both at the first and now, was and is, to hold as 'twere the mirror up to nature: to show virtue her feature, scorn her own image, and the very age and body of the time his form and pressure.

For good measure, Hamlet adds:

> And let those that play your clowns speak no more than is set down for them.

Want to bet that while Hamlet was complaining about clowns there might have been a clown onstage? What if it was the Player Queen? Or any of the other players? There were certainly clowns in Shakespeare's acting company. In *Hamlet* they played the gravediggers. Famously they improvised, and famously Shakespeare didn't like that, but the speech still isn't a sermon. The reaction of the listening clowns and the audience's response to their presence support a major theme of the play: Hamlet wants the truth to be shown, the world around him smirks, including the audience. Shakespeare's plays are not written as slices of life—how could they be, if they were written partly in verse? They're

carefully considered artifices that rely on the audience's awareness of the stage as a stage. They certainly weren't written as stage
pictures, intended to be mistaken for slices of life. Antony and
Caesar didn't wear togas in Shakespeare's original productions;
Elizabethan actors wore Elizabethan clothing, sumptuous out-
fits in fashionable styles of the day. The scenery for the original
Antony and Cleopatra didn't include a Sphinx or columns topped
with lotuses. Shakespeare's stage needed to be kept clear and un-
cluttered so scenes could flow swiftly from Antony's Rome to
Cleopatra's Egypt and back again.

The delusion that illusion was always what was intended by
a playwright, and always appropriate for an actor's choices, justified well-intentioned mutilations to Shakespeare's texts. Even
when the text was left intact it was often sabotaged by naturalistic productions. Shakespeare kept Cleopatra's barge unseen but
well described, the Victorians floated it up onto the stage. This
limits Shakespeare's power rather than expands it because an
audience can't help comparing a description with what's being
described, which is a distraction. The theatrical conventions in
the theater Shakespeare wrote for supported the spoken word's
dramatic impact on the imagination, not the scenery's impact on
the eye or the props. We see Ophelia's flowers and her drowning
more clearly in our imagination because we do *not* see it on the
stage.

Henry Irving, the Victorian actor/manager who was famous
for his attention to detail in production, defended the practice of
stage design as illustration. Once Elizabethan stage practice was
forgotten, illustrating description acquired centuries of its own
traditions. In 1878 Irving wrote a preface to an acting edition of
Hamlet in which he shared the "natural" beliefs of his time.

> It is but natural that, in attempting to place one of Shakespeare's
> works on the stage in a manner worthy of the great master, the
> utmost care should now be exercised with regard to the scenic
> decorations and other accessories of the play. We live in an age

remarkable for the completeness of its dramatic representa-
tions in this respect at least; and it would be showing very scant
honour to the poet...were we to treat his works with less gener-
osity and less artistic care...than the works of inferior authors...
Shakespeare, if well acted on a bare stage, would certainly afford
great intellectual pleasure; but that pleasure will be all the greater
if the eye be charmed, at the same time, by scenic illustrations in
harmony with the poet's ideas.

Good ideas or not, Shakespeare's texts endure separately
from productions and anyone who reads his plays might arrive
at other ideas. Clearing the text of centuries of tradition, like taking yellowing varnish off an old oil painting, was the first chore.
In England, that began with the zeal of William Poel.

William Poel (1852–1934) was the son of an illustrious civil
engineer; his mother was the daughter of an evangelical minister. They were well connected in Victorian artistic and classical musical circles, enough so that Poel, at twelve, was an artist's
model for several Pre-Raphaelite painters. Unlike his two older
brothers who were sent to universities, at the age of seventeen
William was apprenticed to a building contractor. By the time
he was twenty-two, he found a calling and left his trade for a
career in the theater. Perhaps, he thought, he would be an actor.
Poel began with practical measures to begin his new life: taking
classes and watching performances. In 1878 in his first professional stage job a printer's error changed his name from Pole to
Poel. He kept the mistaken spelling of his name to save his family
from embarrassment. Stanislavsky adopted a Polish actor's name
for the same reason.

The Italian actor Salvini fascinated Poel, as much as Salvini
had fascinated Stanislavsky, but with a difference. Stanislavsky's
appreciation was theoretical. Poel joined Salvini's touring troupe
as a nonspeaking extra in order to study the Italian's craft up

close. Where Stanislavsky intuited Salvini's purposes, Poel observed the way Salvini's spoke on stage—rapid, light, rhythmic—and importantly, even though Salvini performed in an Italian translation of Shakespeare's English text, it was a translation of the original text, without the centuries of changes English editors had been making to Shakespeare's punctuation, act breaks, standardized capitalization, and spelling.

The impetus of Poel's long, focused career was the restoration of Shakespeare's original texts, and by extension the idea that the preparation of a theater artist should begin with a study of the text of the play for meaning, before researching the time and place in which the play is set or investigating the psychology of a role. Poel began his life's work with staged readings, moved on to salon performances, coached actors in other people's productions, directed influential productions himself but never had a single theater as an artistic home. More often he rented halls for performances. He preferred to cast amateurs—they had less bad habits to overcome. He was unique as a scholar and historian because he put his research and writing into practice.

Poel prepared by studying architecture, not the architecture of ancient Rome as Stanislavsky did for his disastrous 1903 production of *Julius Caesar*, but the architecture of the buildings in which Elizabethan dramas were performed and how that architecture affected the construction of Shakespeare's plays. There were no act curtains on Shakespeare's stages, which explained why scenes ended with exits, not a curtain coming down on a stage picture. Scenes flowed into scenes, there were no breaks for scenes or acts, which explained the function of the double plots, so characters could leave and return without confusion that the following scene was a new scene at a later time. Poel met the truism that Shakespeare was for all ages with the observation that Shakespeare was of his own age, too.

Poel further prepared by careful analysis of the original texts, comparing versions—the Quartos and Folios—to learn what the words on the page revealed as opportunities for performance. He insisted that speaking Shakespeare's words so that the audience might hear them was essential to performing what Shakespeare wrote. Other aspects of production that competed for attention were to be avoided if the words were to achieve their potential to engage the audience.

In 1881 Poel staged *Hamlet* on a bare stage in London with little more than a red velvet curtain behind the actors, the first of four productions of *Hamlet*, all cheeky challenges to overstuffed Victorian versions. In 1895 Poel founded The Elizabethan Stage Society to uphold his principles with demonstrations on bare platform stages or other simulations of the stage in Shakespeare's time. These allowed for rapid moves from scene to scene and revealed the power of what we would call Shakespeare's cinematic approach, though there was, as yet, no cinema. Speech in Poel's staging was rapid, pauses for thought rare, since thought, for Shakespeare, was more often described than enacted. During soliloquies actors addressed their audiences directly, rather than the ludicrous invention of those who would maintain the invisible fourth wall in which a person talks to himself while being overheard by the audience. Poel differed from original Shakespearean practice in certain significant ways: women played women's roles in his productions, and Poel used electric lights, including footlights. He experimented with putting people in Elizabethan costume in the audience.

Not all of Poel's experiments found favor, neither with critics, audiences, historians, nor his peers, and it is to his credit that none of his dead ends stopped him—for what is the good of experiments if there are no failures to learn from? He put into practice a great deal of what he imagined could be done and was unswayed by popular success or failure. Twice he was offered a knighthood; twice he turned it down. His methods, like the Stanislavsky System, were first considered eccentric but have become part of standard modern practice, preparation, and performance. Better actors, more accurate historians, and more consistent theoreticians have done much less.

Adolphe Appia (1862–1928), a Swiss theorist of theater, also advocated for performances freed from the responsibilities of realistic illustration. Appia was as much a philosopher as anything else. At the age of sixteen Appia saw his first performance and began to form opinions about theater production. He had been drawing and thinking about scenery since he was fourteen.

Unlike the Greek philosopher Aristotle, who in writing the *Poetics* wrote about what had been, Appia wrote about what could be. Appia prophesied how light might become a dynamic part of a theatrical event and how a stage event might be unified by a stage director and designer's concepts. Though Appia's titles make his writing seem abstract—*The Work of Living Art: A Theory of the Theatre* (1921), for example—they were meant as slogans for action. Appia was inspired by the German composer Richard Wagner, who conceived operas in which music, words, and stage pictures would all be part of the meaning of the performance. Characteristically, the first time Appia attended a performance of Wagner he was greatly dissatisfied by the production and imagined his own.

Appia's theories were read about more than put into practice professionally, but he inspired playwrights—who had studied his writing in school—to include stage directions, specify the color, intensity, or form of light, as well as employ music and sound effects. The ambition to write a play that included light—its direction, color, intensity—as an integral part of the script was increasingly realized in the professional theater in America and Europe by technological advances in lighting instruments. Recorded sound made similar advances. The technological advances that enabled the reality-obsessed Stanislavsky or Belasco to achieve convincing onstage illusions could, Appia realized, be the means to achieve something very different than such illusions.

Rather than hold up a mirror to life, Appia abstracted the elements of stage decor reducing scenic elements to their working essence: walls, stairs, ramps, columns. These were composed with geometric simplicity, as much to display the changes in light as tell the audience where the action took place. Appia insisted on three-dimensional scenery rather than painted flats, and he insisted decor for the stage be mindful of time as a dimension of design. Performances unfold in time—and Appia pointed out that as the plot unfolds—the progression, repetition, and contrasts of the visuals build meaning for the audience, just as music or spoken words do. Appia's poetics of theater considered production as essential to theatrical meaning, not secondary to a written text, and not an illustration. Film would come to adopt this way of working, so that a film's director—more often than the person writing the screenplay—would lead a team of artists to create a unified artwork.

The spoken word for Appia was a part of a whole, not necessarily the most important aspect of a performance. For Appia, performers were subordinate to the aims of the production, like parts of a machine. Other people developed this idea by experimenting with ensemble work that aimed for results very different from the life-like crowds of the Duke of Saxe-Meiningen who had inspired Stanislavsky and William Poel. The Swiss composer Émile Jaques-Dalcroze, whom Appia worked with, invented Eurhythmics, rhythmic movements performed by a group of people and occasionally a soloist. The Russian director Meyerhold created Biomechanics, reinventing the acting ensemble as a machine for performance. In photographs, the poses of Eurhythmics and Biomechanics seem arch, but so do other art forms and styles from the turn of the nineteenth to twentieth centuries. Art Nouveau, Symbolist plays, these all seemed new advances in their day, and now seem dead ends. What's a dead end and what's a step forward in history is decided by the winner, in this case Realism.

In 1910 Appia designed the Festspielhaus Hellerau in southern Germany as a school for Dalcroze. The Hellerau theater featured an open stage without a proscenium arch or curtain. Waxed white cotton strips were lit from behind to make moveable scenic elements, and the audience could be moved around, too. Nazis took over the building in 1939 and turned it into a police station. Oddly enough, they kept a yin-yang sign decorating the pediment. When the Soviet army conquered East Germany, the Russians put up a big red star where the yin-yang had been. By 1992, with the collapse of the Communist Empire, the building was in disrepair. Since 2008 the Festspielhaus Hellerau has hosted an international theater festival.

Forty years after Appia passed away, the Czech stage designer Josef Svoboda would make good on Appia's promises by fabricating astonishing scenery from curtains of light shimmering on ionized dust particles. Appia's ideas to reduce scenery to basic "pure" architectural elements was spectacularly realized by Svoboda's scenery for a Polish production of *Oedipus* in which a flight of stairs, the breadth of the stage, ascended as high as the proscenium and beyond.

Edward Gordon Craig (1872–1966) was an English theater visionary with just as much personal theory to expand on as Appia. Craig worked in the professional theater in America, England, and Russia. Well-placed socially for his career, he was the illegitimate son of Ellen Terry, Henry Irving's leading lady and acting partner. Craig had grown up in the upholstered Victorian theater and lived to rebel against it.

For Craig, as with Wagner and Appia, the theater was something in which human beings were part of a composition. Craig was particularly interested in masks and puppets. As with Appia's theories, it is startling to read what Craig wrote about at the same time Stanislavsky and the pioneers of filmmaking were working to create the illusions of realism and psychological nuance.

Craig lived to be ninety-four but stopped working as a designer for actual productions when he turned forty, supposedly because of an inability to compromise. He wrote well and persuasively. He had a good platform to publicize his ideas in *The Mask,* the first international magazine of theater, which Craig founded and edited from 1908 to 1929. Using over sixty false names, he wrote all the articles himself. Like his mother, he was not overly concerned with social conventions, and took a series of lovers, among them the great American choreographer, Isadora Duncan, whose work was similarly clearing away Victorian excess from dance. Duncan, who was worshipped like a goddess in Russia, introduced Craig to Stanislavsky.

In 1908 Stanislavsky invited Craig to Russia to direct and design a production of *Hamlet* for the Moscow Art Theatre. This was typically bold of Stanislavsky, whose love of experimentation continued throughout his life, though records of it were later removed by Soviet authorities bent on reinforcing Social Realism. Craig's idea for Moscow was that, aside from Hamlet himself, all the other roles were phantoms of Hamlet's imagination. Craig argued that Hamlet should be onstage constantly, watching scenes in which he didn't appear. Stanislavsky, who staged the landmark production of *A Month in the Country* that same year, was unpersuaded. Hamlet did not watch all the scenes. Craig kept true to his idea in another way: at the end of the play the figures onstage disappeared, as if they had been the phantoms of a dream from which the audience—and Hamlet—was waking. The French press and the German press loved it, and the production sounds great, but among Russian critics at the time it was disliked. Craig wasn't invited back, and his approach wasn't followed up in other MXAT productions.

Appia championed simple steps, ramps, and other basic architectural elements. For *Hamlet*, Craig used a series of screens that slid, rotated, carried shadows, and gleamed. Unfortunately, they also jammed, and jammed often. It wasn't until several years had passed that the value of the production's innovations surpassed the unpleasantness of sitting through it in a theater.

Craig's abstractions found great realization with the work of choreographers: Martha Graham in America, Mary Wigman in Germany, and other creators of dance theater. Craig was interested in puppets as moving physical objects, along with moving light to make theater. American choreographers Alvin Nikolais and Murray Louis realized Craig's dreams and those of Appia too, in pure form and light that made dramatic spectacles, if not literary drama. Craig, like Appia, downplayed the dominance of the spoken word in performance. In his essay "On the Art of the Theatre," written in 1911, Craig argued that performers created theater before dramatists. This may or may not be so, but William Poel would argue that because of the text, theater endures, as could be said of the many texts that waited for inspired interpreters: *Peer Gynt, A Month in the Country, Woyzeck,* and *Hamlet.*

Poel, Appia, and Craig were not ignorant of what was popular, nor did they ignore what was popular. They were provoked by what was around them—and would probably not have come up with their ideas without the realistic theater's popularity to annoy them. They were the avant-garde, in advance of their time, and very unusually for the theater, in advance of other arts: cinematic before there was cinema, abstract before abstract art, blatantly theatrical and unsuited for the naturalism that film and television would come to demand. Their theories still confront the domination of realism and naturalism. The live chickens at the Théâtre Libre caught the eye and Stanislavsky-trained actors caught the heart. The ideas of Poel, Appia, and Craig continue to capture our imaginations.

Chapter Sixteen

MELODRAMA AND POPULAR THEATER IN AMERICA

George S. Aiken (1830–1876)
Fanny Brice (1891–1951)
George M. Cohan (1878–1942)
John Augustus Stone (1801–1834)
Royall Tyler (1757–1826)
Bert Williams (1874–1922)

Theater in the United States of America began, as it began
in other European colonies, as one more way—along
with uncomfortable shoes and unnecessary lace—for
the homesick seventeenth century British colonials to remind
themselves *who* they were despite *where* they were. In Colonial
America, performances of plays by Shakespeare or performances
of witty eighteenth-century comedies popular in London were
proof of high culture and civilization, as much proof as the performance of "classical" music or even just the difficulty and expense
of importing a piano from Europe. Performances of plays were
signs of prestige. Rich people paid for such performances just
as they paid for and enjoyed other displays of power: fur, pearls,
itchy wool, and nice buttons on the uniforms of their servants and
slaves. In any British colony, to be able to perform Shakespeare,
or watch his plays with understanding, demonstrated refinement.
The performance and enjoyment of what Shakespeare wrote still
demonstrates refinement in former British colonies.

Distinctly *American* theater began with less refined forms, though American character types appeared first in conventional colonial plays. Royall Tyler's *The Contrast*, written ten years after the American Revolution, introduced one of the first of American types: Jonathan, the cunning stage Yankee. *The Contrast* is otherwise a formulaic British comedy of wit, though not so witty. After John Augustus Stone wrote *Metamora; or, The Last of the Wampanoags* in 1829, audiences met and enjoyed a new American type: Metamora, the Noble Indian. As a play, *Metamora* is otherwise forgettable. The role of the pretentious Mrs. Tiffany in Anna Cora Mowatt's *Fashion*, written in 1845, is an American variant of a stylish type seen in London comedies, as are the names and roles of other characters in *Fashion*: Snobson, a conniving clerk, and Trueman, an honest farmer.

American playwrights characterized their types in the same way roles were characterized in the Italian Renaissance commedia. Though you couldn't prove a direct line of origin or a family tree, the wily Jewish pawnbroker of American comedies follows in the path of Pantalone, the commedia's clever Venetian with a hooked nose and clinking purse. The saucy black maid with the polka-dot do-rag who graces or disgraces, depending on your point of view, American drama, could claim a close cousin in Columbina, the commedia's flirt in a patched apron who hails from the wrong side of Bergamo. The characterization of American types, as in commedia, as elsewhere and in other times, caricatures recognizable accents. In early American theater, the rolled r's, elongated vowels, and mistakes in grammar made by immigrants, former slaves, foreigners, country bumpkins, and city slickers were considered funny and laughable or pathetic and moving, and a reminder that these types, abnormal as they were in speech, were less-than-fully-normal human beings. The Athenians had done the same thing with the Spartans in Greek comedies written two thousand years before.

When American theater begins to take itself seriously, by its own definition, it kept to conventional forms and recognizable types, but enrolled these crowd-pleasing clichés in a serious cause—to abolish slavery. *Uncle Tom's Cabin*, the 1852 novel by Harriet Beecher Stowe, is credited with influencing the abolition of slavery in America by depicting black people with compassion. Stage adaptations of the play were even more influential in America because stage adaptations toured widely and were seen by people who couldn't or wouldn't read a book—and there were many such people. George S. Aiken's version of *Uncle Tom's Cabin* was one of the most popular. That Aiken's play is silly and the dialogue awkward is beside the point for those savoring the importance of the moral purpose. The confusion of aesthetic value with moral excellence and purpose is not particularly American, but it holds special (and continuing) power in America, a country founded by Puritans who thought of theater as time wasted, time that could have been better spent in church or, better yet, at work. Theater was prohibited by law in several of the British colonies in America. At the time of the American Revolution theatrical performances were banned by both sides. What performances there were of plays in colonial America were illegal, slightly naughty if not outright immoral, and paid for by aristocrats who could afford to flout the current prejudices—prejudices proffered as morality.

After the American Revolution, Americans uneducated in the higher culture but with need for diversion, made up a new potential audience. There were no longer laws prohibiting theater, but for commercial theater to develop in America, for respectable people to come regularly—that is to say, to buy tickets—theater in America still had to pass as something good for you, like medicine or Sunday School. Popular melodramas in nineteenth century America entertained in the ways Puritan sermons roused congregations: a crowd titillated by the presence of evil could sit safe in the expectation that evil would be punished and good would prevail. If good didn't prevail in the theater, as in *Uncle Tom's Cabin*, at least good people ascended to a heaven of plucked harps and fluttering white robes.

Harps, or some other musical instruments, were essential. The French word *mélodrame*—a French word that passed directly into the English language as melodrama—comes from melody drama. The presence of music organized the meaning of the text in performance. Music signaled to the audience the emotional significance of the scene, much the way music does in action or suspense films. At a melodrama, the audience is united emotionally by music telling them how to respond, individually and as a group, a very nice thing in an emerging democracy. Even if you couldn't follow too closely or hadn't the education to understand the cultural references of a play, you would at least know when to hiss at the villain and cheer on the hero. In George S. Aiken's version of *Uncle Tom's Cabin*, when the nasty slave-owner Simon Legree enters, the first thing he does is spit on a black man's clean boots. When he kills Uncle Tom, the last thing Tom does is beg pardon:

[*(Rises feebly on his hands.)*]
There ain't no more you can do. I forgive you with all my soul.

These kinds of words and actions made it easy for the audience to understand who was who, what was going on, and how, as an individual audience member, one was supposed to react as part of the group.

Aiken's *Uncle Tom* toured the country for decades with lavish productions including live horses, dogs, comic slaves, and miserable villains to satiate audiences' expectations of spectacle, moral superiority, and emotional stimulation. Aiken's *Tom* continued touring well after the Civil War was over and slavery was abolished. With its moral campaign concluded; it lived on by virtue of its thrills.

In the cities large and small, Industrial Age factory workers and others who lived emotionally restricted lives found themselves stimulated in the theater. Something similar happened in twentieth century Soviet Russia and other communist countries where popular theater offered escape from dreary, soul-numbing daily life and state-stifled expression. In nineteenth century Europe, melodramas placed characters who might have come right up out of the audience—shop girls, factory workers, sailors—in heightened emotional situations. Female characters in the popular theater forms of the nineteenth century, especially melodrama, suffered publicly, displaying emotions hidden by women in polite society.

Melodrama plots were satisfyingly predictable: the villain threatened the good guys, the villain lost, or if the heroes lost, they would be vindicated by going to heaven. Suspense and stage spectacle kept the audience's interest. That the experience followed a formula was comforting. There was nothing like Ibsen's subversion of expectations. Just as Renaissance theater paid for by kings flattered kings, the popular theater paid for by the general public offered the general public a vision of itself as heroic. Otherness was safely exotic, enticing, and laughably funny.

In an increasingly industrialized nineteenth century America, tours by train or horse-pulled coaches rolled theater productions out of the cities and into mining camps or wherever a hall could be found or a tent set up for the occasion. Better lighting in American cities, at first gas lamps on the streets, ultimately electric streetlamps, meant middle-class audiences felt safer going out at night. Tickets were priced to be available to a wider range of ticket buyers than ever before. To maintain financial support from as broad a base as possible, theater buildings in America were large. Performers necessarily used loud voices and large gestures in order to be seen and heard. As technology advanced, flaming gas jets lit up the stage much more brightly than candles had done before. Brighter lighting meant there could be larger audiences. Gaslight provided more lurid colors and shed more intense shadows, accentuating the lurid style of acting. Even so, subtle acting was praised; psychological nuance was possible within the context of the clichéd roles.

Virtuoso stars in America enticed audiences into theaters more effectively than the reputations of famous authors. Plays were commissioned by actors, and sometimes actors bought the exclusive legal right to perform certain crowd-pleasing plays. *Metamora; or, The Last of the Wampanoags,* for example, won first prize in a contest set up by Edwin Forrest who was twenty-two at the time. Forrest bought the rights and played The Noble Indian for the next forty years. The author, John Augustus Stone, died penniless.

Distinct from plays, there had always been popular entertainment in America without significant text: juggling, acrobatics, dancing, animal acts, singing—all can be very dramatic, if not dramatic literature. A collection of such entertainments presented together for an audience's pleasure was called, among other names, a variety show, a vaudeville, a burlesque, or a revue. Notice the spelling in revue and vaudeville—the hint of something exotic, naughty, unusual, "Frenchy." In England the tradition is called music hall and began as entertainment performed in taverns where money was made on drinks not ticket sales. In America, gold rush saloons did the same with dancing girls, though the gold rush girls were advertising their legs as much as touting the beer. The American variety show is similar to the British music hall performances, but in America variety shows played in theaters, not bars.

The Black Crook, often claimed as the first musical comedy in America, is a better example of a revue. In 1866, at a theater in New York called Niblo's Garden, the show curtain rose on a beautiful painted backdrop of a mountain forest in Germany. Two lovers met by moonlight, there was a dance, according to the stage directions, of "female villagers with garlands, followed by males, two of whom bear a rustic chair, festooned with flowers." In the third scene, the evil hunchbacked alchemist from whom the text gets its title entered. Moonlit lovers! Dancing maidens! An evil hunchbacked alchemist! Crookback…evil: *The Black Crook!* Subtle it wasn't. *The Black Crook* included a lot of songs and a lot of dances, since the idea for doing it at all began in desperation when a French ballet company was stranded in New York. You don't need to read it, though you could. You might want to know about it to understand commercial success in the American theater.

Niblo's Garden, the New York theater where *The Black Crook* opened on what was then Lower Broadway, sat 3,200 people. The show ran for five and a half hours, which was a great diversion for that part of the audience who would otherwise have had to be working. The first New York run lasted an astonishing 474 performances. Touring versions and a revival spun on for decades. And *The Black Crook* was an opportunity to see a girl's legs. In nineteenth century America, women's sexuality was publicly controlled and the delights of a body were displayed in codes, never overtly. Onstage at a revue you could ogle women's legs and necks—and arms. The original playbill for *The Black Crook* boasted, in letters bigger than any of the star's names, "A Corps of Seventy Ladies."

With an emphasis on spectacle, producers accumulated great importance within the commercial theater. It was easier to produce cheaper and shorter shows than *The Black Crook*. You didn't always need a corps of seventy ladies. A plot was unnecessary, too, and independent sketches could be just as entertaining. Presenting unconnected acts meant more power for producers because acts could be replaced and so could headlining stars. The development of the transcontinental train system after 1869 meant it was possible to set out on longer tours, up into English-speaking Canada, from the coast of the Atlantic to the Pacific and back, as well as on boats up and down the Mississippi river.

Over time, the most powerful producers were called, half-jokingly, impresarios. The term impresario (from the Italian word *impressa*, an undertaking) bears a direct connection to the word emperor. In the Italian opera the impresario is the person who hires the composer and other personnel. In the American theater, impresarios were enterprising people with an aesthetic or social agenda of their own, but rarely an interest in plays as literature. David Belasco was an especially influential impresario who led the field by his example of producing shows with detailed realistic scenery and elaborate lighting effects lavished on lackluster texts. Tony Pastor, B.F. (for Benjamin Franklin) Keith, and E.F. Albee assembled collections of theatrical venues around the country where they could send out touring shows, guaranteed, by virtue of these producer's reputations to provide clean entertainment suitable for women, without profanity, and without slang. Florenz Ziegfeld was an impresario famous for a tableaux of beautiful women posed like statues. Known as "the Glorifier of the American Girl," he was born to German immigrants in Chicago in 1867. The Ziegfeld Follies, as Ziegfeld billed his extravaganzas, began in 1907 and continued every year until 1931, the year before Ziegfeld died. These impresarios, whose names on a program guaranteed ticket buyers value for their money, used their great power to make theatergoing socially acceptable in America, though at the cost of making popular theater into little more than pleasant entertainment.

Clever producers publicized polite "vaudevilles." Vaudeville is a word so unconnected to its French origins, the meaning of the French is debatable. In America, vaudeville meant mixed entertainment, a combination that might include animal acts, male and female impersonators, as well as comedy sketches—and sometimes class acts: Sarah Bernhardt, for example, performed tirades from *Phèdre* in vaudeville. Onstage and off there was an appeal, alternately soothing and titillating, to middle-class sensibilities.

Importantly, people who did not have a classical background or opportunities for classical training could take part in vaudeville performances: in particular, black people, Jews, and Irish immigrants. The stage Irishman—drunk, witty, clog dancing, womanizing, with his thick brogue and checkered pants—was a part of the assimilation into the United States of the four and a half million people from Ireland who came to America between

1820 and 1930. In the cities where they lived, the Irish, specifically the Irish Catholic, were discriminated against, formed gangs,
created their own separate world, and took on the reputation of
an urban underclass. They were not invited into polite society.

At the same time, Irish singers and dancers were welcome
onstage. The Irish way of crooning made words easier to understand than the elongated vowels and foreign languages heard in
operas. Irish dancing was comic and livelier than ballet. Vaudeville programs often included Irish numbers, and there were
early Irish stage stars, culminating with George M. Cohan, born
in 1878 in Providence, Rhode Island, who created many of the
iconic images of what it is to be American, including the songs
"I'm a Yankee Doodle Dandy," "Give My Regards to Broadway,"
"It's a Grand Old Flag," and the American anthem of the First
World War "Over There." Cohan, who began playing violin at the
age of eight, grew up in a vaudeville family as one of the Four Co-
hans. By stringing his songs together with a narrative, he wrote
plays in the tradition of *The Black Crook*.

Immigrant Jews, most of whom came to America from Eastern Europe about forty years after the Irish immigration, were
also unwelcome in polite American society but accepted happily in American theaters as comedians and songwriters. Some
immigrant Jews had their own tradition, the Yiddish-speaking
theater, but this—essentially another refined colonial theater—
sent few if any writers or performers to cross over to the coars-
er English-speaking theater. Jewish immigrants willing to play
into popular stereotypes could enter American show business
if they wanted. Some Jews disguised their origins and changed
their names to assimilate. Some Jewish performers, especially
comedians like Fanny Brice (born Fania Borach in New York to
a family of Hungarian Jews) took advantage of their otherness,
accentuating their accents. Sometimes, Jews like Al Jolson (born
Asa Yoelson in what's now Lithuania) so exaggerated their difference from "white" Americans that they performed in blackface,
speaking in what passed for "Black" dialect. Jewish songwriters

gave America dozens of definitively American songs. Irving Berlin (born in Russia as Israel Isadore Beilin) wrote the words and music to "God Bless America" and "White Christmas."

Black Americans could not assimilate in the same way as Irish or Jewish immigrants. In nineteenth century America, the projection of singing and dancing onto the "Other," the "Black Man," was satisfied by the minstrel show with its banjo-strumming, high-stepping, or shuffling, caricatures of African Americans who sang mournful or jubilant tunes, and drawled stupidities. There were other characters in minstrel shows: Jim Crow the carefree slave, Mr. Tambo and Mr. Bones—the jolly musician and his straight man—and the ludicrously pretentious Zip Coon. These cartoons defused a white public's fear of Black anger and revolt by having Black people dance and sing and act foolishly. This was done symbolically when white actors smeared their faces with burnt cork or black grease paint, known as blackface. Black actors were forbidden to perform in minstrel shows until after the Civil War, though African-American plantation dances, jigs, music, and songs were repurposed for minstrel shows and eventually by other forms of popular American entertainment.

Even before the Civil War, some Black men put on minstrel makeup and pretended to be white men pretending to be black men. Black performers in America continued to perform in blackface as late as the 1930s. Some became celebrated stage stars. Bert Williams, who did much to push back racial barriers during his career, was born in Nassau, the Bahamas, and came to New York when he was ten. He teamed up in vaudeville with George Walker. Walker played the wise guy; Williams played the slow drawling fool. Williams and Walker wore blackface but advertised to emphasize they were "really" black. They were later criticized for reinforcing racist stereotypes, but working within the system as it then existed, they devised a strategy that brought personal respect, professional respect, and success. Before 1920, the voice of Bert Williams was the most recorded in the world.

Williams and Walker wrote their own comedy material, their own songs, and created their own musical revues. Their biggest success, a revue titled *In Dahomey*, opened in 1902 on Broadway, with segregated seating; it then went on to acclaim in London without segregated seating. In 1908 George M. Cohan asked Williams and Walker (who were starring on Broadway) to appear in a charity benefit. An Irish monologue artist tried to organize a boycott, but only two other acts went along with the boycott, which failed. Ziegfeld, in 1910, was faced with those in his company who didn't want to share the stage with Bert Walker because he was black. They felt his presence would lower their own social status. Ziegfeld announced, "I can replace every one of you but him." They all stayed. A fragment of Walker's act survives in *A Natural Born Gambler,* a silent film Williams made in 1916. The last few minutes include a silent poker pantomime right out of his old vaudeville act. In 1922 Bert Williams collapsed onstage in Detroit. "That's a nice way to die," he said, as the audience laughed. A week later he was back in New York to recuperate but passed away six weeks later at the age of forty-seven.

Another way the culture tamed the terror of otherness was by staring at it from a safe distance. P.T. Barnum, the circus impresario, displayed dwarves, giants, albinos, bearded women, and pinheads, but given a stage to do so, also showcased natural talents like Jenny Lind, the Swedish singing sensation. The price of Barnum's ticket was made cheap enough to encourage a mass audience, which would become the business model for the development of the cinema.

It would take decades to assimilate stereotypes and freaks into American literature, but the great change from staring at freaks to compassion for freaks—and a respect for the consequence of who was considered marginal in America—can be considered a starting point for the achievement of American playwrights such as Eugene O'Neill, Clifford Odets, Tennessee Williams, Arthur Miller, and August Wilson. At first, writers of American theater took pains to publicly distance themselves from the popular theater. Over time, more confident, American playwrights could come to embrace their theatrical heritage, and the musical revue, freak show, minstrel show, and the inclusion of the immigrant or African-American experience would make for truly American theater.

As with most theater traditions, America's has a mix of low and high forms. What is specifically American, however, is the eventual incorporation of the low, retaining its low identity, as part of national identity and the infiltration of outsiders who composed, constructed, and performed what it means to be American.

Chapter Seventeen

AMERICAN CLASSIC: EUGENE O'NEILL AND MARTHA GRAHAM

Martha Graham (1894–1991)
Eugene O'Neill (1888–1953)

E ugene O'Neill, literally a child of the American theater, was born in a hotel room off Times Square in New York City in 1888. His father was starring in *The Count of Monte Cristo*, a romantic melodrama or, if you like, a melodramatic romance based on the novel by Alexandre Dumas. Whatever you want to call the play, it was a windy vehicle for an actor to show off fancy talk, fancier swordplay, period costumes from rags to ruffles: in short, a play meant to distract middle-class Victorian audiences from their own preoccupations. O'Neill's father had been playing the Count since 1882. He racked over six thousand performances in a little over thirty years.

As in a novel or a play, Eugene O'Neill's beginnings would determine the rest of his life and his artistic career. It is inherently dramatic that O'Neill, the person who killed off melodrama in America, was the son of an American melodrama star. Much of the O'Neill family history resembles a novel or a play. The family's relationship to alcohol abuse is epic; their relationships to each other echo as tragedy. At the beginning of Eugene O'Neill's great fame when he was in his early thirties (1920–1923), all three members of O'Neill's family died slowly and painfully: his mother, father, and his older brother who committed suicide by literally drinking himself to death. Both of O'Neill's sons committed suicide, and he stopped talking to his only daughter after she turned eighteen. All of this is memorable gossip, but what does it have to do with the words on the page written by a playwright? Just this: the circumstances of O'Neill's life are significant to his work because he raised them past gossip into a high mythology of the modern age. The then recent theories of Sigmund Freud about thwarted desire—ideas about obstacles, repression, and personality that parallel the acting theory of Stanislavsky—opened up a channel for O'Neill to think of his family beyond despair and desperation. Freud offered a resonant vocabulary of Greek mythology, including Greek tragedy, which O'Neill claimed as his artistic inheritance and personal property.

O'Neill's explorations of tragic form and his self-examination of conflicting emotions culminate in his one undisputed masterpiece: *A Long Day's Journey into Night.* Written between 1939 and 1941 but hidden and unperformed until 1956, three years after O'Neill's death. The play isn't light reading, and it wasn't easy to write. The family he imagined in a fog-smeared Connecticut country house mirrors O'Neill's family. In the play, James Tyrone—one of the all-time great roles for an actor—is, as was O'Neill's father, James O'Neill, a well-rewarded hack of a stage star who in his youth had shown promise playing Shakespeare. In the play, as in O'Neill's family, there are two brothers. The older brother is a drunk; O'Neill's older brother drank himself to death. The younger brother in the play is doomed to die of tuberculosis as Eugene would have died had he not survived after contracting tuberculosis when he was twenty-four. At the heart of the matter is the sad scandal that O'Neill's mother was a morphine addict. In the play, as in life, the mother's addiction began when her husband hired a cheap doctor to attend the birth of her second child. Eugene believed these were the circumstances of his own birth.

O'Neill lifted his family secrets high: the haunting of the house, the death of hope, the doom of a child, the curse on an entire family became in his greatest play neither confession nor memoir, but myth. The tragedy that Aristotle describes the Greeks achieving, O'Neill achieved: pain that leads to awareness. What O'Neill learned about his personal history is what the blind Argentine author Borges suggests about misfortune:

> the ancient food of heroes: humiliation, unhappiness, discord. These things are given to us to transform, so that we may make from the miserable circumstances of our lives things that are eternal, or aspire to be so.
> (Borges, "Blindness," *Seven Nights*)

All great playwrights have a vision of how human beings relate to each other. Ibsen saw the smothering of individual spirit by society countered by the unstoppable sometimes destructive impulse for freedom. Strindberg conceived the idea of soul murder. For Strindberg, the world was made up of vampires and their victims: there were those who stole life force from others and those from whom it was stolen. O'Neill was inspired by the writings of Ibsen and Strindberg, but his revelation was his own. O'Neill's insight was shame. The author of *Long Day's Journey into Night* is ashamed of himself, of his father, of his mother; he fears and pities them—and himself. In this way O'Neill lifted guilt—an idea at the heart of Greek tragedy and Shakespeare's tragedy—onto the modern stage.

The play almost didn't get published or performed. O'Neill wrote it in secret, weeping as he wrote it, according to his wife who kept him apart from the world in a mansion on a mountain in what is now the Las Trampas Regional Wilderness (the Spanish word *trampas* means snares) overlooking the Pacific. Aware that *Long Day's Journey into Night* would change his father's reputation, not to mention his mother's, when O'Neill finished the manuscript, he melted a wax seal onto it and specified in his will that the seal remain unbroken until twenty-five years after his death, which would have been in 1978. This is as theatrical as any novel or play.

Of course, his wife and publisher cracked the seal. After his death they were worried about the drop in his reputation. They had read the manuscript and knew it would seal O'Neill's reputation for all time. Cautiously, the play was performed first in Sweden in 1956 where O'Neill had been honored with the Nobel Prize in 1936. The world came to Stockholm to see the play. The reaction was such that within nine months *Long Day's Journey into Night* played on Broadway in New York and won the playwright a posthumous Pulitzer Prize, his fourth. Assessments of O'Neill changed immediately. Had *Long Day's Journey into Night* been lost or burned or kept in a vault twenty-five years, O'Neill's place in history might have been the vast ambition of his theatrical experiments. That ambition was nothing less than to convert the purposes of theatergoing and playwriting in America from the diversions of melodrama and musical revues to a communal search for meaning, including the meaning of the most profound pain.

Martha Graham (1894–1991), born six years after O'Neill, had similar ambitions to transform dance. Graham aimed to take an art form enjoyed in America as an excuse for leering at women's legs—or gawking at fairies on tippy-toes—and extend its reach beyond divertissement to create American dances that celebrated the heights and depths of passion, self-knowledge, and remorse. Graham was born in what's now Pittsburgh, Pennsylvania. Her father was what was then called an "alienist," an early job description for a psychologist. As a teenager she began to study at Denishawn, the dance school in Los Angeles run by Ruth St. Denis and her husband Ted Shawn. Denishawn was intent on reforming dance, and its students went on to establish world-class American dance theater. In search of the spiritual sources of movement, Denishawn students studied the religious dance traditions of Asia. Ruth St. Denis, who was born on a farm in New Jersey, reproduced Japanese and Indian dances decked out in elaborate wigs and costumes accompanied by exotic music played on exotic instruments. St. Denis imagined what ancient

Egyptian dances were like, and it says something that her dances were sometimes part of vaudeville programs. St. Denis's husband, Ted Shawn, did much the same. Martha Graham got her professional start as a burlesque performer in *Xochitl* an "Aztec dance" created by Shawn.

After seven years at Denishawn, Graham came to New York City to become a dancer in the Greenwich Village Follies revue. By 1927 she began her own ensemble and established her own approach to dance, an approach very different from what had gone before her. Graham's dance was modern, American, challenging, and alarming in its jagged beauty. By 1929 the *New York Times* recognized Graham's status.

> Bitter, intellectual, cold, if you will, her art is arresting, even aggressive, with a hard beauty as of sculptured steel. It is difficult to imagine any one's being indifferent to Miss Graham, but, whether she inspires enthusiasm or intense dislike, the evidences of greatness are inescapable.
> (Martin, *New York Times*, Jan 21, 1929)

Graham and O'Neill, the leaders in their fields in America, had freedom to experiment which they accepted playfully and seriously. Both used masks, choruses, unresolved endings, and untraditional forms. O'Neill and Graham, who both grew up in the professional American theater, had an intuitive understanding of how to entertain an audience. Both knew how to publicize their work so that a paying public came to the theater already prepared to enjoy themselves.

Aware that theater and dance in America were considered low and seedy or, even worse, confined to small audiences in a ghetto of artiness, O'Neill and Graham had ambitions to escape being marginalized. They both wanted to participate on the world stage and in the commercial world. They prepared themselves by learning what they could in classrooms. Graham took a two-year hiatus to go to the Eastman School in Rochester, New York. She studied there with the film director Rouben Mamoulian, known for his mastery of rhythm in storytelling. In 1914, O'Neill enrolled in the famous playwright's class taught by George Pierce Baker at Harvard University. O'Neill lasted a year at Harvard.

O'Neill moved to Provincetown, Massachusetts in 1916, a small fishing village at the tip of Cape Cod. The place was known for its artists' colony—and radical politics. There was a small community theater that played on a wharf there, calling themselves the Provincetown Players. O'Neill, who arrived in the second year of the Provincetown Players, became their star playwright beginning with a production of his one-act *Bound East for Cardiff*, in which the fog rolled up out of the bay onto the wharf, the actors, the action, and the audience during the first performance. O'Neill's small sea plays were fresh dramatic progressions of revelation and perception rather than well-plotted potboilers. The Provincetown Players successfully brought their work to New York City's Greenwich Village, staging plays in the Provincetown Playhouse named after their venue on the Cape Cod wharf. New York, after the First World War, was commencing its role as cultural capital of America. Inspiration and work might happen elsewhere, but it was in Manhattan, and often in the pages of New York newspapers, that reputations were made, including Eugene O'Neill's reputation. When *Beyond the Horizon* played on Broadway in February 1920 it won the first of O'Neill's Pulitzer Prizes. In November that same year, *The Emperor Jones*, a fantasia in eight scenes based on the slave revolt of Haiti, opened downtown at the Provincetown Playhouse, which was too small for the crowds that gathered to see the play. The production moved to a larger building, ultimately running for 204 performances. The son's reputation in the theater now eclipsed that of the father, who died in August of the same year.

O'Neill's writing ranged from one-act plays set at sea, nine-act plays that ran for hours, plays with spoken subtext, plays with poetry, and slices of life with realistic dialogue. Throughout O'Neill's writing career, he tried to make artistic use of American vernacular speech: the accents of Swedish immigrants, New England farmers, Irish maids and an African-American man studying for his law exam. Much, if not most, of his work is less than successful, but he is all the more important for trying. He was not a natural lyrical writer, and much of his experimentation was as borrowed as Denishawn's Oriental trappings. No matter the style, O'Neill's vision of relationships between people is genuine.

O'Neill's sensibility was rooted in literature, something he dramatized in his relatively late play *Ah, Wilderness!* The exclamation point is part of the title. It's O'Neill's one comedy, his childhood as he wished it had been, he once said. The central character is a teenage boy—a young playwright in the making—inspired to silliness by reading *Hedda Gabler*, the plays of Bernard Shaw, and the twelfth century poetry of Omar Khayyám, whose quatrain about satisfaction is the source of the title:

> A Book of Verses underneath the Bough,
> A Jug of Wine, a Loaf of Bread—and Thou
> Beside me singing in the Wilderness—
> Oh, Wilderness were Paradise enow!
> (*The Rubáiyát of Omar Khayyám*, Edward FitzGerald, trans.)

The great Broadway Irishman, George M. Cohan, starred in the original 1933 production as the father in the play, a wonderful link between the popular theater and a tip-off to the public that this was meant to be funny, not another tragedy, not another of O'Neill's nine-hour experiments.

Martha Graham courted her audience in her own way for over fifty years with plotless, abstract dances, narrative dance theater, imagistic dance theater, fifteen-minute dances, and three-hour programs. Her inspirations were wide-ranging: Greek myth, Catholic legends, Hopi Indian rituals, American history, the Bible, lyric poetry, and modern music. She created her own movement vocabulary, the Graham Technique, based on a dynamic of contraction and release related to breath. Her use of music was unique: her dancers reacted to the structure of the score as if moving through a landscape. Graham also experimented with spoken words in dance, most successfully with comedy, but also in dances meant to be tragic, not just sad.

Though O'Neill and Graham experimented in many varied ways, they were each consistently working towards something. The cumulative effect of Graham's experimentation resulted in the Graham Technique, the first consistent vocabulary for dance since classical ballet. By teaching classes and founding a school, Graham made sure her work would have future interpreters. Graham dancers need to act as well as dance to be able to embody their roles properly.

O'Neill's lessons to future interpreters culminated emotionally in *Long Day's Journey into Night* and concluded with his insight in other plays that delusion is an anesthetic that wears off, leaving his dreamers awake and in pain. His experiments with large ensembles paid off in O'Neill's late realistic play *The Iceman Cometh* (written 1939, first performed 1946) set in a crowded bar. Unlike the dead-on Naturalism of Gorky's squalid *Lower Depths*, O'Neill turned squalor into poetry as part of a dramatic composition in a dynamic juxtaposition of cigarette smoke and pipe dreams.

The evidence of Graham and O'Neill's success is their influence, along with public acclaim. Graham was given many honors: the Key to the City of Paris, the Japanese Imperial Order of the Precious Crown, and the United States Presidential Medal of Freedom. O'Neill's 1936 Nobel Prize was an impressive achievement. Though the Nobel Prize is conferred by the Swedish Academy, the greatest Swedish playwright, August Strindberg, had not been thought worthy of the honor. In his acceptance speech to the Swedish Academy, O'Neill made much of his debt to Strindberg:

> I am only too proud of my debt to Strindberg, only too happy to have this opportunity of proclaiming it to his people. For me, he remains, as Nietzsche remains in his sphere, the Master, still to this day more modern than any of us, still our leader.

O'Neill understood what the Nobel Prize signified at home.

> This highest of distinctions is all the more grateful to me be-
> cause I feel so deeply that it is not only my work which is being
> honored, but the work of all my colleagues in America—that
> this Nobel Prize is a symbol of the recognition by Europe of the
> coming-of-age of the American theatre.

As O'Neill hoped to do for American playwrights, Martha
Graham led the way for a group of American choreographers
who aspired to—and achieved—legitimacy in the world of their
art. Other choreographers who created significant dance dramas
in the 1930s and 1940s include Doris Humphrey and Agnes de
Mille, both of whom, like Graham, got their start professionally
working in variety shows and revues.

Agnes de Mille (1905–1993) changed the role of dance in
the commercial Broadway theater. The dances de Mille choreographed for the 1943 Broadway musical *Oklahoma* filled out
the psychology of the characters and advanced the story. Before
Oklahoma, dances in musicals were interludes, not part of the
dramatic action. De Mille also created dances outside of musicals, taking on American motifs ranging from the notoriety of
Lizzie Borden in *Fall River Legend* to the delight of a tomboy
cowgirl at a hoedown in *Rodeo*.

Doris Humphrey (1895–1958), who also studied at Denishawn and, like Graham, began dancing professionally in
vaudeville. Humphrey conceived a theory of life as an arc between standing and lying down. For Humphrey, dramatic action
meant resisting gravity or giving in to its inevitability—and dying. The through-line of her theatrical choreography was the-
matic rather than driven by character or plot. Other American
choreographers who followed in Graham's wake include Eugene
Loring, famous for his ballet *Billy the Kid*, and Katherine Dunham who researched the dance heritage of the African diaspora
to inspire the unique body of her own choreography. Dunham

built a school to pass her inspiration along in, among other places, East Saint Louis.

Women had opportunities in dance theater they did not have in the theater of the spoken word. O'Neill's contemporaries among the Provincetown Players included women, notably Susan Glaspell, whose short play *Trifles* is still performed, a play in which a crime is solved by women in a small village when they notice what the village men think insignificant. But Glaspell, consumed by family responsibilities, ended her public career as a playwright after winning the Pulitzer Prize. In the late 1920s, Boston-born Marita Bonner, who was black, had the daring to imagine surreal dreamscapes onstage. Her plays went unperformed and unappreciated, and she stopped writing them after 1929. Compare the encouragement given to O'Neill's fantasies onstage for his 1928 *Strange Interlude* in which asides offer an audience the entertainment of eavesdropping on the character's subconscious thoughts. *Strange Interlude* took over four hours to perform and won O'Neill his third Pulitzer.

O'Neill and Graham chose their colleagues astutely. O'Neill would pencil sketch while writing plays, and these sketches would be shown to Robert Edmond Jones in order to engage the set designer in the earliest part of constructing the performance. The scenery for *Desire Under the Elms,* written in 1924, resembled a head in the disguise of a house cut open. The house as a disguised head was O'Neill's idea, Robert Edmond Jones gave the concept shape, specifics, and the harmony of a design.

Graham centered a galaxy of collaborators, first among them the Japanese-American sculptor Isamu Noguchi (1904–1988), who designed scenery, masks, and sculptural costumes for her dances. Noguchi's organic forms—made from such varied materials as rocks, sticks, and string—placed the world of Graham's dance theater outside of ballet fairyland or the burlesque stage. Jean Rosenthal (1912–1969), a pioneer in the field of light, met Graham in 1929 at the Neighborhood Playhouse School of Theater in New York City. The two women would collaborate for

thirty-six productions. By flooding the area upstage of the performers with light, Rosenthal removed the shadows that were
a part of vaudeville and melodrama, resetting Graham's dances
and dancers like jewels.

The entrance of O'Neill and Graham into mainstream art and
acceptance was only possible because of who and what held power in the professional American theater as the nineteenth century turned into the twentieth. Advertising and publicity played an
increasing role in achieving professional success. Influential critics at daily newspapers and weekly and monthly magazines had
power over their readers to muster support for what was challenging the status quo in theater and dance. O'Neill's rise in the
commercial theater was championed by critics George Jean Nathan and H.L. Mencken, using the power of national magazines
The Smart Set and *The American Mercury* to encourage readers
to buy tickets. Nathan waged a successful witty war against the
mendacity of American plays. Dance theater was supported by
John Martin in the *New York Times* and Walter Terry in the New
York *Herald Tribune*, both of whom championed Martha Graham and other modern choreographers. Such theater and dance
critics, rather than simply reporting what pleased or thwarted
an audience's expectations, encouraged audiences to appreciate
what was new and worthy of attention.

As part of a desire to reach the highest levels of esteem and in
a sincere effort to create timeless work, O'Neill and Graham took
on the motifs of classical Greece. O'Neill moved the situations
of Greek tragedy to America. O'Neill's trilogy of plays titled,
Mourning Becomes Electra, closely parallels the ancient Greek
Oresteia by Aeschylus. The *Oresteia* begins just after the Trojan
War ends; O'Neill's trilogy begins just after the American Civil
War ends. A victorious general is murdered in both plays, setting
off the action summarized by O'Neill's titles *Homecoming*, *The
Hunted*, and *The Haunted*. O'Neill's *Desire Under the Elms* places
Euripides' *Hippolytus* on a farm in Vermont. The text of *Phèdre*,
Jean Racine's 1677 version of same play by Euripides, is bejew-

eled by the incestuous stepmother's elegant outpouring in French
verse. O'Neill restricts her and the object of her desire to a spare
New England dialect and speech so terse that when bare declarations of desire erupt the simplest words turn voluptuous and
powerfully raw. Sometimes O'Neill borrowed the conventions of
a Greek tragedy rather than its story line: *Lazarus Laughed*, for
example, has a chorus of forty-nine masked figures who comment on the action as O'Neill supposed they might have in an
ancient Greek drama.

For Graham, classical Greek motifs were a part of her cultural inheritance. They were also, for Graham, signs of prestige,
power, and displaying a woman's mastery of male-dominated
stories. Graham's version of the Oedipus story, *Night Journey*,
is from the point of view of Jocasta. Medea's side of the story,
not Jason's, inspires *Cave of the Heart*. The largest of Graham's
Greek-inspired work is a full-length version of the Oresteia titled
Clytemnestra.

The American choreographer Isadora Duncan took up the
spirit of Ancient Greece in dance well before Martha Graham
and Eugene O'Neill looked for inspiration in classical Greek
forms. In 1904 when Martha Graham was ten and Eugene
O'Neill was sixteen attending boarding school in the Bronx, Isadora Duncan, who was then twenty-seven, danced alone on the
stage of the Metropolitan Opera House in New York while the
New York Philharmonic played Beethoven's Seventh Symphony.
Born in San Francisco, Duncan's dances were inspired by what
she intuited from classical Greek sculpture, paintings on Greek
vases, and visits to the Parthenon in Athens.

Rather than dance steps, Duncan embodied essences, the impact undeniable, to judge from contemporary descriptions and
the respect given her. She claimed she had no technique beyond
nature. Her solo work was improvised. That's hard, though, for
anyone else to reproduce. Compare the fate of jazz improvisations,
which were preserved by recordings that still inspire listeners and
other musicians. Isadora Duncan's greatest improvised dances

went unrecorded, and the specifics of her accomplishment have dimmed in memory and history. There is a Duncan school, but its effects are not the same as the school Graham founded to pass on the Graham technique. Graham's choreography (and the scenery, lighting, costumes, and props designed for her dance) can be reassembled and reinterpreted. Similarly, as long as O'Neill's dialogue and stage directions can be read, later generations will have the opportunity to put into practice how his words live in performance. Classical theater, to claim the definition of classic as timeless excellence, proves its value by reinterpretation by audiences and artists over decades, over centuries.

Along with the prestige of classical Greek form, O'Neill and Graham actively sought American themes. O'Neill went as far as to outline a saga of eleven separate plays that would tell the story of America from the colonial period up to the modern age. He was dissatisfied with most of them, and his notes and drafts were burned, though one that survived, *The Moon for the Misbegotten*, is performed with success. Graham's American sources ran deep. Her dances *Primitive Mysteries*, choreographed in 1931, and *El Penitente,* created in 1940, are possibly the first respectful treatment of American Indian themes onstage. Graham's *Appalachian Spring*, perhaps her greatest work, was first performed in 1944. Graham, who did not believe film could capture dance, reluctantly agreed to allow *Appalachian Spring* to be filmed, but panicked the day before shooting and had to be talked back to set by, of all people, Agnes de Mille. The 1958 version, first shown on television, preserves Graham's genius. In *Appalachian Spring* a chorus of four bonneted young women become a new sprouting field, then a church full of young worshippers. A preacher in a black tailcoat twirls and struts, a bride, unforgettably played by Graham with tenderness and passion, focuses the story like a pioneer guiding settlers across a prairie. The music is extraordinary and was Graham's only collaboration with the American composer Aaron Copland (1900–1990). The best of Copland's work in *Appala-*

chian Spring might be his distillation of the Shaker hymn "Simple Gifts," the first line of which might as well be the motto of the modern aesthetic: "'Tis the gift to be simple, 'tis the gift to be free."

Chapter Eighteen

EXPRESSIONISM TO EPIC

Bertolt Brecht (1898–1956)
Vsevolod Meyerhold (1874–1940)
Eugene O'Neill (1888–1953)
Erwin Piscator (1893–1966)
Sophie Treadwell (1885–1970)

S purred by his dissatisfaction at what he was asked to study in a college theater seminar, Bertolt Brecht began writing his first play when he was twenty. Born in 1898, in the midsized city of Augsburg in southern Germany, Brecht enrolled for medical studies at a university in Munich in 1917, so he could obtain a student deferment and avoid a stint in the army during the First World War. Even so, in October of 1918 he was drafted as a medic into a military clinic specializing in venereal diseases. The war ended a month later. Brecht did not return to medical studies. He did return to writing.

Brecht named his first play *Baal* for the pagan idol of the Old Testament who demands human sacrifices, a clever way to refer to the war without putting battles or soldiers onstage. His hero, or rather antihero, Baal is a poet so hungry for all that life might offer he seizes and devours what he wants omnivorously. He repeatedly seduces and abandons young girls, though he eventually runs off with a man who he kills in a brawl.

> Vice is not so bad, says Baal. Don't spit
> Either on the men who practice it.

Don't say no to any vice as such
Pick out two, for one will be too much.
("Chorale of the Great Baal," William E. Smith and Ralph Man-
heim, trans.)

Baal resembles Henrik Ibsen's antihero Peer Gynt, who is as hungry for love as he is empty of a heart, and Alfred Jarry's King
Ubu, who might be uninterested in love but reaches out insatia-
bly for power. All three of these bad boys rebel against worlds
that would rule them. Peer is a peasant and Ubu is a boor. Baal,
though, is fashionably stylish—and the style is Expressionism.

The Expressionism movement began as a rebellion in art and
literature in the late nineteenth century, especially in Germany,
where writers and visual artists revolted against classical decorum. The harmony so carefully sought by nineteenth German
classicists—along with the sublime beauty cherished by German idealists—was mocked, if not simply ignored after the First
World War as no longer relevant in a country that was broke and
broken, too hungry, too dirty, and too poor to hang on to middle-class morality or high-minded ideals. Classic forms could no
longer express the fragmentation, horror, and ecstasy of life.

Expressionism carries forward the Romantic ideal that an
artist's impulse creates its own forms. Expressionism does not
subdue creativity to balance or harmonize. An Expressionist artist avoids idealization, especially the idealization of forms that
classic art enjoys. Expressionism willfully escapes the discipline
that demands the submission of content to form, avoiding, too,
the disciplines of realism and believability. Expressionist paintings show the green face of jealousy, the blue shadow of sorrow,
and, sometimes, the aura of power. Baal declares the sky above
his head is yellow, green, orange, and in a rare moment of calm,
blue. As Baal's friend Ekart, who Baal will later murder, says:

I've got a kind of sky inside my skull, very green and terribly
high, and under it thoughts move, like light clouds in the wind.

In no particular direction. I've got all that inside me.
(*Baal*, scene 11, Smith and Manheim, trans.)

To shake the European habit of copying Greek and Roman Art, Expressionists pursued sources that were considered in Europe to be primal and primitive. Expressionist writers and artists looked to pagan and pre-Christian culture and found inspiration in Norse sagas, African masks, Egyptian friezes, Polynesian carvings, German legends, and other alternate mythologies to the twenty-five-hundred-year-old Greco-Roman tradition.

Expressionist artists and writers had a hunch that beneath a thin veneer of civilization the people of the then new twentieth century were still as ever savage, ruthless, passionate, impulsive, and pleasure-loving in all ways, including sexually, without concern for consequences. Improved machinery didn't so much mask, ironically, as accelerate a return to savagery by making life more exciting, dangerous, exhilarating—and crueler.

Along with *Baal*, a modern-day avatar of a pagan malevolent god, the titles of Brecht's earliest plays announce the preoccupations of Expressionist theater. *Drums in the Night* (1919) is set in Berlin during postwar looting. *In the Jungle of Cities* (1921) takes place in Chicago where human life, as Brecht understood from American pulp fiction, was reduced to the survival of the fittest. For purposes of Expressionism, there was no need for Brecht to see Chicago for himself in order to set a play there. Since the time of Columbus, Europeans projected ideas of barbaric savagery onto America and Americans.

Though he intended to avoid the formulae of Expressionism, the aesthetic of Expressionism suited Brecht, who styled himself as an unshaven rough guy with a leather jacket and tough talk. More importantly, the force of art stripped to its essence powered Brecht's transformation of what theater could do to communicate the essential connectedness of things, as Brecht saw them, politically, historically, and economically.

Epic Theater is what Brecht called this approach, taking on the term and the idea from his Berlin mentor, Ervin Piscator, the radical leftist stage director. Beginning in 1922 Piscator was creating an aggressively political theater adapting texts from newspaper accounts, novels, and folk tales. Epic theater refers to the word "epic" in the sense of the *Iliad* or the *Odyssey*, epics that were recited for an audience. Piscator and Brecht thought to revive ancient storytelling techniques, mingling narrative with enactment on the modern stage, telling modern stories and adding modern technology to the mix.

The original idea began in Russia, two decades before Piscator and Brecht's efforts in Berlin, at the Moscow Art Theatre where Vsevolod Meyerhold, who was part of Stanislavsky's acting ensemble, chafed under the restrictions of realism. As an actor under Stanislavsky's direction, Meyerhold created the roles of the suicidal Treplev in the 1900 Moscow Art Theatre's *The Seagull* and the doomed Baron Tuzenbach in the 1904 premiere of Chekhov's *The Cherry Orchard*. During the Moscow Art Theatre rehearsals, Meyerhold wrote to Chekhov complaining that the birdcalls and paraphernalia of Stanislavsky's realistic staging were unnecessary and distracting. Chekhov agreed.

Stanislavsky respected Meyerhold and generously set him up in a separate studio where Meyerhold could experiment without the pressure of public acceptance or commercial success. Meyerhold's most radical work, which Piscator and Brecht knew about, began with the study of Greek and Elizabethan theater and the Italian commedia dell'arte from all of which Meyerhold derived perhaps his most important contribution to theatrical practice, the idea of the episode and episodic structure.

Plays, Meyerhold concluded, were not necessarily connected by plot, as in melodramas, or by the actor's motivations intuited by an audience, as in the theories of Stanislavsky and the practices of the actors of the Moscow Art Theatre. Episodes onstage can be simply self-contained events put together in a string of events that the audience, rather than the author or the director or an actor, might put together for meaning beyond psychology or plot. Read and performed this way, plays that had been considered unfinished or crude—Georg Büchner's *Woyzeck*, for example— were understood, enjoyed, and successfully staged.

The word episode comes from the Greek language. Meyerhold, Brecht, and Piscator consistently claimed they hadn't invented such a thing; instead, they had perceived it in older forms of theater, including classical Greek theater, and put it into play in their own modern forms. Up-to-date machinery might be used in their productions along with the crudest materials and primitive stagecraft: turntables powered by modern motors and hand-lettered placards from out of the Middle Ages mixed with new materials such as Mylar and steel assembled in overtly non-illusionistic ways. The stage was meant to be understood as a stage and the actors as performers, not people in another world or in a realistic portrait of life.

In Berlin, Piscator added his own spin constructing episodes as theatrical translations of the German philosopher Hegel's theory, *thesis + antithesis = synthesis*. Hegel's idea had been percolating in Germany for a hundred years before Piscator applied it in ways that would have appalled its creator. Hegel's original theory, which he lectured about from 1821 to 1831, proposed that human relationships, including the process of history and the structure of tragedy, could be explained by the mechanics of a thesis meeting its antithesis and in doing so, creating something new in and of itself: a synthesis, not simply the clash or compromise of opposites. The easiest way to think of this is how water and fire combine to make steam, and how steam is something different from either water or fire. Applying his theory to theater, the clash of two different ideas of good made a tragedy. Applying his theory to history and aesthetics, Hegel posited that the thesis of classical rational Greco-Roman culture encountering the antithesis of wild Germanic tribes along the Rhine, achieved a fine synthesis in neoclassic Germany. Art that synthesized opposed extremes was the best art of all to Hegel, an idea that appealed to the rising middle class in Germany and elsewhere. Passion subdued to form yielded something sublime and uplifting, like the Alps.

Piscator held his own theories of opposition, a combination of thesis and antithesis of behavior in which action onstage would be played reluctantly or eagerly despite hesitation. A cruel man could be ashamed of what he does and does it anyway. Someone could be foolishly wise or happily and unknowingly destructive. The synthesis of opposites is not always brought about by the actor or by the person the actor portrays. Often it is the audience who resolves the opposition or is left with the attempt to try to do so. Sometimes opposition could be constructed with stage effects: someone walking on a turntable going nowhere, or soft music playing during a violent scene.

Brecht first realized, or rather recognized, his own ideas for epic acting—distinct from epic theater—when he was in Moscow in 1935 attending a performance of the Chinese actor Mei Lanfang. Stanislavsky, Meyerhold, and Piscator were there too, but it was Brecht who appreciated that an actor in the Chinese tradition was telling a story at the same time he was playing a character. He realized that Mei Lanfang commented on his own actions even as he performed those actions. By interpolation Brecht realized that the contradiction of this could provoke an audience into completing or at least consider the meaning of contradictory actions onstage and off.

From Chinese acting, Hegelian theory, Piscator's example, a radical rethinking of ancient Greek theater, and a radical rethinking of much else in theater history, Brecht set out certain principles of the epic theater forcefully challenging the ancient Greek rules for dramatic theater laid down by Aristotle in his *Poetics*. Aristotle's rules had been defining theater for 2,500 years. To establish a modern aesthetic, a new *Poetics*, Brecht drew up charts comparing his ideas of an Epic theater to Aristotle's dramatic theater. He put his theories into practice as a playwright and director. These are central to his practice:

Alienation—Brecht's translator in Moscow used this word, passing on the term coined by the Russian literary critic Viktor Shklovsky, to identify how something familiar taken out of context could be made strange, fresh, and newly significant. Despite creative misinterpretation, alienation doesn't mean getting the audience angry—it means paying close attention to something overlooked in everyday life, so that it might be perceived in a new way. Watching performances of his play *The Life of Galileo*, Brecht noted with approval the way drinking a glass of milk was alienated, so that the audience noticed Galileo's capacity for sensual enjoyment.

Opposition—This is an idea taken directly from Hegel in theory and Piscator in practice. In Brecht's play *The Caucasian Chalk Circle* (1944), a judge's mistakes are just. Had the judge been paying more attention and following the law, he would have ruled unwisely. In Brecht's *Mother Courage and her Children* (1939), the mother's courage contributes to the death of her children.

Open Theatricality and Skepticism—The audience is provoked to question the believability of the scene. At the end of Brecht's play with music, *The Threepenny Opera* (1928), the gentleman rogue Macheath is about to be hung when a purposefully fake policeman trots onstage astride a horse that Brecht specifies should look fake. The Policeman saves the day, mocking the apparatus of the happy ending and the deus ex machina.

Unresolved Contradictions—The synthesis of thesis and antithesis is left undone onstage to be completed by the audience. In *The Good Soul of Setzuan* (1941, the German title is *Der gute Mensch von Sezuan*) three Chinese gods have come to Setzuan province to find a moral person. The person they choose has a secret life as a cruel gangster. The good woman asks the gods, "Did my life as a gangster get rewarded? Why, when I was good, was I taken advantage of? Why have you made the world this way?" The Gods evade such questions, and their clumsy return to the sky via squeaking pulleys and a shaky ladder is all the better for the audience to think about the answer—and perhaps conclude that people on earth might change the way things are, rather than wait for the gods to return.

Above all, Brecht wanted to rearrange the relationship of performance to the audience. Instead of an opiate, intended to distract or relax, Brecht wanted theater to be an incitement to judgment and action. Everything onstage was part of a machine to do this, including the actors, who are meant to demonstrate and give testimony rather than sway an audience to shallow short-lived empathy. Brecht launched a red-hot assault on emotional immersion, the glory of Stanislavsky and realistic acting. Brecht's repugnance for empathy was prompted by the rise to power of the Nazi party, which manipulated the German population at public rallies. Brecht urged theater to do something besides training mobs to fall for propaganda. Theater could teach people to judge, not empathize, with all that passed before it. The public might get just as angry or happy or annoyed as before, but theoretically in Brecht's theater the audience would not share the emotions of Shakespeare's Iago—or the historical Hitler—or Brecht's Mother Courage—they would condemn them. Brecht had passed beyond identification with the central character as in Baal.

In his notes "On Looking Through My First Plays" Brecht wrote:

> Baal is a play which could present all kinds of difficulties to those who have not learned to think dialectically...I admit (and advise you): this play is lacking in wisdom.
> (Ralph Manheim and John Willet, editors, *Brecht Collected Plays*, Volume 1, quoting "Bei Durchsicht meiner ersten Stucke")

The spirit of Expressionism had become a dead end for him; rebels without a cause were a romantic delusion, possible to those with free time, impossible for effective revolutionaries. He still held to the expressionist conviction that civilized men were inherently feral, but now Brecht hoped to show the audience this was not evitable but a function of feral civilizations.

In America, apart from Brecht or Piscator, several playwrights toyed with Expressionism in the 1920s before they too abandoned it. In Eugene O'Neill's Expressionist play *The Emperor Jones* (1920) in which an African-American ex-convict named Brutus Jones (classical brute, get it?) is running to escape the rebellious subjects of his self-created Caribbean empire. Like Baal, Jones ends up dead in the forest. As he flees, he abandons the trappings of civilization. He tears off his splendid Emperor's uniform and his shining spurred boots. He tosses away his pants and, wrapped in a loincloth, howls in the wilderness. O'Neill's Expressionist play *The Hairy Ape* (1922) shows that below the shining deck of an ocean liner working men shovel coal as if they were the greasy cogs of a machine. When Yank, the ship's stevedore, arrives in New York, the city reduces him to the status of a gorilla in the zoo.

Elmer Rice's Expressionist play, *The Adding Machine* (1923), shows the trial, execution, and afterlife of Mr. Zero, an accountant replaced by the machine of the title. After a time in Purgatory and what passes for Paradise, Mr. Zero learns his soul is to be recycled and sent back down to earth, where it has been enslaved for centuries: building the pyramids or working in an office, exchanging an iron-collar job for a white-collar job. Six years after *The Adding Machine*, Elmer Rice wrote the hyperrealistic *Street Scene* (1929)—a play that won a Pulitzer Prize for its depiction of slum life in details similar to Gorky's *Lower Depths* (1902).

Machinal, by Sophie Treadwell, is a definitively American Expressionist play, written in an episodic style based on a true-crime story. We follow a sort of dis-assembly line as a young woman goes from office drudge to murderer. *Machinal* made a splash when it opened on Broadway in 1928 and is still performed, but Treadwell was dabbling in Expressionism. The rest of the three dozen plays she wrote (some before and some after

Machinal) were conventional comedies or realistic dramas organized around social issues.

After the collapse of the American economy in October 1929, Expressionist plays were no longer appreciated by American audiences looking for reassurance. As a style, Expressionism continued on in American film, thanks to German cinematographers who fled to Hollywood. In America, Expressionist shadows and the reversion to feral behavior in Expressionist plays was channeled to film noir.

Back in Germany, although German filmmakers had been using Expressionist visual vocabulary since the dawn of film to create alternate distorted realities, Hitler's culture minister declared Expressionist film—and Expressionist novels, paintings, and plays—to be decadent. Art that advanced the Nazi cause was scrubbed and sunlit. Anything else was forbidden.

At the same time as Expressionism was condemned in Germany, Meyerhold's practice of what would become Epic theater was declared decadent by Communist culture tsars in Russia. Meyerhold was praised by Communist Party leaders, at first, for his innovations in form and content. At Meyerhold's 1920 production of *Dawn*, which included announcements from the battlefields of the ongoing Russian Civil war, audiences sometimes stood spontaneously to sing revolutionary songs. In 1923, Meyerhold was declared People's Artist of the Republic.

In theory, audiences new to theater going were easier to radicalize than the middle-class audience of Stanislavsky's Moscow Art Theatre. In practice, many peasants, factory workers, and theater administrators were baffled by untraditional art. Intent on useful theater, communists decided Social Realism, which extolled previously oppressed people's lives in familiar old-fashioned realistic forms, would be the only style tolerated in totalitarian Russia. In 1939 Meyerhold protested the monopoly of Social Realism at a meeting of the Soviet Director's union. He was taken from his home the next day, tortured (he was sixty-five), and soon enough shot against a wall. Meyerhold's image and achievements were erased from Soviet theater history, which is why Epic theater was defined by Brecht from the safe havens of first Denmark, then Paris, then Finland, and then in America where he settled in Santa Monica, California.

Piscator tried unsuccessfully in the 1930s to start a German-speaking theater in Russia. By 1940 Piscator was in New York where his creativity was channeled into the practicalities of establishing The Drama Workshop at New York City's New School. While Piscator prepared for large-scale professional projects (that never came about), he taught classes to children and to adults. He lectured and what he had to say was passed down by oral tradition, but he did not write about theory in the way that Brecht wrote.

Brecht found little else to do in America besides theorize and scheme for the future. Projects were proposed, but few were realized. He waited out the Second World War in Santa Monica, California where he reworked drafts of the plays now considered to be his masterworks: *Galileo, Caucasian Chalk Circle, Good Soul of Setzuan,* and *Mother Courage.*

Galileo, first written in 1938, was translated into rough English with hopes that it might make a screenplay. A Hollywood film star with intelligence, talent, and free time, the large and lumbering British character actor, Charles Laughton read *Galileo* and proposed that he would star in a stage version. According to Brecht's account, he and Laughton worked together for two years on a new English translation for America. Laughton lived within walking distance and Brecht would stroll over.

> ...because he spoke no German whatever and we had to decide the gest of dialogue by my acting it all in bad English or even in German and his then acting it back in proper English in a variety of ways until I could say: That's it...This system of performance-and-repetition had one immense advantage in that psychological discussions were almost entirely avoided. Even the most fundamental gests, such as Galileo's way of observing, or his showman-

ship, or his craze for pleasure, were established in three dimensions by actual performance.

Brecht noted with approval that Laughton understood the craft of opposition.

> In such a case an actor's greatness can be seen in the degree to which he can make the character's behavior incomprehensible or at least objectionable.
> (*Aufubau einer Rolle/Lauhgtons Galilei*, John Willett, trans.)

If Brecht intended in 1919 that the original audience for *Baal* would cheer the rebellious energy of his antihero, thirty years later Brecht wanted the audience to reject the amoral drive of Galileo as antihero. Galileo's "pure" pursuit of science was linked by Brecht with the German scientists whose pursuit of pure knowledge had led to efficient crematoria and the atomic bomb. Great men had the power for great betrayals. At the same time, Brecht wanted his audience to consider the circumstances of societies, including their own, in which selfishness was necessary for survival.

> Unhappy the land that has no heroes!

Galileo's disappointed follower, Andrea, calls out, immediately after his teacher renounces the truth. The great astronomer can't help but overhear Andrea, nor does he miss Andrea's disgust. Galileo responds.

> No. Unhappy the land where heroes are needed.
> (*The Life of Galileo*, scene 13, Charles Laughton trans.)

The play, starring Laughton, was staged in Los Angeles and New York in the summer of 1947. America critics dismissed it, though anti-Communist investigations ramped up. In late October 1947 Brecht accepted an invitation by the House Un-American Activities Committee to answer questions about his politics and writing. His testimony is so witty a transcript of it has been made into a play. Asked if he was a member of the Communist Party, he replied, he never had joined. This was true. When congressmen quoted sections of his work that seemed to support the Communist Party line, Brecht pointed out that he wrote in German, these were translations. The committee thanked him for his cooperation. He left the next day for Europe.

He waited in Switzerland to return to Berlin. As a sort of bait, he staged an Epic theater adaptation of *Antigone* in Switzerland. According to legend, the West German government offered Brecht a theater while the East German government offered him a theater and salaries for the actors. Brecht went to East Berlin but retained an Austrian passport and kept his money in a Swiss bank. The Berliner Ensemble, the company he founded in East Berlin, toured Paris and London setting off a revolution in theater practice as profound as when the Duke of Saxe-Meiningen toured Europe in the 1880s.

Brecht died in 1956 at the age of fifty-eight. It says something that the toilet that he sat on at home in East Berlin faced the cemetery where he is now buried. Piscator, who was five years older than Brecht, died in 1966. Piscator's move in 1951 to West Berlin left Piscator as mired in the practicalities of production as he had been anywhere else in the world.

Brecht's productions and plays and theorizing were among the rare high points of Communist culture respected as significant outside of the Communist world. For decades Brecht's plays were performed throughout the Soviet Empire from Cuba to Mongolia. Unlike Meyerhold (or rather, learning from Meyerhold's example), Brecht made an accommodation with Social Realism—claiming that Epic theater and Stanislavsky had much in common, both called attention to the overlooked significance of everyday behavior. With the fall of the Soviet Union, Brecht's work has been produced much less regularly. The value of the Epic theater, though, needs to be assessed separately from the political system Brecht, Piscator, and Meyerhold believed in. We appreciate the Catholic Church's concept of Grace without being Christian; without being Marxist we can appreciate the Epic Theater's insight that human relationships are a series of transactions. The economic forces shaping men's lives are certainly worth considering as much, if not more, than the will of the gods or a character's childhood traumas and subsequent psychology.

Chapter Nineteen

AMERICAN AGITPROP (OVERT AND DISGUISED)

Stella Adler (1901–1992)
Harold Clurman (1901–1980)
Hallie Flanagan (1890–1969)
Margo Jones (1911–1955)
Elia Kazan (1909–2003)
Eva Le Gallienne (1899–1991)
Arthur Miller (1915–2005)
Clifford Odets (1906–1963)
Paul Robeson (1898–1976)
Lee Strasberg (1901–1982)
Thornton Wilder (1897–1975)

J anuary 1935. The Great Depression is in its sixth year. A quarter of the American work force is unemployed. The efforts of the federal government to improve or simply alleviate the hardships brought on by the collapse of the economy have not so far succeeded. What is to be done? The audience enters the Civic Theater at Sixth Avenue and Fourteenth Street in Manhattan to find a union meeting underway. Taxi drivers are sitting in a semicircle onstage deciding whether to strike. Lefty, the union leader in favor of the strike, hasn't yet arrived. While the drivers wait for him, they give testimony, acting out in short scenes the events from their lives that justify a strike. A corrupt union leader named Harry Fatt—subtle this isn't—tries to persuade the workers to cave into the demands of their bosses. News arrives that Lefty has been killed, murdered by the bosses. The meeting and the performance conclude simultaneously when the audience joins in with the last words of the play, "Strike! Strike!" Actors have been planted in the house to instigate responses from the audience throughout the performance.

This is agitprop, agitation propaganda. The word passed into English directly from the Russian word coined at the start of the Russian Revolution in 1917 to describe the efforts of the Communist Party to radicalize peasants, many of whom could not read. While Bolshevik armies were still in battle, Communist acting troupes crisscrossed Russia by rail, tossing posters out the windows of the train to announce free performances for whoever gathered.

Agitprop theater meant to agitate its audience by inciting anger at oppression and then, sharing a belief in the necessity of social revolution, inciting political action. The word propaganda was taken from the Catholic Church where it had been used since 1622 to refer to whatever materials, from pictures to pamphlets, missionaries used to propagate the faith. Propaganda, in its original form, was meant to propagate Christianity like a crop of corn to non-Catholic countries. Agitprop theater was by design meant to inspire and was easy to understand with easily identifiable characters. Like the plays of the Middle Ages in Europe, the structure of the performances was episodic, so that audiences who saw even only a part could understand something, even if they missed the whole.

Waiting for Lefty was written by Clifford Odets, who was born into an immigrant Jewish family in Philadelphia. Odets dropped out of high school after two years to become an actor. At nineteen he moved to Greenwich Village in New York City where he joined the Poet's Theater under the direction of the Provincetown Players' Harry Kemp. After a few years scratching out a professional actor's career, including a stint as perhaps the first radio disc jockey and walk-on roles for Broadway shows, Odets auditioned for The Group Theater, a theater collective inspired by Stanislavsky and the Moscow Art Theatre. Odets was the last person hired for the Group Theater ensemble and, as on Broadway, he had walk-on roles in their early productions. He was encouraged to write by the ensemble's directors Harold Clurman and Lee Strasberg.

Seeking a playwright who wrote for their ensemble the way Anton Chekhov had written for the Moscow Art Theatre, the Group Theater wanted realistic plays by Odets and, on their terms, got them. A month after *Lefty* opened, they produced *Awake and Sing!* (which Odets had written first) then *Paradise Lost* (1936), both directed by Harold Clurman. Heavily indebted to Chekhov, *Awake and Sing!* and *Paradise Lost* dramatized the wonder, confusion, pain, and stoicism of the American middle class. This was good material to demonstrate the Group Theater's superlative realistic acting.

Waiting for Lefty was the Group Theater's first public success. After opening downtown in Manhattan in January of 1935, *Lefty* moved to Broadway that March and played until July. Performances were staged in other American cities where the hardships of the working poor and local labor troubles, including strikes, were ongoing. With its simple setting and poster-like characterizations, *Lefty* was requested by union halls and community centers, as well as theaters. Anyone who produced the play invited attacks from those with other biases, as happened to the Seattle Repertory Theater in 1936 which was blacklisted by the *Seattle Times* after a single performance of *Lefty*.

There was no tradition for overtly political theater in America where social advocacy had relied on sentiment, as with *Uncle Tom's Cabin*, or the appeals of the picturesque poor in American imitations of Gorky's *Lower Depths*. *Waiting for Lefty* was transparently political: scene six included a discussion of the *Communist Manifesto*.

Chekhov's plays had always been constructed with apolitical irony. Chekhov was careful to maintain the ambiguity of the forces that undo his characters. Hard truth announced in a play by Chekhov is made human by who speaks it. The student who prophesies the future in the *Cherry Orchard*, for example, is, if not a fool, foolish; his language is a collection of clichés out of pamphlets. None of the Group Theater hotshots read or spoke much Russian. In translation much of Chekhov's irony is lost, and Odets' prophets or bad guys are just that, with their goodness or badness assigned with little ambiguity.

When Odets wrote his plays—encouraged by Clurman and Strasberg—he was convinced of the importance of being earnest, not ironic. His plays are often terse slangy bursts from inarticulate characters at odds with their own feelings and need of expression under pressure. In plays by Odets, such characters burst out, however clumsily, in a white-hot torrent of words.

In *Paradise Lost*, a minor character named Pike, a veteran of the First World War who is now practically a derelict, shuts off a bloodthirsty Armistice Day broadcast after hurling his glass of red wine at the radio. Under the artifice of realistic theater, he speaks to the other characters onstage, but he is essentially addressing the audience.

> PIKE: If we remain silent while they make the next war—who then are we with our silence? Accomplices, Citizen! Let me talk out my heart! Don't stop me! Citizens, they have taken our sons and mangled them to death! They have left us lonely in our old age. The bellyrobbers have taken clothes from our backs. We slept in subway toilets here. In Arkansas we picked fruit. I followed the crops north and dreamed of a warmer sun. We lived on and hoped. We lived on garbage dumps. Two of us found canned prunes, ate them and were poisoned for weeks. One died. Now I can't die. But we gave up to despair and life took quiet years. We worked a little. Nights I drank myself insensible. Punched my own mouth. Yes, first American ancestors and me. The circle's complete. Running away, stealing away to stick the ostrich head in sand. Living on a boat as night watchman, tied to shore, not here nor there! The American jitters! Idealism! (Punches himself violently.) There's for idealism! For those blue-gutted Yankee

Doodle bastards are making other wars while we sleep. And if we remain silent while they make this war, we are the guilty ones.
For we are the people, and the people is the government, and tear them down from their high places if they dast do what they did in 1914–18.
(Slowly sits tremblingly.)
LEO (softly): We cancel our experience. This is an American habit.
(*Paradise Lost*, Act 1)

The source of this anger is unambiguous. After the 1929 stock market crash, misery in the United States was undeniable and widespread. Prompted by the crash and the fragmentation of society, American theater rediscovered the ancient Greek impetus to watch a play. For socially aware American theater in the 1930s, the function of the theater was to represent the *demos*, the people of the community who, in a democracy, held ultimate power. By revealing to audiences what they had in common, performances of plays created a community. There was entertainment besides agitprop that flourished with gusto in America in the 1930s, but throughout the decade and on into the late 1940s, socially aware American theater set itself a task to affirm and redefine—rather than reflect or distract—America.

Hallie Flanagan was the most influential and powerful theater-maker figure in America at this time. Neither an actress nor a playwright, but a visionary producer, Flanagan ran theater departments at two women's colleges, first Vassar from 1925–1942, then Smith. At Vassar she presented an encyclopedia of world drama with productions ranging from ancient Sanskrit plays to the world premiere of T.S. Eliot's first verse drama *Sweeney Agonistes*. Thanks to a Guggenheim Fellowship in 1926, the first ever given to a woman, Flanagan traveled to Europe to see the work being done by Stanislavsky and Meyerhold in Russia. On her trips she also met Edward Gordon Craig and Pirandello—but missed out entirely on what Piscator and

Brecht were doing. Their theaters were not where a lady would go at that time.

At Vassar she staged productions of plays by Italian Futurists and German Expressionists, casting faculty and student actors. For her production of Chekhov's *The Proposal*, she demonstrated Stanislavsky's approach to the play; then, on the same bill, she repeated the text in the manner of Meyerhold's Biomechanics.

In 1935 the President of the United States, Franklin Delano Roosevelt, established the Works Progress Administration—renamed in 1939 the Works Program Administration. It was and is invariably referred to by its initials as the WPA. The WPA hired people for public work: building roads, train stations, and post offices. Art—and theater especially—was considered public work, and under the Federal Theatre Project, the WPA hired actors, designers, directors, and other theater artists. From 1935–1939 Hallie Flanagan staged almost one thousand plays in fifty thousand performances produced by twelve thousand actors, directors, and stagehands in forty theaters in twenty states to an audience of twenty-five million Americans.

This was a truly national theater. Regional units originated productions in New Orleans, Oklahoma City, Detroit, and Tacoma, Washington, among other cities, breaking up the cultural dominance of New York and the Eastern seaboard states where New York-bound shows previewed. Black Americans were provided resources to create theater, there were puppet troupes, and troupes performed original plays in immigrant languages. The Federal Theatre Project (FTP) presented innovative director's versions of Shakespeare, Aristophanes, and the Living Newspaper—a form of theater Flanagan learned about in Russia—which dramatized the events of the day and was unafraid to assign complicity, if not blame, for joblessness and hunger, to powerful forces in America, including bankers and newspaper owners. That is to say, the Living Newspaper was agitprop which would become an even more damning label than melodrama in the vocabulary of American theater criticism.

In 1939 the FTP was dismantled. Fast. Not coincidentally, a Living Newspaper report on the disgrace of race relations in America from slavery to lynchings, all too aptly titled "Liberty Deferred," was being prepared for production, though it was never actually performed. This assault on the unapologetically racist strongholds of the country was overt, and it was felt that the government of a democracy should not be using taxpayers' money to subsidize one point of view or set one group of people against another. Flanagan's 1938 testimony defending herself to a gang of sanctimonious politicians who called themselves The House Committee to Investigate Un-American Activities (HUAC) was made into a play and a movie. One of the more unintentionally theatrical moments was when a member of the House of Representatives asked Flanagan if Christopher Marlowe (1564–1593) and Mr. Euripides (who died around 400 BC) were Communists. To questions about communist propaganda and propaganda in general, Flanagan replied without hesitation:

...We have never done plays which [were] propaganda for communism, but we have done plays which were propaganda for democracy, propaganda for better housing.

Dramatic as Flanagan was, she didn't change any minds among those who understood better than she did how dangerous to their own power a populist American theater might become. A few months before, the same committee, which had been looking to see if the Ku Klux Klan was in league with the Nazis had decided, no, the Klan was not. This possibility of a connection between white supremacists wasn't worth investigating further because, as a congressman said, "After all, the KKK is an old American institution." The HUAC took away Flanagan's funding. Let's be clear, however, if Flanagan had been talking back to the government in Russia in 1939, she would have been executed or worked to death in a gulag. In Germany, if she hadn't had the chance to flee the country when the Nazis came to power, Flanagan would have been taken away to a concentration camp.

Many German theater artists who fled Nazi Germany found places for themselves in America. Erwin Piscator, Brecht's mentor, had toyed with establishing a German-speaking theater in Russian Central Asia but abandoned that fantasy and in 1939 moved to America where he was invited to begin a training program at the New School in Manhattan. As with Flanagan at Vassar and Smith colleges, American university and college theater departments—confident in ticket sales from campus audiences—became laboratories for an evolving sophisticated cosmopolitan American theater. Piscator's workshop in New York began in January 1940 with twenty students. By 1947 there were almost a thousand. Thwarted in his attempts at professional stage work in America, Piscator returned to Germany in 1951, but his students would come to dominate American theater—and film, though they would learn to cloak the social activism Piscator passed on to them. Actors who studied with Piscator included Marlon Brando, Harry Belafonte, Elaine Stritch, Walter Matthau, Sylvia Miles, Judith Malina, Tony Curtis, Bea Arthur, and many others.

Arthur Miller, who was a student of Piscator at the New School, is the first enduring American playwright of social protest. Miller was from a prosperous Jewish family who manufactured coats. The family business tanked during the Depression, and the Millers lived haunted by the collapse of their ambitions as much as any family described by Odets in his plays *Paradise Lost* and *Awake and Sing*.

Miller wrote plays that still speak to audiences and offend those in power. Miller's *Death of a Salesman* (1948) and *The Crucible* (1953) have achieved a place in the world repertory. *Death of a Salesman* follows Willie Loman (notice the connection Lowman has to the medieval Everyman), to whom, as his wife Linda says, "Attention must be paid." That's the most famous line in the play, a sentiment right out of Brecht. Willie is a traveling salesman who has worked all his life. Now that he's old and worn out and of little use to his company, he's fired—tossed aside like an old shoe. In a flashback we learn Willie had a mistress. He betrayed his loving wife, just as the business he believed in betrayed him. If there is a pattern in Miller, it is crushed hope, and in this way *The Crucible* and *Death of a Salesman* work as tragedies, with a dispassionately profiteering social system taking on the role that Fate (with a capital F) played in classic Greek tragedies.

In *The Crucible*, Miller demands audiences pay attention to American history. Here the Salem witch trials of 1692 are used as a parallel for what were called the witch hunts of the early 1950s with their reckless allegations that Communists had infiltrated the American theater made by HUAC, the same committee attacking Hallie Flanagan. *The Crucible*'s plot twines sexual temptation with the temptation of betraying the truth in order to survive. An audience skeptical of social protest coming from unadulterated heroes can be more easily engaged by flawed characters such as the bellowing bewildered Willie Loman or *The Crucible*'s morally compromised John Proctor.

The Federal Theatre Project (FTP)—whose emphasis was on hiring people, not elitist ideas of artistic excellence—left few if any scripts that are still performed, nor did the FTP further the career—or even recognize—any significant new playwrights, including Arthur Miller, whose first play, produced by the Federal Theatre Project in 1937 in Detroit, was praised by some readers on the committee that judged such things as an "exceedingly promising play, just fitted for the Anglo-Jewish Theatre" despite "weaknesses in dramatic structure" and "often heavy" dialogue. For the FTP, inclusion and representation boosted the value of minimum competence. Along with that dubious practice, the Federal Theatre Project adhered to the sorry American tradition of apologizing for theater to the Puritans who had damned it as a waste of time better spent in church or chopping down trees.

The descendants of the Puritans maintained their traditions. In 1910, the United States Consul General to Shanghai, Amos

Wilder, whose family settled in Massachusetts around 1636, wrote a letter from China to his son and daughter, who were living in Oakland, California with their mother. The consul general was responding to reports that his fourteen-year-old son had so fallen under the spell of what was going on at the Greek Theater outside of Berkley—outdoor productions of Shakespeare, Aeschylus, Sophocles, and Mr. Euripides—that the boy was climbing trees to spy on rehearsals.

> As for Greek plays, you know Papa has only a limited admiration for "art"... Some of it—pictures, drama, music—is good as an incidental and diversion in life—but character is the thing in life to strive for. There are people who know all about pictures and Greek tragedy and the latest opera who are not interested in the poor and know little about kindness...I want you to appreciate all good wholesome things of every age, but don't get side-tracked by dramatic art or Wagner music or postage-stamp collecting from present day living, throbbing problems and needs.

Thornton Wilder, to whom this letter was written, responded over time. Decades later, asked by Georg Wagner in a 1953 interview about sources for his great novel *The Bridge of San Luis Rey*, which won a Pulitzer Prize in 1928, Wilder volunteered what set him off.

> The central idea of the work, the justification for a number of human lives that comes up as a result of the sudden collapse of a bridge, stems from friendly arguments with my father, a strict Calvinist. Strict Puritans imagine God all too easily as a petty schoolmaster who minutely weights guilt against merit, and they overlook God's 'Caritas' [love], which is more all-encompassing and powerful.

Our Town, written by Wilder in 1938, defines American identity as much, if not more, than any agitprop theater, and with even bolder and obvious theatricality. The play won Wilder a second Pulitzer. It begins disarmingly. A narrator saunters onto a bare stage with a script in his hand. He identifies himself as the stage manager. Scenery is assembled and taken apart onstage. A boy meets girl story is told and ends in a cemetery, with the graves represented by chairs. Wilder reassures an audience that a life cycle from birth to death familiar to small town Americans will prevail, no matter what the passing sorrows of economics or personal life. *Our Town* does not share the Federal Theatre Project's critique of American values. The play wasn't funded by the FTP—it didn't need to be. *Our Town* was produced on Broadway and made money doing so. *The Skin of Our Teeth,* written by Wilder in 1942 just before America entered the Second World War, takes a hilariously long view of how families survive disaster, tracking close escapes from extinction back to the time of the dinosaurs. *The Skin of Our Teeth* was also a commercial success.

With wildly anarchic imagery and truly American subject matter, Wilder's theater practices parallel traditional Chinese theater—a bare stage, symbolic scenery, a narrating stage manager, and masks. Wilder lived in China for a few years during the early 1910s, but what seems to have been his inspiration was seeing the great Chinese actor, Mei Lanfang, perform in 1930 in New York. Mei Lanfang had similarly inspired Bertolt Brecht. In a 1937 letter to a friend Wilder describes "*Our Town*—a New Hampshire village explored by the techniques of Chinese Drama." The wild swings of passion in O'Neill's plays or Odets' or Miller's are nowhere to be found in Wilder's work. The culture he grew up in and chose to stay within—he never married, he lived with his sister—prized discretion, unlike the immigrant cultures of Kazan, Strasberg, Miller, and Odets, for whom complaint and self-revelation were essential steps to changing society. Wilder upheld less noisy communal values of trust, hope, and fidelity. *Our Town's* advocacy for self-recognition, not change, starts with the celebratory first word of the title. The limitations of Wilder's thoughtful, tasteful, funny writing are deliberate, but his plays, especially *Our Town*, it seems, will be performed in America as long as there are high schools.

Born in 1911, Tennessee Williams is often grouped among other American playwrights with roots in the Depression. Like Miller, Williams studied with Piscator—who chastised Williams for his lack of political commitment. Initially a poet, at age twenty Williams aspired to write plays after he saw the Russian actress Alla Nazimova perform in O'Neill's *Mourning Becomes Electra*. Five years later he saw Nazimova again, this time the play was by Ibsen—the same experience that inspired Eugene O'Neill twenty years earlier. As playwright, Williams remained a poet. His dialogue, even his stage directions, for such plays as *The Glass Menagerie* (1945), *A Streetcar Named Desire* (1947) and *Cat on a Hot Tin Roof* (1955) evoke for readers and theater audiences a parallel world charged with lyric beauty and terror. These plays have their social concerns, not least of all sexual liberation, yet Williams' indirect approach disappointed politicos throughout his life, not just Piscator but, forty years later, gay activists who wished him to be as outspoken in his plays as he was in the short stories he had been publishing since the 1940s.

Though there were women playwrights who did well commercially, they mostly did so by adapting to the existing conventional theater, rather than changing it. More forceful changes in the American theater during the 1930s and '40s came from women who were directors and producers. Along with Hallie Flanagan, the American theater could boast of the actress/director Eva Le Gallienne, whose Civic Repertory Theatre and Acting Ensemble brought Ibsen and Chekhov to American audiences. The director Margo Jones, known as "The Texas Tornado," sparked the American regional theater system when she established *Theatre '47*. Started in 1947, the name of the theater changed every year.

The most significant male stage directors, Elia Kazan and Harold Clurman, were both members of the Group Theater. Clurman, the son of Yiddish-speaking immigrants, who did not himself speak that language, directed Odets' *Awake and Sing!* and *Paradise Lost*. Clurman staged over forty productions, wrote theater criticism for thirty years for the weekly magazine *The Nation* and, in 1945, passed on an invaluable frontline report about the Group Theater with his stirring book *The Fervent Years*. Kazan, the son of Greek immigrants from Istanbul, was the actor in *Waiting for Lefty* who set off the famous shouts of "Strike! Strike!" Kazan's premieres as a director were game changers: Wilder's *The Skin of Our Teeth*, Williams' *Streetcar*, and Miller's *Death of a Salesman*. Kazan and Clurman were especially fortunate to work with actors who they themselves had trained. American approaches to acting flowered, altering the way plays were written, rehearsed, and understood.

The American understanding of Stanislavsky's approach to acting that inspired the Group Theater was systematically passed on in classes taught by Lee Strasberg, Elia Kazan, and Stella Adler (who had created the roles of the mothers in *Paradise Lost* and *Awake and Sing!*). Lee Strasberg, in particular, emphasized a psychological theory of blocked emotions and taught exercises for actors to confront their blocks and fuel performances by releasing the powerful emotions of repressed memories. This is as old as Oedipus, and the connection with Freud and the Oedipal complex gave the intellectual underpinnings to the idea. Direct address (as in *Waiting for Lefty*) was disguised. Characters would testify at a trial or look out a window in order to set up the same relationship as before. As in the eighteenth century when opera composers wrote arias for sopranos who were trained to trill, American playwrights, writing for Strasberg-trained actors, wrote bravura monologues for which the action was the revelation of some past psychological trauma.

In 1936 Stella Adler tracked down Stanislavsky in the south of France. When she asked him about emotional memory, he denied its importance. Considering such exercises a distraction, Stanislavsky's company had abandoned their use by 1904. When Adler reported this back to the Group, she was expelled.

Strasberg insisted his Method would replace Stanislavsky's System. That happened in America because the raw emotions the Method delivered were raw material out of which film directors and editors might construct their own art.

Aside from the Group Theater and the Federal Theater Group, there were important commercial producing organizations responding in their own way to the times. Broadway productivity peaked in the late 1920s with 250 shows presented in a season. Despite a sharp decline in production after 1929, the commercial theater continued to gather an audience, often bringing people together with shared laughter rather than outrage. Listening to the radio sensitized people to the spoken word. Popular songs with witty lyrics readied an audience to enjoy the wit of George S. Kaufman and Edna Ferber's *Dinner at Eight* (1932) or Clare Booth Luce's *The Women* (1936). Beginning in 1920, the subscription-based Theatre Guild, whose board of directors met in committee to choose what they presented, raised standards on Broadway—and on national tours—by producing eighteen plays by Bernard Shaw, seven by Eugene O'Neill, as well as *Porgy and Bess* (1935).

Black writers and performers continued to be marginalized in all-Black productions, like *Porgy and Bess*, often written by white people. There were a few African-American stars in the mainstream theater, Paul Robeson, first among them. Robeson graduated Rutgers University in New Jersey in 1919. Because of his skin color, he was not allowed to live in the dorms or eat in the cafeterias. He was class valedictorian and the captain of the football team. He had a deep singing voice and a strong resonant speaking voice, valuable onstage before the invention of microphones. Robeson starred in O'Neill's *The Emperor Jones*; he was the stevedore who sang "Old Man River" in the 1932 *Show Boat* revival and the 1936 film. In the 1930s, in London and then later in New York, he appeared as Othello, in the path of Ira Aldridge, the nineteenth century African-American actor who mastered classical roles. New plays were not written for Robeson, though, and it was unthinkable at the time to cast him in *Death of a Salesman* or *Streetcar* or *Skin of Our Teeth*.

Suspicious that reports of Stalin's atrocities were American propaganda (they were not), Robeson considered communism an acceptable alternative to racist capitalism. His sympathies were trumpeted by the Soviet government, catching the attention of the House Un-American Activities Committee. Robeson's 1956 response to a question asked on behalf of the committee after he had given his prepared statement is worth repeating:

INVESTIGATOR: Will you just tell this Committee, while under oath, Mr. Robeson, the Communist who participated in the preparation of that statement?

PAUL ROBESON: Oh, please. The reason I am here today, from the mouth of the State Department itself, is: I should not be allowed to travel because I have struggled for the independence of the colonial peoples of Africa. The other reason I am here today, again from the State Department and from the record of the court of appeals, is that when I am abroad, I speak out against injustices against the Negro people of this land. That is why I am here. I am not being tried for whether I am a Communist; I am being tried for fighting for the rights of my people, who are still second-class citizens in this United States of America. My mother was born in your state, and my mother was a Quaker, and my ancestors in the time of Washington baked bread for George Washington's troops when they crossed the Delaware. My own father was a slave. I stand here struggling for the rights of my people to be full citizens in this country. And they are not. They are not in Mississippi. And they are not in Montgomery, Alabama. And they are not in Washington. They are nowhere, and that is why I am here today. You want to shut up every Negro who has the courage to stand up and fight for the rights of his people, and the rights of workers, and I have been on many a picket line for the steelworkers too. And that is why I am here today.

This reads like a speech by Clifford Odets. Dissent has been treasured enough in America to be staged or, like Paul Robeson's righteous anger, preserved for later generations to read and consider. The periodic abuses of capitalism, with its cycle of thieves and scoundrels, has a history of raising the rhetoric of protest, not always as literature or drama, more like cries of "Thief! Thief!" at a Renaissance market. As a tool of totalitarian states where dissent was suppressed, agitprop theater reversed its original purpose. In capitalist America, agitprop fostered debate—and, though its texts might be ephemeral, still does.

Chapter Twenty

POETRY OF THE THEATER

Antonin Artaud (1877–1948)
André Breton (1896–1966)
Jean Cocteau (1889–1963)
Eugène Ionesco (1909–1994)
Daniil Kharms (1905–1942)
Gertrude Stein (1874–1946)

Theater is public and communal and commercial. The way anyone learns about a play or a playwright if they don't read the work—or go to see and hear performances—is filtered through criticism, word of mouth, and advertising. Through these filters over time reputations build, decline, disappear, or erupt. What's radically new might become stifling dogmatic or might be dismissed someday as old hat. Clifford Odets, who wrote *Waiting for Lefty* in 1934, was acclaimed for his use of working-class vernacular to rebuke the ruling class. When a voice in the dark asks "Where's Lefty?" the answer from the stage is "I honest to God don't know, but he didn't take no run out powder." For sure Odets' language has grown stale and productions of Odets are out of fashion now. When some decades have passed, 1930s slang might become fresh again—and the play might be performed more frequently in the future. Sometimes, forgotten plays and neglected playwrights have been lifted out of obscurity to serve as inspirational touchstones. Turgenev's *A Month in the Country* and Büchner's *Woyzeck* were both written in the first half of the nineteenth century. Only until the twentieth century, thanks to productions staged decades after these two plays were written, decades after the death of the authors, were *A Month in the Country* and *Woyzeck* given their due as prophetic visions. Turgenev is now understood to have written the formula for achieving psychological action onstage, well before Chekhov. Büchner is now considered to be the forerunner of Brecht's episodic Epic Theater. Are Shakespeare's plays forever radical or are they an obsolete idea of excellence? Through six centuries Shakespeare's writing has been fashionable and out-of-fashion, inspirational, derided (by the Russian novelist Tolstoy!), and intentionally ignored (by those seeking to cast off colonialism in all things, including literature).

The twentieth century writers, who for purposes of discussion let's agree to call poets of the theater—Jean Cocteau, Gertrude Stein, Daniil Kharms, and Eugène Ionesco—have each and all been fashionable and out-of-fashion, inspirational, derided, and intentionally ignored. Despite their evolving or devolving reputations and the frequency with which their works are performed, these poets of the theater retain a lasting significance and influence. Their theoretical writings are sometimes more persuasive than the plays they wrote, but in theory and in practice they are, in their own way the passers-on of the restless spirit, if not the forms, of Henrik Ibsen, Bertolt Brecht, and Alfred Jarry.

Unlike Ibsen or Brecht or Clifford Odets whose plays investigate society and the workings of the world in which recognizable men and women suffer or triumph, the texts of Cocteau, Stein, Kharms, and Ionesco create an alternate reality that rises like Atlantis out of the sea whenever the dialogue they wrote is spoken or their stage directions are followed.

Jean Cocteau was born in France in 1889, a year after Ibsen wrote *Hedda Gabler*. Cocteau died in 1963, the same year Clifford Odets died. Cocteau was as desperate to escape bourgeoise expectations as Ibsen's heroine and as articulate about the need for revolution as the union workers imagined by Odets. Cocteau wanted the theater itself to be liberated.

Cocteau declared he wanted "poetry of the theater, not poetry in the theater." Poetry *in* the theater is easy to recognize: the rhymes of Racine, Corneille, Molière or any other subsequent author working in the refined classical tradition of wit and eloquence. Poetry *of* the theater is something elegant rather than eloquent, misshapen rather than misspoken. Poetry of the theater could be a swinging door, a flickering light, an awkward gesture, an oversized costume, gaps in speech, or breaks in cause and effect between events. The occasion for Cocteau's pronouncement about poetry of the theater was his published preface to *Les Mariés de la Tour Eiffel* (*The Eiffel Tower Wedding*), a theatrical event Cocteau devised for a 1921 performance in Paris by the Ballets Suédois (the Swedish Ballet). The Ballets Suédois was briefly fashionable in Paris in the wake of Sergei Diaghilev's Ballets Russes (the Russian Ballet) for whom Cocteau had conceived a previous spectacle, *Parade*.

Parade was danced theater. Diaghilev assembled a dream team in Italy where the Ballet Russe rehearsed: Leonid Massine choreographed, Erik Satie wrote the music, and Pablo Picasso created décor and masks. The origin of *Parade* is a good story, perhaps true: Cocteau approached Diaghilev with the suggestion of a ballet. The impresario responded, "Astonish me." Cocteau took up the challenge.

In performance, Satie's score for *Parade* swoopes and tinkles as three hucksters tempt passersby to enter a circus tent onstage. Massine's choreography echoed tap-dancing, gymnastics, classical ballet attitudes, and Charlie Chaplin's penguin walk. Picasso created body masks for the dancers—a cubist sculpture of a pipe smoker, for example, out of which legs emerged. The cubist smoker carried a cane, and its knocks echoed the knocking of a smoking pipe. Two dancers animated a vaudeville horse costume with a Picasso-made horse head. One grand costume by Picasso topped a collection of tall buildings with a megaphone. The audience never did get to see what was inside the circus tent. The poet Guillaume Apollinaire wrote the program description for *Parade*, coining the word *surrealism* to describe the happenings: beyond realism, a parallel reality. Cocteau wanted to include spoken words but was overruled by Diaghilev, who thought speech had no place in a ballet.

Cocteau's scenario for *The Eiffel Tower Wedding*, first performed in 1921, contains snatches of dialog and fragments of conversations broadcast out of two megaphones on behalf of all the characters. A wedding party assembles for a marriage on the Eiffel Tower observation platform: a photograph is taken, after a lion eats a general, and exits into the camera, then the megaphones react:

> PHONOS I AND II. Ahhhh! Ahhhh!
> PHONO I. Poor General!
> PHONO II. He was so lighthearted, so eternally youthful! Nothing would have amused him more than this death: he would have been the first to chuckle over it.
> (Dudley Fitts, trans.)

The party resumes. A character called "the Child of the Future" assassinates everyone while a fugue plays. There is a funeral march. The party continues, not so much resurrected as oblivious to death. The other characters include an ostrich.

In his preface to *The Eiffel Tower Wedding* Cocteau described his aims:

> Sunday vacuity, human beastliness, ready-made expressions, disassociation of ideas from flesh and bone, the ferocity of childhood, the miraculous poetry of daily life: these are my play...
> (Dudley Fitts, trans.)

Cocteau, inspired by styles as varied as melodrama, Greek tragedy, and boulevard comedy, wrote many more plays though none so original as his scenarios for *The Parade* and *The Eiffel Tower*

Wedding. He also wrote novels and poetry. He painted frescoes. His drawings are remarkable. Among many of his contemporaries he was dismissed as facile. In certain circles he was despised for his lack of a principled stand against the Nazis occupying France and envied for his ability to land on his feet. After the Second World War, he made important movies, including his 1946 surreal masterpiece *Beauty and the Beast.* The film begins with Cocteau writing on a chalkboard, first the credits, and then, just before the action begins Cocteau speaks—in English!— "Wait, a minute!" Instructions for the audience follow, written in French, concluding with an appeal.

> C'est un peu de cette naïveté que je vous demande et, pour nous porter chance à tous, laissez-moi vous dire quatre mots magiques, véritable mots magiques, véritable « sésame ouvre-toi » de l'enfance :
> Il était une fois…

> (*I ask of you a little of this childlike sympathy and, to bring us luck, let me speak four truly magic words, childhood's "Open Sesame": Once upon a time…*)

For better or worse, Cocteau's art—in film, onstage, or anywhere else—sparkles with playfulness. This made him seem shallow to those perpetually adolescent critics who confuse being grim with being serious.

Poetry of the theater, as Cocteau defined it, had already been imagined in 1901 when August Strindberg wrote stage directions for *A Dream Play* calling for a castle to transform into a chrysanthemum. Another scene change in *A Dream Play* requires petty squabbles inside a wall-papered room to dissolve into the sounds of a waterfall within a cave. The surreal shape-shifting is excused by the frame of a dream. Poetry of the theater provides no such reassuring frame as a dream but rather requires a more complete giving over of the audience to the roller coaster ride of inexplicable events.

Years before, Adolphe Appia, Edward Gordon Craig, and the composer Richard Wagner had dreamed of a unified artwork of the theater. But for poets of the theater, music would not be what unified the spectacle, as Wagner wanted, nor light as Appia hoped, nor the dominating persona of the auteur director, as Craig achieved. Nor does the poetry of the theater answer Antonin Artaud's 1931 "Manifesto for a Theater of Cruelty," which advocates, as translated by Mary Caroline Richards, the display of "truthful precipitates of dreams, in which [man's] taste for crime, his erotic obsessions, his savagery, his chimeras, his utopian sense of life and matter, even his cannibalism, pour out on a level not counterfeit and illusory, but interior."

For poets of the theater, music and light and words and the director's intention or a performer's efforts combine as if they were parts of a machine, ironically a machine with no purpose aside from its own existence A story might unfold or it might not. An audience might or might not understand the intentions or obsessions of those who create such theater. Neither the audience's reaction nor the artist's impetus to create can ever be a summation of the performed event's meaning or significance, which remains the event itself. There are a number of adjectives applied to such theater, including absurd, illogical, paradoxical, and Apollinaire's word, surreal.

On his way out of Paris to collaborate with the Ballet Russe in Rome, Picasso stopped by the apartment of his friend, Gertrude Stein, to introduce Cocteau to her. Miss Stein, an expatriate American, lived in rooms crammed with her collection of paintings by Picasso and other modernist painter friends. Stein assembled words as a sculptor or collage artist for the pleasure of the assembling and the pleasure in beholding the assemblage. Her practice was to recite aloud, and what she spoke was written down by her companion, Alice B. Toklas. In this way Stein created what she called "geographies or plays," by which she meant landscapes of language through which performers and audiences might move, as if touring. Did Stein or Toklas mention these word landscapes to Cocteau? Maybe. Maybe not.

Well before she moved to France, even as a little girl in Oakland, California in the 1880s, Stein enjoyed theater and good company. Stein liked sitting and watching people speak and move about. That speaking and moving about onstage could have a purpose—to propagandize some faith or push some politics or offer role models—didn't much interest her. Wealthy from family investments, Stein didn't need to sell theater tickets, appeal to critics, or have her plays accepted for productions. As had Ibsen when he wrote *Peer Gynt*—or Strindberg, *A Dream Play*—Stein supposed that someday someone would stage what she imagined. If that didn't happen, it didn't. Unlike most women in her time, she didn't have a family to bring up or defer to, and in this way, among many others, she is rare and unrepresentative. To understand what she wrote requires close attention while reading. Skimming won't do. It's often easier to understand what she wrote while listening to the words spoken aloud.

Stein had the words "Rose is a Rose is a Rose" printed as a circle on her letterhead, its form as important as the meaning of the words. Her plays work the same way. For Ms. Stein's play *Short Sentences* over four hundred named characters speak one line each. The text on the page begins with the title, which might or might not be spoken as part of the performance. A stage direction follows, though it isn't set off by brackets. Is it also meant to be spoken? Stein's writing offers many possibilities of meaning. Considering the possibilities is part of the inviting charm of what she wrote—especially for those who would stage what she put down on paper.

SHORT SENTENCES
The scene is one in which nicely they go:

Madame Bucher. Will you come
Nathalie. Oh yes will you come
Amelia. But I know you will come

Barbette. I ask you to come
Eugene. Will you
Joseph. I have been able to come
Edmund. Is he better because you bring what you bring when
you do come
Chorus. And so they are all not alike.

Stein's repetitions—she preferred the term *insistence*—resemble thought itself and when spoken aloud turn musical. It was natural she would write opera librettos—*Four Saints in Three Acts* for the American composer Virgil Thomas and the libretto for *Dr. Faustus Lights the Lights*, which Stein completed even after the intended composer dropped the project. She poured out words like an oracle while Alice faithfully transcribed them. Stein's facility can be exhausting, yet what she wrote is often effervescent. Here's a speech from *Dr. Faustus Lights the Lights* with the original punctuation. As often with what Stein wrote, it's helpful to read aloud to make sense of it, which should tell you something about Stein's dramatic writing.

SCENE II
I am I and my name is Marguerite Ida and Helena Annabel, and then oh then I could yes I could I could begin to cry but why why could I begin to cry.
And I am I and I am here and how do I know how wild the wild world is how wild the wild woods are the wood they call the woods the poor man's overcoat but do they cover me and if they do how wild they are wild and wild and wild they are, how do I know how wild woods are when I have never ever seen a wood before.

I wish (she whispered) I knew why woods are wild why animals are wild why I am I, why I can cry, I wish I wish I knew, I wish oh how I wish I knew. Once I am in I will never be through the woods are there and I am here and am I here or am I there, oh

where oh where is here oh where oh where is there and animals
wild animals are everywhere.
She sits down.

Yes, the heroine is lost in the woods! Might you read the stage
directions as part of the text? Yes, you might. Does the lack of
punctuation allow you to create your own interpretation? Yes, it
does.

Stein created a cult of personality for herself as a lesbian
sphinx. This had its uses, but it has also obscured the depths of
her achievement as a writer and a thinker. Stein anticipates performance art, the music of Philip Glass, the theater of Robert
Wilson, the rhythm of hip-hop, and the irony of Andy Warhol.

Unlike the mysteries of Gertrude Stein's writing, the short
plays of the Russian hooligan Daniil Kharms speak for themselves. Here is the first of "Four illustrations of how a new idea
dumbfounds a person who is not ready for it" written in the late
1920s.

The Writer: I am a writer!
The Reader: And I think you are shit!
(The Writer stands still for a few minutes, shocked by this new
idea, and falls dead as a doornail.
(Matvei Yankelevich, trans.)

In the next three "illustrations" the same words are relayed to an
artist, a composer, and a chemist, each of whom drops dead and
gets the heave-ho.

Kharms was born Daniil Ivanovich Yuvacho in 1905 in St.
Petersburg, Russia. His Kharms name—one of many he invented
for himself—is a combination of the English words *charms* and
harms, pronounced with the guttural KH that sounds, in English,
like preparation to spit. Dan-Dan (another of his self-invented
names) was a red diaper baby, what Communists called the off-

spring of parents who advanced the red flag of the Russian Revolution. His father helped found the radical collective that assassinated Tsar Alexander in 1881, twenty-six years before Russian revolutionaries assassinated Alexander's brother, Tsar Nicholas. Like Alfred Jarry, who began his masterwork *Ubu* by mocking a high school physics teacher, Kharms knew his own mind early on and followed respectfully where it led him past respectability, well past the conformity of non-conformity. Thrown out of a communist college for his lack of community spirit, Daniil became a public eccentric, dressed as an English dandy and carried a curved pipe in imitation of Sherlock Holmes. His first play *Elizabeth Vam* (1926) includes illogical sequences of words and nonsense sounds.

In 1926 Daniil Kharms founded the OBERIU, or Union of Real Art collective, unintentionally the last of the avant-garde Russian artists' groups. The OBERIU staged what we would now call Happenings: non-logical, non-linear, non-verbal, yet still somehow voiced, theatrical events, not always in theaters, sometimes on a roof or in the street. The Kharms performance texts are often short narratives. The Kharms performance texts are often short narratives without spoken words. This is from the text of *An Optical Illusion*:

> Semyon Semyonovich, having put on his spectacles, looks at
> a pine tree and this is what he sees: In the pine tree sits a man
> showing him his fist.
> (Matvei Yankelevich, trans.)

Sometimes Kharms included dialogue and stage directions as in *An Unsuccessful Show*, in which six people come out onstage one after another to vomit and run off until a little girl enters to announce the actors all feel sick and the theater is closing. Curtain.

Though full-frontal assaults on realism were repressed in Russia and other Eastern European countries under unapologetically totalitarian Communist rule, the traditional genre of satire channeled non-realistic theater, as long as the object of derision was not the communist system itself but its imperfect practitioners. The constructivist artist Kazimir Malevich, notorious in icon-worshipping Russia for a canvas painted solid black, lent rehearsal space to Kharms and the OBERIU, telling them, according to a Russian anecdote, "You are young trouble-makers, and I am an old one. Let's see what we can do."

They had little time to do much. By the early 1930s, whatever previous stage experiments had been going on in Russia had reached a conclusion, at least for those in power. Socialist Realism, which upheld easily understandable role models and positive images, often of previously oppressed members of society, advanced the revolution. According to Socialist Realism, social, political, and economic forces explained behavior. Anything else that might confuse an audience was not only bad taste, or poor craft, but was counter-revolutionary and a bad example to be curtailed—and erased from Soviet history—before anyone else got confused, or worse, followed along in error. Social and artistic revolution followed by stagnation is nothing new. Egyptologists can trace such a thing back before the pyramids were built.

Arrested in 1931, Kharms was sent into exile for a year then rehabilitated to write children's literature, though he detested children and made no secret of it. Even so, about twenty of his books have become Russian children's classics. In 1941 Kharms was arrested again and died in prison during the Siege of Leningrad (the Soviet name for St. Petersburg), probably of starvation.

Only two poems by Kharms were published in his lifetime. Aside from his children's books, he wrote "for the drawer" as Russians put it. After he died, his sister and an OBERIU friend— the musical theorist Yakov Druskin—carried the Kharms manuscripts around in suitcases to keep them safe.

Beginning in the 1960s, the radical writings of Kharms circulated secretly in Russia. In the 1980s when the history of Soviet avant-garde theater was disclosed, along with the accomplishments of the radical director Meyerhold, Kharms' work was published in Russian and, for a while, achieved a cult-like following—its cultural colonies a welcome alternative to Social Realism, now so unrealistic as to be laughable. As Russia has entered a new cycle of cultural repression and pushback from radical artists, Kharms' name and caricature appear in graffiti and OBERIU has been cited in Russian courts as the tradition from which current protest and twenty-first century hooliganism derives.

Eugène Ionesco—like Cocteau, Stein, and Kharms—piled on clichés, puns, non-sequiturs, and noise to construct plays. Yet Ionesco managed to tell stories onstage, develop plots, and provided actors unexpected, fresh ways to establish emotion and relationships. The ecstasy of martyrdom climaxes in Ionesco's *The Lesson* (1950) when a young student sacrifices herself to comprehend the meaning of the word "knife." Adolescent rebellion is unforgettably snarled out by the title character of *Jack, or the Submission* (1955), who rejects the bride chosen for him by his family because she has two noses. He wants a girl with three.

Though Romanian by birth and self-definition, Ionesco wrote mostly in French, inviting actors and audiences devoted to French classical stage traditions of dramatic recitation and oratory to pursue such tastes to their ultimate refinement in Ionesco-created exchanges of sonorous air. Ionesco's first play *The Bald Soprano* (1949) was inspired by inane repartee in a textbook meant to teach English conversation. Here's a sample of Ionesco's dialogue:

> MR. SMITH: One walks on his feet, but one heats with electricity or coal.
> MR. MARTIN: He who sells an ox today, will have an egg tomorrow.
> MRS. SMITH: In real life, one must look out of the window.
> MRS. MARTIN: One can sit down on a chair, when the chair doesn't have any.

Not all *The Bald Soprano's* exchanges fall at cross-purposes. The Martins—Mr. (*He who sells an ox...*) and Mrs. (*One can sit down on a chair...*)—are sitting beside each other in an English drawing room when they discover that they both live on the same street (*Comme c'est curieux! Et quelle coincidence! Comme c'est bizarre!*), in the same apartment (*Comme c'est bizarre! Et quelle coincidence! Comme c'est curieux!*), have the same children and are married (*Quelle coincidence! Comme c'est curieux! Comme c'est bizarre!*). Ionesco was a master of comic structure, the proof being his plays are funny in translation: *How bizarre! How curious! What a coincidence!*

The term "Theatre of the Absurd" was coined, in part, to describe Ionesco's writing, but his dramas are not absurd in the sense of nonsensical or purposeless. In his memoir, written in Romanian and included in an English language collection of his prose titled *Notes and Counter Notes*, Ionesco revealed that at the back of his work was a fear of death. The words in his plays and the act of speech itself can be understood as ways to ward off death, like a charm—or, just as powerfully, to alleviate the pain of death. In Ionesco's *Exit the King* (1962), a dying man's embittered first wife lovingly teaches him to let go of life by naming his failing body parts.

Behind the acceptance of death is the threat of violence and pain. André Breton, who claimed leadership over Surrealism, suggested in the *Second Surrealist Manifesto* (1930) that a random shooting into a crowd was the ultimate surreal act. The first published version of *The Bald Soprano* ended with stage directions for machine-gunning the audience, taking to extremes what comedians say when they "kill." Taken as metaphor, the surreal means to annihilate the audience's reality. Ionesco's annihilations are into bliss, celebration, and mystery.

Ionesco was thrown out by Breton from official Surrealist circles because of the Romanian author's refusal to accept the atrocities of communism under Stalin as an alternative to Hitler's Fascism. Cocteau was denounced by Breton, too, supposedly for the same reason, though it can be argued homophobia towards

Cocteau had a lot to do with Breton's anathema. Kharms was criminally apolitical in communist Russia. As the Nazis overran France, they left Gertrude Stein and Alice B. Toklas, not only Jews, but gay Jews, untouched while millions of others, gay or Jewish, were rounded up and slaughtered. Stein, after her death, was accused of collaboration—for not protesting.

Poetry of the theater, like a shaman's ritual or the altar of a temple, draws its power as art and as a spiritual force by separation from the shared world, including a separation from politics. Even so, Ionesco gives the sadistic professor in *The Lesson* an option to put on a Nazi armband and Ionesco's play *Rhinoceros* was one of his most popular for a while because the metamorphoses of men to bestial monsters in a provincial town could be reduced to a metaphor for Romania turning communist or fascist, depending on who you asked, communist or capitalist.

Ionesco's claim that at the back of his work is a fear of death suggests something beyond metaphor: the speaking of words can create a spell that holds the world, and fear of its annihilation, at bay. In realism we speak of the suspension of disbelief—poetry of the theater, when successful, achieves that and something more potent: the momentary suspension of mortality.

Chapter Twenty-One

PERSONAL MYTHOLOGY

Jean Genet (1910–1986)
Federico García Lorca (1898–1936)
Yukio Mishima (1925–1970)
August Strindberg (1849–1912)

S ome playwrights link human affairs to Heaven and Hell in such comprehensive and original ways that their vision may be called a personal mythology. Unlike playwrights who establish alternate, surreal worlds onstage—Ionesco or Cocteau, for example, or playwrights who seek to mirror or depict the recognizable world, as did Ibsen or Chekhov—playwrights with a personal mythology are not so much creators of myth as testifying witnesses, caught up in their own damnation or salvation, survival or disaster.

August Strindberg, born in Stockholm in 1849 to an upper-class family, was a writer with just such a personal mythology. At the time Sweden was begrudgingly modernizing, Strindberg wrote over sixty plays: panoramic histories of Swedish kings and queens, as well as realistic plays that helped define what realism could be. Strindberg's surreal collages of stage directions and dialogue are meant to create images onstage more like X-ray plates than photographs. Soul-murder is often the action in a play by Strindberg. Whether goddesses, cooks, or countesses, his characters are divided into vampires and their victims: those who steal the life force from others and those from whom it is stolen. In *Miss Julie*

(*Fröken Julie*), written in 1888, the daughter of a count falls for her father's valet, Jean. He succeeds in dragging her down to his level, the cook's bed in the lowest floor of her father's estate. Miss Julie may be a count's daughter, but in a man's world whatever physical satisfaction there might be between them is inevitably Jean's conquest of Julie. As a dumbwaiter descends, conveying the count's boots down to the kitchen for Jean to polish, the heel of the class system crushes down on them both. An upstairs bell rings, and Jean bows towards the dumbwaiter and explains:

> It's not the bell—it's someone behind the bell, the hand that sets the bell in motion—and something else that sets the hand in motion. (Edith and Warner Oland, trans.)

Jean has whispered something into Julie's ear and hands her a razor. Julie, as mechanical as the dumbwaiter, goes off, presumably to kill herself.

Razors, guns, poison, even axes, figure in the wars Strindberg believed men and women wage with each other. He believed—in his heart—that women gathered secretly to hatch their plots to steal power from men. His play *The Father* (1887) depicts a Prussian cavalry captain, proud and cocky, spurs jingling. The captain's authority is sabotaged by his wife and daughter. When he tries to resist them, he's committed for insanity against his will and is ultimately undone by his old nurse who coaxes him into a strait jacket by reminding him how she used to dress him as a small child. *The Dance of Death* (1900) observes a husband and wife as if they were a pair of squabbling scorpions. *The Pelican* (1907) demonstrates how a mother might steal the life force from her children.

Strindberg's mythology melds personal experiences: his unhappy marriages, selfish stepmother, severe drug and alcohol abuse, and feigned or genuine madness, along with the theories of the German philosopher Nietzsche who believed a superman (or woman) would inevitably dominate weaker men and women. Add to the mix Strindberg's simplified understanding of Darwin's ideas about survival of the fittest, the tedious sexism of nineteenth century capitalism in which women were legally property, and the novels of Émile Zola who sought to explain character and action as a function of larger economic and social forces. Strindberg wrote quickly, with a quill pen, throwing the pages on the floor as soon as the ink dried, rarely editing or revising.

His psychological theories and his interpretations of history might be grotesque distortions but, like the Expressionist paintings by his friends Edvard Munch and Paul Gauguin, what's seen onstage in a Strindberg play is not meant to be confused with a mirror. Ibsen, who was twenty years older, kept a painting of Strindberg at his desk and referred to him as "that madman." If Strindberg was mad, his madness, like many illnesses, left him tender and sensitive, for better or worse, to other people's feelings.

His writing is often sour. He had an obsession (as did Shakespeare's contemporary Ben Jonson) with filth, greed, and lust in its animal aspects. He held a low opinion of people in general, heightened by cynical laughter. A little of this goes a long way.

Yet Strindberg's *Ghost Sonata* (*Spöksonaten*), written in 1907, five years before he died, reveals disgust with human animality as a path to compassion. In *Ghost Sonata* the dead walk, the past and the present and the future coincide. A character called The Mummy, who squawks incomprehensibly like a parrot, stops the ticking of a grand onstage clock to speak in a clear voice:

> We are miserable human beings, that we know. We have erred and we have sinned. We like all the rest. We are not what we seem; because at bottom we are better than ourselves, since we detest our sins.
> (Elizabeth Sprigge, trans.)

That we can be disgusted by ourselves means we know better.

A Dream Play (*Ett drömspel*), written by Strindberg in 1901, reveals celestial connections. The daughter of the god Indra, herself divine, descends to earth as a soul in various incarnations—unhappy wife among them. She returns to heaven with the sorry knowledge that human life is suffering. Indra and his daughter are powerless to change that. The implication of the play as a dream bestows the gods' awareness of suffering onto the audience, but also renders the audience, at least while watching the stage, just as powerless as Indra and his daughter to end any suffering they witness. As Indra's daughter returns to oblivion in heaven, the sleeper—that is to say the audience—wakes from the spell of the dream/play, leaves the theater, and goes out into the street with the possibility of a power to allay suffering, a power Indra and his daughter will never have.

Strindberg was a self-taught painter of seascapes, inspired by a love of the sea and its storms. He slathered thick dark oil paints onto the canvas with a trowel. We see abstractions swirl around a single flower or beneath the silhouette of trees. Born at the dawn of the new art of photography, Strindberg experimented with original ways to capture images. He invented the celestograph, for which a glass plate coated with light-sensitive salts is exposed to the night sky. In this way, lit by the light of the stars, images form over time on paper. The process continues after Strindberg's death thanks to unknowable ongoing chemical processes. This is as good a metaphor as any for what he was trying to do as a playwright, record the dark night of the soul, in inexact ways, with results that continue to develop over time.

Photographs taken in the dark are also good metaphors for the plays of Jean Genet (1910–1986), that convey his audience to an underworld lit by the flashbulbs of a crime scene.

Genet's one-act thriller *The Maids* was inspired by the real-life crimes of the Papin sisters, whose double-portrait photographs taken before and after their arrest in 1933, electrified French tabloid readers more than a dozen years before Genet began to write about the Papins.

In their first double portrait printed in the tabloids, the sisters appear a little shy in front of the camera. Their hair is neatly coifed and curled. Their clean well-scrubbed necks are exposed by the scoop of matching lace collars, their eyes reserved, their faces plump blank, asexual ovals—dowdy, polite, and dull. The second portrait is the work of police photographers following the sisters' confession to hammering two other women to death before dismembering the still quivering bodies. The sisters appear as wild beasts, hair in disarray. Their necks in the second of photographs are wedges of flesh framed by the collars of what look like kimonos. What circumstance transformed these two respectable servants into mad killers?

Genet's answer to that question is free will—the sister's heroic choice to stoke the fire of madness, to accept the burden of tragedy, to live up (not down) to the responsibilities of outlaw insanity and infamy. Collapsing the details of the tabloid news, the plot of *The Maids* has two sisters, who are servants, rehearse the ritual murder of their mistress. The girls take turns playing murderer and victim. The victim always masquerades as the mistress of the house, imitating Madame's affectations while wearing Madame's discarded wigs and soiled gowns. One night the maids attempt a genuine murder and poison Madame's tea. Despite her servants' polite insistence, Madame avoids even a sip before she gaily departs for a romantic rendezvous. Claire, the younger sister, decides to drink the poison herself and die. The play ends as both sisters envision the fame their murder will achieve, what a grand parade there will be for Solange on her way to the hangman, how headlines will beatify the murderer on the scaffold.

Besides Genet's play, there have been at least two other theatrical versions of the Papin's story, dramatizations in which the double murder is motivated by the real-life petty cruelties of the mistresses that drove the Papins to extremity. For Genet the mistress is kind, if condescending, to her servants. She treats her maids like dolls with presents, kisses, and shared confidences. The servants are demeaned but not degraded; the maids' lives are dull but not cruel, predictable and banal but not tortured. In *The Maids*, a beautiful, if evil, dream replaces dull, if nice, reality. This is something other than logic, realism, or psychological portraiture. It is a vision of a road to glory in which sacrifice while revolting against authority bestows sainthood.

Genet was in Algeria when the case of the Papins broke. He had enlisted in the French Foreign Legion the year before, an early way to leave his French provincial reform school, which is where he ended up after he was thrown out of an orphanage. As an infant he had been abandoned by his mother, who was a prostitute. Before and after his army stint, he was an inept petty thief, so consistently arrested for lifting books and small bolts of cloth that he received a life sentence.

In the early 1940s, according to Genet, he was in a French jail cell cutting out photographs from tabloid newspapers of handsome criminals, most of them murderers. With glue made from chewed bread, he would stick the handsome faces to the wall behind his bed. There at night he would spin erotic fantasies involving his gallery of rogues in adventures intricate enough to weave into a novel, *Our Lady of the Flowers*. Thanks to influential friends, he was pardoned, and the book was published, yet for the rest of his life he identified himself as a criminal.

The central characters in Genet's plays are haloed by their crimes: theft, insurrection, treason, and murder. In Genet's *The Blacks,* written between 1955 and 1959, a group of Black people perform the ritual slaughter of a white woman. The play, subtitled *a clownerie*, is set up as a minstrel show, ironically performed by Black people who mean to distract a white audience and keep them in the theater while a revolution rages in the city in which the show is performed. Genet's *The Screens* (1964), a vast text takes over seven hours to perform, introduces Said, a poor Arab who steals from other Arabs. As the Algerian war for independence from French colonization unfolds, Said betrays the revolution. He is the outcast of the outcasts and hailed as a hero by outcasts among the dead for refusing to do anything that would serve a purpose. In *The Balcony* (1957), figureheads of power—a queen, a bishop, and a judge—are assassinated in an ongoing revolution and then replaced on the balcony of a bordello by the people who assume the identities of queen, bishop, and judge for sex play. At the play's end the madam of the bordello turns off the stage lights. She complains about the cost, then points out to the audience where the exits are, so they may leave and, as she says, assume their own disguises at home.

Genet's words glitter, still enticing elite French audiences, critics, and performers to submit to the unnerving wonder of gloriously baroque prose dropping out of the mouths of those whom the French elite traditionally considered subhuman: servants, thieves, whores, and people of color. Genet, and the words he gave to his creations, turned all such identities—the elite and the despised, audience and performer, critics, and criminals—into aspects of the underworld.

> Milk will be black, sugar, rice, the sky, doves, hope, will be black.
> So will the opera to which we shall go, blacks that we are, in black
> Rolls Royces to hail black kings, to hear brass bands beneath
> chandeliers of black crystal...
> (Bernard Frechtman, trans.)

In a note that precedes the published text, Genet explains the origins of *The Blacks*:

> One evening an actor asked me to write a play for an all-black
> cast. But what exactly is a black? First of all, what's his color?

In fact, the untranslated title of *The Blacks, Les Nègres,* is not so polite in French. In Genet's personal mythology there will always be "les nègres," whoever they are, dark-skinned or not.

This mythologizing robs human misery of historical reality, another way to objectify human beings rather than change the social conditions that oppress them. Enrolling himself directly into the social revolutions of the late 1960s in France and America, Genet abandoned playwriting, identifying it as a part of his life that was over. He died more than twenty years later, in 1986.

Spain—where African tribes known in the West as Moors built an Islamic civilization for over seven hundred years until they were forced out by Catholic Europeans—has its own theatrical traditions. Churches in Spain hosted performances in the aisles of their sanctuaries and on the steps leading out to church squares a few decades later than in England and a few decades earlier than in France. Performances of plays were held in Spanish courtyards and inns at roughly the same time that Marlowe and Shakespeare's plays were performed in similar circumstances in late sixteenth century England. By the 1600s buildings were constructed in Spain for performances by professional theater companies. This was a few years later than theaters in England. In Spain, however, women performed in plays a hundred years before they did on English stages.

The plays of the Spanish-language repertory remain segregated by tradition and choice—as much as Chinese theater or the dramatic repertory of the Indian subcontinent. Spanish theater enjoyed a Golden Age of classics, including *Fuente Ovejuna* written by Lope de Vega (1619), in which a village takes responsibility for a crime, and Pedro Calderón de la Barca's *Life is a Dream* (1635) in which a princely hero locked in a tower, learns that what he has been told of the outside world is a deceitful illusion. During the nineteenth century, theaters in Spain and its overseas colonies, as in theaters throughout Europe, performed classics out of duty, but were overrun with melodrama, musical reviews, and operettas.

It is then a marvel that Federico García Lorca, a self-taught poet-playwright born in 1898, emerged as a significant figure in world theater. He was hauled away by local thugs and shot dead at the age of thirty-six in the first weeks of the Spanish Civil War. Though he was fascinated by theater since childhood, Lorca channeled most of his visions into incantatory poetry and concentrated on writing plays only during the last four years of his life, while he was directing and adopting Spanish Golden Age plays for La Barraca, a touring theater company. He fortified his texts for the stage with imagery and dramatic structure so potent as to survive translation—and decades of political suppression in his own country. Here, for example, is what the moon says in *Blood Wedding*:

> Round swan of the river
> Eye of the cathedral
> False dawn on the leaves
> No one can escape me.
> The moon hangs like a knife in the air.
> (James Graham-Luján and Richard L. O'Connell, trans.)

That the moon speaks is unthinkable in a play by Ibsen or Chekhov but in the world Lorca created onstage and in his verse, inevitable. Famously, the wind is green in Lorca's poetry. In his plays, the colors onstage—of a flower or a dress or a curtain—are as active and alive as any character. In his plays, musical sounds—bells, guitars, animal horns turned into trumpets, out-of-tune pianos—played onstage or heard offstage, are as meaningful as the sound of the spoken word. In his own way Lorca realized both aspects of Cocteau's poetry *in* and *of* the theater.

Blood Wedding (1932) has a plot as familiar as a folk song: a woman marries someone other than the man she loves, and on the night of her wedding the true lover carries the new bride away. As their pursuers on horseback draw close, the runaways exchange vows in a shadowy thicket, escaping the sound of the approaching hoof beats. The silences between impossible promises are pierced by the inexplicable squeaks of a pair of violins. When the moon arrives in the person of a young, fresh-faced woodcutter, the dark wood is irradiated with a spectral blue.

No one can escape me.
The moon hangs like a knife in the air.

If Genet's plays occur in the underworld, Lorca's run on ground beneath the shadow of a storm or in the light of an ominous moon, with rumbling underneath and the sounds of unreachable pleasure in the distance. What rooms there are in Lorca's plays have walls that tremble, though the doors are locked tight and the windows tighter still. In *The House of Bernarda Alba*, finished but not performed at the time of Lorca's death in 1936, a stabled stallion kicks hard against the thick whitewashed walls behind which a stern mother keeps her five unmarried daughters imprisoned. The youngest daughter, who escapes to make love, hangs herself. Her mother commands the corpse be laid out and mourned as a virgin. An older sister considers the dead girl a thousand times blessed for having possessed the pain of love.

In all of Lorca's plays, love is a means to gain pain: "glass splinters in the tongue," as the bride of *Blood Wedding* boasts. In Lorca's mythological world, pain is a means to a transcendent death, often a long lingering death-in-life. In *Doña Rosita the Spinster or The Language of Flowers* (1934), a woman waits thirty years for a man who will never return to her:

I want to run, I want not to see; I want to be left calm, empty…
Yet hope pursues me, circles me, bites me, like a dying wolf.
(Graham-Luján and O'Connell, trans.)

That love is pain, that pain exalts, is a mythology, certainly not a fact. As with Strindberg, the life Lorca led is refracted in visions of heaven and hell. Lorca was gay and, out of what he considered respect for his traditional Catholic family, closeted for most of his life. He believed he had Jewish and Arabic ancestors who were never spoken of openly. When he was ten, his father moved the family from the southern village where they grew sugar beets to a townhouse in Grenada, a few short yards from where the ancient river Genil emerged into sight—in all other parts of Grenada the ancient Genil is paved over.

In all aspects of Lorca's plays, in words, stage pictures, lighting, and music, there is something like the Genil running under the ground, as in the grand Spanish—and Moorish—idea of passion twisting beneath a smooth exterior. His craft writing plays is demonstrated by his use of silences and the dramatic importance of what is offstage to determine the meaning of what is seen and heard onstage. We miss in translation Lorca's irony and humor. What we get is the vision that offstage there is inevitably death, betrayal, and heaven.

Lorca was a slow student in high school and in college. He gained theater savvy on tour. He learned from the classics of the Spanish theater by staging them. The women washing clothes at the river in *Yerma* are descendants of the choruses of *Fuente Ovejuna*, which toured Spain in an adaptation by Lorca. The uses of illusion and time in his unrealized "impossible plays"—the last thoughts of a young suicide in *As Five Years Pass* is one such "impossible play"—derive from the preoccupations of *Life is a Dream*, in the La Barraca production of which Lorca played the character of Shadow while covered in black gauze.

Lorca, Strindberg, and Genet, considered outside of history and alongside each other, reveal certain similarities as artists and thinkers in and out of the theater. All these writers thought in images. Strindberg made paintings and took photographs, García Lorca drew and painted with watercolors. Genet made collages and a film. For all the difference in their cultures, what these visionary playwrights have in common is the staging of damnation and exaltation. The vocabulary put into use for these purposes is often a mix of coarse and eloquent, subverting the traditional genres of tragedy, farce, and comedy.

That they brought forth personal mythologies, rather than repeat conventional orthodoxies, was made possible by the weakened authority of the church and European society after

World Wars I and II, or in the case of Strindberg, the collapse of a medieval world into the industrialized nineteenth century.

A similar collapse occurred in twentieth century Asia. Japan's admission of defeat in the Second World War left Japanese identity as shattered as any bombed Japanese city. In the psychic ruins amidst the visible rubble, the playwright and novelist Yukio Mishima, born Kimitake Hiraoka in 1925, lived his life as the creator and devotee of a mythology of annihilation. His vision fused the European romantic ideal of exploding in ecstasy with the Buddhist idea of Nirvana as the extinction of desire. For Mishima, frustration, fear, and pain were means to enlightenment.

Like Genet, the personal turns of Mishima's life and politics distract attention from the achievement of his writing and the depth of his thought. Born into an upper-middle class family with aristocratic connections, his talent as a writer was recognized and cultivated beginning with the haiku he wrote as a child. The publication in 1949 of his novel *Confessions of a Mask* brought him fame in Japan. It's the story of a man who discovers his attraction to men. In the same year, 1949, Mishima's career as a playwright began successfully with the premiere of *The Lighthouse,* a one-act play in which a stepson and stepmother confess their love for each other at a seaside resort. When writing fiction or when writing for the stage, Mishima considered the pleasure and pain of transgressive behavior to be beautiful decadence rather than sexual identity or sin.

As a spectator and as an author, theater appealed to Mishima as a spectacular sham. Performing a play written by Mishima manifests what is beneath the surface, especially a splendid surface. His writing for the stage makes public what is hidden and private. Sometimes what's hidden is hidden out of shame, sometimes hidden out of modesty, or hidden out of cunning. He mocks mechanical systems like Freud's or Darwin's that offer mechanical explanations of unseen mystery. His especial metaphor for the revelation of what's beneath the surface is blood spilling out from a living body. He was fascinated by ritual suicide and chose to die that way in 1970 on the morning he finished the last of a series of novels, *The Sea of Tranquility*. He was forty-five.

In all, Mishima wrote over sixty plays in different styles. In 1955 he had nine plays premiere in Japan. Nowadays, his most accessible plays in English are the twentieth century Modern Noh plays where, as in traditional Noh, ghosts haunt the living. An eerie sailboat glides into a hospital room in Mishima's modern *The Lady Aoi* (1954), the sound of a drummer in hell assaults the audience of Mishima's modern *The Damask Drum* (1951) but remains unheard by the person onstage for whom the drumming is intended. Mishima also wrote realistic Western-style plays, as shadowed by unseen spirits as Noh.

He wrote grand historical pageants, in which the most splendid events are compromised for audiences who learn the secrets of historic glory. A parade of war elephants with gilded tusks in *The Terrace of the Leper King*, written in 1969 and set in twelfth century Cambodia, marks the triumphant return of victorious King Jayavarman VII. At the end of the day's festivities, as the king leans back to relax on his golden throne, the sleeve of his gown rolls down to reveal a red blemish like a rose petal on his upper left arm, the first sign of leprosy. In *The Rokumeikan* (in English, *The Pavilion of the Baying Stag*) first performed in 1956 and set in 1886, the heroine, Asako, is a former geisha married to a crooked politician. She presides over a grand ball in celebration of the emperor's birthday. The waltzing is interrupted by a gang of revolutionaries demanding social reform. Asako appears at the head of a grand staircase, audaciously confronts the rebels, and dares them to use their drawn swords on her. Seemingly shamed by her audacity, the gang backs down the staircase at Asako's command and runs away. Mishima specifies she is to wear a beautiful, hooped shirt with startling décolletage, allowing views not possible if she was wearing a kimono. It's all wildly theatrical, but the revolutionaries are not what they appear to be.

They are thugs, hired by her husband, pretending to be political supporters of Asako's former lover. In all of Mishima's plays an audience is confronted with the unexplainable power and truth of what is false and, often, deliberately deceptive.

In Mishima's *Madame de Sade* (1965), the action is rhetorical, modeled on the techniques of the French neoclassical master Jean Racine. The story depicts the Marquis de Sade's wife, Renee, waiting twenty-five years for her husband to be released from prison, scheming for his pardon, then refusing to see him when he is freed, and effectively divorcing him by entering a convent.

Renee explains what fascinates her about the Marquis de Sade, though she knows firsthand that he is in some sense evil:

> He has built a back stairway to heaven...Alphonse is not a scoundrel. He is a kind of threshold between me and the impossible, or perhaps between me and God.

And then later:

> You and your kind when you see a rose say "How pretty!" And when you see a snake you say "How disgusting!" You know nothing of the world where the rose and the snake are intimates and at night exchange shapes, the snake's cheeks turning red and the rose putting forth shining scales...

Mishima, Strindberg, Lorca, and Genet—from disparate cultures and social backgrounds—use the words and images of their plays to shift shapes—snakeskin to rose petals, maid to mistress—and to unite opposites—black rice, a living mummy. Such a mystic vision of unity: all time, all space, and all identities combined as aspects of a vision, is neither real nor unreal but, according to its own values, true.

Chapter Twenty-Two

TWO MASTERS: SAMUEL BECKETT AND TENNESSEE WILLIAMS

Samuel Beckett (1906–1989)
Tennessee Williams (1911–1983)

On January 5, 1953 at the seventy-five-seat Théâtre de Babylone, and every time since, when the curtain rises on Samuel Beckett's *Waiting for Godot*, two men meet as planned at a country crossroads marked by a small bare tree. The shabbily dressed pair call one another Didi and Gogo—"dee dee" not "die die" (though the latter would make sense). Didi is short for Vladimir and Gogo for Estragon. Beckett specifies bowler hats, baggy pants, and laced boots. The men have been called, though not by their author, tramps; the costumes could also identify them as British music hall comedians. They are waiting for someone they call Godot. How that name is said aloud, now that Beckett is dead, is open to debate. Either it's pronounced God-o (as if they're waiting for God to arrive and are on such familiar terms with God that they've given Him a nickname) or, as in the original French title, *En attendant Godot*, stressing the second syllable, Gu-DOH, which is someone and something less familiar. Whoever he (or He) is, he doesn't arrive by the intermission. In the second, final act, the pair waits some more. The tree has sprouted four or five leaves. The sun sets; the moon rises. Godot never does arrive.

VLADIMIR: Well? Shall we go?
ESTRAGON: Yes, let's go.
[They do not move.]
[Curtain.]

Beckett's original title, *En attendant Godot,* literally means *while waiting* for Godot. What people do while they wait is the subject of the play: sing, tell jokes, quarrel, makeup, grow bored, brood. Despite expectations, the audience's and their own, they do nothing but wait, even though they say (and perhaps decide) that they'd prefer to go.

That nothing happens is what happens. As in a play by Chekhov or Turgenev, the interior life of the characters is where to look for the dramatic action of Beckett's plays. Unlike Chekhov or Turgenev's plays, just who Beckett's characters are and what precisely they want is left ambiguous. As in a play by Brecht, some things are meant to be imagined by the audience or left incomplete. The circumstances of who and why are not, in Beckett's plays, as essential as onstage behavior—especially habits enacted in ceremonies of faith and inertia.

In Beckett's *Happy Days* (1961), the curtain rises on the sight of Winnie, a plump, blonde middle-aged woman buried up to her waist in a mound. Is it sand? The sands of time? Dirt? She cannot move, but she can remember, she can tell herself stories, and she can enjoy the lovely weather while her husband crawls at the bottom of her mound. In the second act the mound has risen. Winnie is up to her neck. She can remember, tell herself stories, and enjoy the lovely weather. The repetition is funny and sad and puts on stage Beckett's essential metaphor that repeating what's mundane is a way of performing, rather than living, one's life. The circumstances are never explained, but again, unforgettably, Beckett's theatrical vision embodies faith and inertia.

To express his vision with greater precision, Beckett refined his theatrical vocabulary over decades. The short plays he wrote late in his life used fewer and fewer words and took less and less time to perform while the stage pictures he insisted on grew more spare. A performance of *Not I* (1972) leaves nothing for the audience to watch but a mouth suspended in the dark and the back of a listener swallowed in shadow. Sometimes Beckett disengages the spoken word from the speaker. In *Krapp's Last Tape* (1957), an old man listens to the voice of his younger unfamiliar self. Sometimes there are no spoken words in a play by Beckett. *Breath* (1969) is meant to be performed in twenty-five seconds. The stage directions call for the sounds of a birth cry, then breathing, then a death cry. The audience looks at a stage "littered with miscellaneous rubbish." Beckett's producer received the *Breath* manuscript on a postcard.

Though Beckett's plays can seem dry and spare, they can also prompt laughs. Beckett's jokes are often physical, including pratfalls and hat tricks. Krapp slips on a banana peel and a second banana peel is comically tossed off the stage into the audience. In *Godot*, when Didi and Gogo consider hanging themselves, the rope of Estragon's belt is too short for the intended purpose and in pulling the belt out to check the length (and ability to hold the weight of a dead body) Gogo's pants fall down like a clown's. In Beckett's *Endgame* (written between 1955 and 1957), which takes place inside what might be a bunker or a silo with a view of a blasted wasteland, the lines between Hamm (a blind man who can't leave his chair) and Clov (younger man, who tends to Hamm's needs) often resemble a vaudeville turn.

> HAMM: She was bonny once, like a flower of the field. (With reminiscent leer.)
> And a great one for the men!
> CLOV: We too were bonny—once. It's a rare thing not to have been bonny—once.
> (Pause.)

What Beckett did with that em dash—a pause that provokes thought and then laughter and then gives space for thought and laughter—could take other playwrights pages. That Beckett knew how to provoke and give space for laughter and thought with an em dash is the end product of craft, wit, and genius. We learn little more about the woman who was bonny—once—other than her name: Mother Pegg.

To understand Beckett's plays, we don't need to know much more about Beckett's life than we need to know about Mother Pegg's. That his mother May paced at night like the character named May in Beckett's *Footfalls* (1975) or that he was part of the French resistance to the Nazis during the Second World War (like no one in any of his plays) is, as far as the plays are concerned, inconsequential. This much is significant: born in 1906 in Dublin, Beckett is part of a lineage of Irish playwrights—Richard Brinsley Sheridan, George Bernard Shaw, and Oscar Wilde—who mastered the language of their English oppressors, so they might say, like Shakespeare's Caliban: "You taught me language, and my profit on't is I know how to curse." Beckett wrote some of his most famous plays—including *Godot* and *Endgame*—in French then translated them into English himself, an indication of the discipline he applied to the language of his writing for the stage.

If Beckett's work spirals into the core of a truth, the writing of Tennessee Williams, roughly Beckett's contemporary in America, spirals out to multiplicities of the same truth. A look at Williams' manuscripts discloses his process of composition. He typed and retyped the same passages with variations in wording, the way scales are practiced on the keyboard of a piano. This attention to rhythm and specificity of word choice resulted in naturalistic speech that sings.

> Blanche: Don't you just love these long rainy afternoons in New Orleans when an hour isn't just an hour—but a little bit of Eternity dropped in your hands—and who knows what to do with it? (Williams, *A Streetcar Named Desire*)

That is said by a woman with a weakness for young men, which ruined her reputation and got her thrown out of town. Her name is Blanche, meaning white, as she explains, but she's no lily, as the brother-in-law who uncovers her ruined reputation declares to Blanche's sister, Stella. Williams, who studied under Erwin Piscator in New York at the New School, mastered Piscator's theory of opposition. The beauty to be found in tawdry situations is, for Williams, the most beautiful of all. First and always a poet—as a teenager he won a prize for his poetry—Williams' stage directions are often as lyrical as his dialogue.

> The scene is memory and is therefore non-realistic. Memory takes a lot of poetic license. It omits some details; others are exaggerated, according to the emotional value of the articles it touches, for memory is seated predominantly in the heart. (Stage direction, Williams, *The Glass Menagerie*)

Often the names of Williams' characters—Chance Wayne, Blanche DuBois, Rosa delle Rosa, Flora Goforth, Mrs. Peacock, Fräulein Haussmitzenschlogger—are fragmentary poems. Combinations of the names in Williams' plays are poems. Blanche's sister is Stella ("for star"), Chance's former girlfriend is Heavenly. Vieux (which means *old* in French) is paired with Beau (the French word for *beautiful*) in *The Traveling Companion* (1981). The names of the estranged friends in *The Mutilated* (1966), which takes place during the Christmas season, are Celeste and Trinket.

Borrowing Piscator's technique of titling scenes for an audience, ironic titles projected above the scenes in *The Glass Menagerie* (1945), such as "THINGS HAVE A WAY OF TURNING OUT SO BADLY," cut against the dim and poetic story of a mother struggling for her family's happiness during the Depression.

Williams affirms (with Beckett) that life flares between vast expanses of darkness. For Williams, though, that life and love and youth and beauty are ephemeral makes it necessary to cherish them all the more, to recall them onstage—and celebrate them—

because they last so briefly. At the heart of play after play by Williams, a match or candle or bare light bulb is lit in the dark to shine and then go out. What's glorious in his plays flares up and dies down: a parade is heard passing by at a distance, sparkling glass gets broken, the heat of summer love fades in the winter of life. Pride, beauty, and love fly, float, and flaunt while they can with the audience aware of an inevitable burst or crash or worse. Williams often ends his plays with dramatic situations that resemble bubbles just before they burst. At any time in the trajectory of the action, the buoyancy an audience sees, hears, and feels is shadowed by future collapse. Laura, the crippled, shy girl, dances in *The Glass Menagerie*; Blanche the outcast finds Mitch, a good man who loves her, in *A Streetcar Named Desire*. That Laura will be abandoned by her partner and that Blanche will lose not only Mitch but will be taken away from her beloved only sister are griefs still to come. Williams makes the brief glories memorable. "Sometimes there's God so quickly," says Blanche. And sometimes, suddenly, there isn't any more glory. At the end of *Streetcar*, Blanche is led off to a state asylum while her sister ignores her and the man who loved her looks away crying.

Williams experimented audaciously with dramatic form. Williams' earliest plays, written for and performed by a St. Louis amateur theater group in the mid-1930s, call for large casts to include as many group members as possible. These early sprawling works borrow generic characters and clichés from 1930s movies and popular plays with styles ranging from expressionism to social protest, but in the same 1930s and until he died in 1983, the short plays Williams wrote—there are at least seventy-five of them—with smaller casts and more focused action, refined his technique through and beyond borrowed genres, beyond formulaic realism, expressionism, and social protest. In the spring of 1945 Williams had a hit with an episodic "memory play" in seven scenes: *The Glass Menagerie*. The play was so unusual as to be thought without structure and so life-like some contemporary critics claimed the dialogue was improvised by the actors.

The published text of *The Glass Menagerie* lays out the tight construction of a play in which every aspect of the theater—lights, scenery, costumes, music, and text—contribute to its meaning. After explaining that he's also a character in the play, the narrator (whom Williams gave his own name, Tom) is called in to supper by his loquacious Mississippi-born mother, Amanda. Turning from the audience, Tom joins his painfully shy sister, Laura, in the St. Louis tenement where the action takes place, presided over by a framed photograph of the smiling father who abandoned the family. Tom works in a factory to support his mother and sister, and like his father, he too will run away. Before he does, he'll fulfill his mother's wish that he brings home a suitor for his sister, a gentleman caller who, it turns out, is engaged to someone else and must leave soon after dinner. What memories Tom has of his sister glisten, like an open wound, with guilt.

Unlike Beckett, Williams was open enough about his life—in interviews, essays, and his published memoirs—to invite biographical interpretation of his plays. *The Glass Menagerie* has more than a few names and situations corresponding to Williams' own life. The mother putting on Southern airs in *Menagerie* echoes Williams' mother, Edwina. Williams was brought up in the northwest part of Mississippi known as the Delta, where small towns rise, like the islands of an archipelago, out of fields as flat and vast as an ocean. The towns are far from each other: each one had its town doctor, town beauty, town bully, town sissy. When Williams was seven, his father moved the family to St. Louis. As an adult, the South was a lost paradise to him; the summer to be remembered "in the winter of cities" as his first book of his poetry is titled.

But *Menagerie* is not a slice of life. To begin with, Williams' father, who was an executive at a factory, lived in the house, which was well furnished and large, not a tenement. Williams' sister, Rose, was popular as a young woman; later in life she became as shy as Laura. Williams never joined the merchant marines, as does Tom in the play. Williams was living in a Brooklyn hotel when his mother arranged for Rose to be lobotomized in 1943. The operation left Rose mentally impaired for the rest of her life. For the rest of his life, Williams blamed himself for not being around to argue against the operation—his personal guilt was as much an open wound as Tom's guilt in *The Glass Menagerie*.

Williams was gay—openly so to friends and colleagues, openly so in his fiction and poetry, not so in his early plays. In *The Glass Menagerie*, Tom's sexuality is deliberately enigmatic, not as an evasion—and certainly not out of Williams' guilt or shame—but, like Beckett, an ambiguity to engage an audience.

> TOM: You say there's so much in your heart that you can't de-scribe to me. That's true of me, too. There's so much in my heart that I can't describe to you! So let's respect each other's—
> AMANDA: But, why—why, Tom—are you always so restless? Where do you go to, nights?
> TOM: I—go to the movies.
> AMANDA: Why do you go to the movies so much, Tom?
> TOM: I go to the movies because—I like adventure. Adventure is something I don't have much of at work, so I go to the movies.
> AMANDA: But, Tom, you go to the movies entirely too much!
> TOM: I like a lot of adventure.
> [IMAGE ON SCREEN: SAILING VESSEL WITH JOLLY ROG-ER.]

Beckett thought it a sign of integrity that the theater was half empty at both performances of Strindberg's *Ghost Sonata* when he went to meet the director Roger Blin, the original director of *Godot*. Williams was eager for public acclaim and thrilled to be teamed up with the unapologetically ambitious director Elia Kazan to stage the original production of *Streetcar Named Desire*. Kazan and Williams, by outwitting and acquiescing to Hollywood censors (who especially objected to open displays of a woman's sexual desire), managed to transmute *Streetcar* from a 1947 Broadway hit to a 1951 Hollywood blockbuster, setting the pattern for plays written by Williams over the next ten years to be made into films watched by millions of people.

Even as Williams sought and won approval, he continued to experiment. In 1953, after the acclaim of *Streetcar, Menagerie,* and *The Rose Tattoo* (1950), he expanded a short play called *Ten Blocks on the Camino Real* (1948) into the full-length play *Camino Real*—pronounced American style: *KAmino Reel,* the real road, as opposed to the Spanish pronunciation: *CaMEEno Ray-AL,* which means the royal road. Kilroy, the 1940s American version of Everyman, has followed the Camino Real to where it dead-ends in the plaza of a fanciful Latin American town populated by crooks, petty and grand, from pickpockets to the police. Figures out of history, like Casanova, and characters out of fiction, like Marguerite Gautier, wait for each other by a waterless fountain. The town echoes with the sound of street cleaners who collect dead bodies and bring them to the morgue to be dissected. After Kilroy is collected while still alive, he interrupts his own dissection to run off with his heart in his hand and to woo the gypsy's daughter he's fallen in love with. She ignores Kilroy, and he is as dejected as Gogo and Didi before he finds new purpose by joining up with the dreams of Don Quixote as a new Sancho Panza, forever questing. *Camino Real* baffled those who expected tales of the Deep South from Williams, and the play closed its Broadway run relatively quickly. Williams returned to lyric realism and popular success in 1955 with *Cat on a Hot Tin Roof,* which won him a second Pulitzer and spawned another hit movie. Until late in 1962 he continued most of his experimental writing without offering it for production. After one last hit for Broadway and Hollywood, *The Night of the Iguana* (1961), he stepped away from realism by including Kabuki stagehands for a Broadway flop, *The Milk Train Doesn't Stop Here Anymore* (1964). Though he lived to write until 1983, he never had another popular success. His sojourn into respectability lasted less than twenty years.

Excess and an impulse for self-examination had always fueled Williams' power as a writer. Once he started writing openly about his sexuality and after his drinking and drug abuse became public knowledge, he offered himself as a target to critics, social and theatrical, who blamed his changed aesthetic on a disintegration of his faculties. Even his popularity was held against him. The notes from the Nobel Prize committee considering his nomination reveal a suspicion that Williams' popularity meant his work was trivial. Homophobia also played a part in Williams' diminished reputation. Beckett kept his private life private. His work, as spare and elegant as a beach-washed pebble, spoke for itself and resonated to the core of a world so scoured by Auschwitz and Hiroshima as to find ornament trivial. Williams was in and then out of fashion; Beckett had never been in fashion, but he became stylish among intellectuals (whether they understood what he was writing about or not) and won the Nobel Prize in 1969, though he did not attend the ceremony.

In favor or out, Beckett and Williams each maintained a consistency of vision through all their work, in novels, poetry, and plays. Each offers a vision as mythic as the personal mythologies of Strindberg or Mishima. Along with hats and birds, Beckett and Williams mythologized color. For Beckett, gray is the point in the spectrum where life and death meet, the color of dawn or sunset, and there is little that Beckett can't unpack from gray (or ash, as he calls it sometimes), nor is he afraid of mocking himself for his focus on colorless color. In *Endgame*, Clov has climbed a tall ladder to look out the windows and report to Hamm what's left in the desolation. The exchange is typically vaudevillian.

> HAMM: Is it night already then?
> CLOV (looking): No.
> HAMM: Then what is it?
> CLOV (looking): Gray.
> (Lowering the telescope, turning towards Hamm, louder.)
> Gray!
> (Pause. Still louder.)
> GRRAY!

(Pause. He gets down, approaches Hamm from behind, whispers in his ear.)
HAMM (starting): Gray! Did I hear you say gray?
CLOV: Light black. From pole to pole.
HAMM: You exaggerate.
(Pause.)

For Williams blue is the sign of the otherworld, associated with night and death and sex. A blue (not blues) piano in *Streetcar* plays just around the corner, though never seen. A blue guitar haunts the plaza of *Camino Real*, and there is the blue before Blanche exits *A Streetcar Named Desire* when she imagines she will be dropped overboard after she dies, into an ocean "as blue as my first lover's eyes."

In gray or blue both Beckett and Williams elevate the power of memory and dramatize the simultaneity of past, present, and future. Krapp listening to his younger self on tape has a counterpart in Williams' autobiographical character August from *Something Cloudy, Something Clear* (1981) in which a twenty-nine-year-old playwright working at the beach in 1940 intermittently turns into a seventy-year-old playwright speaking directly to the audience:

Life is all—it's just one time. It finally seems to all occur at one time.

Like Chekhov, the use of silence for Williams and Beckett is as much a part of their technique as the spoken word. Beckett sometimes offers blarney, but the impulse characters have in his plays to blather on is mocked, or broken, often with qualifications or self-corrections, spoken or behavioral. Williams came to believe that his own lyric ability was glib. As he grew older the lyricism of his youth no longer corresponded to his experience of the world. Williams' experiments with broken dialogue were often incorrectly attributed to dementia and drunkenness by critics. It could be fairly said that Williams was picking up the rhythms of Beckett. When *Godot* first played in America, the production premiered in Coconut Grove, Florida not far from where Williams was living in Key West. Williams invested in *Godot* and attended rehearsals. Bert Lahr (best known as the Cowardly Lion in the film of *The Wizard of Oz*) played Estragon. When Lahr was going to drop out, it was Williams who explained the play to Lahr and gave him the confidence to return, according to John Lahr, in the biography he wrote about his father, titled *Notes on a Cowardly Lion*.

After 1962, Williams set more and more of his plays outside of the Deep South: in Mexico, New York, Tokyo, the North Carolina asylum where Zelda (wife of Scott) Fitzgerald burned to death, and often in post-apocalyptic worlds as blasted as Beckett's.

> We're abandoned or we're put away, and if put away, why, then, fantasy runs to riot, hallucinations bring back times lost. Love you'd frightened away returns in dreams. A remission occurs. You fall out of a cloud to what's called real—a rock! Cold, Barren. To be endured only briefly.
> (Williams, *Clothes for a Summer Hotel*)

Williams and Beckett share a vision of beauty that flowers and is seen most clearly in sordid settings. Williams offered compassion to those he has the gypsy's daughter bless in *Camino Real*:

> All con men and hustlers and pitchmen who hawk their hearts on the street, all two-time losers who're likely to lose once more, the courtesan who made the mistake of love…

Beckett offered, if not compassion, at least commiseration to all who are born and must inevitably die.

> One day he went dumb, one day I went blind, one day we'll go deaf, one day we were born, one day we shall die, the same day,

the same second, is that not enough for you?
(*Waiting for Godot*)

Where they part company is flesh. Williams celebrates the body in the grand tradition of American romantics, Walt Whitman, for example:

I have said that the soul is not more than the body,
And I have said that the body is not more than the soul...
("Song of Myself," *Leaves of Grass*, 1892)

Physical beauty and sexual enjoyment are as real as pain to Serafina, the widow of Williams' *The Rose Tattoo*:

I remember my husband with a body like a young boy and hair on his head as thick and black as mine is and skin on him smooth and sweet as a yellow rose petal...I count up the nights I held him all night in my arms, and I can tell you how many. Each night for twelve years. Four thousand—three hundred—and eighty. The number of nights I held him all night in my arms. Sometimes I didn't sleep, just held him all night in my arms. And I am satisfied with it.

Beckett's writing views the body as a distraction or worse, at least onstage. The producer of *Breath*, who received the postcard with the text of the play, was Kenneth Tynan, the one British critic who had championed *Godot* in 1952 when it was first performed in London. In 1969, Tynan was soliciting plays for *Oh! Calcutta!,* an all-nude theatrical revue of erotica. Where Beckett had specified twenty-five seconds of:

RUBBISH No verticals, all scattered and lying

The director opted for trash, rather than rubbish, and added some scattered lying naked bodies. This did not strike Beckett as witty;

he objected and after a single preview the play was not performed again. There are no young girls onstage in any play by Beckett, except as memories—sneered at, usually. What we see onstage between husband and wife or between friends is, in a play by Beckett, sexless. Beckett describes winter and autumn with relish; spring was beyond his inclinations to detail or elaborate.

Williams' stage directions are explicit. In *Streetcar*, Blanche stands in her slip behind a sheet with a light behind her, as in a carnival girlie show. Maggie in *Cat on a Hot Tin Roof* is forever identified with the slip she wears for most of the first act. The burlesque business of putting on and taking off stockings is specified as behavior to accompany dialogue in several plays by Williams. The beautiful Brick comes out of the shower wet at the top of the first act in *Cat*, handsome Chance Wayne sits up in bed wearing silk pajama bottoms in *Sweet Bird of Youth* (1959), in *The Milk Train Doesn't Stop Here Anymore* two mature women spy appreciatively on a sleeping naked poet. In several late plays by Williams, men and women are naked or expose genitalia. Shoulders, waists, breasts, butts, and crotches are as much objects of contemplation—along with the pride, shame and power of sexuality—for Williams as are the ash heaps of Beckett's barren landscapes.

Both Williams and Becket created the poetry of the theater that Cocteau sought. Beckett insisted on keeping his stage pictures as he had composed them, deliberately enigmatic. He famously closed down a production of *Endgame* set in a Manhattan subway station: too specific, not what he intended. Williams' stage poetry is precise. Consider Blanche's final exit from *Streetcar*, where dialogue, stage directions, setting, lights, sound, and costumes work together like the parts of a machine.

Dark laughter erupts from both these visionary playwrights and their plays—as a survival mechanism, but also as a response to the world's despair. Williams was known for his cackle in the back of the theater as Blanche was led away to the madhouse. Beckett's characters laugh hard and often.

Nothing is funnier than unhappiness, I grant you that...Yes, yes, it's the most comical thing in the world.
(from *Endgame*)

In essential ways they are both followers of Chekhov. The paradox "I can't go on, I'll go on" might be spoken by any of Chekhov's three sisters, or Anya in *The Cherry Orchard*, or Sonja and Uncle Vanya, but it is, in fact, the last line of the narrator of Beckett's novel *The Unnamable* and could just as well be a confessional aside slipped into the dialogue of such Williams characters as Blanche, Tom, Amanda, or Kilroy. Williams and Beckett also share with Chekhov the knowledge that if we cannot assuage each other's pain, at least by listening, we can offer comfort. "What am I to do?" asks the doctor (and Chekhov was himself a doctor) at the end of the second act of *The Seagull* to a sobbing young woman, very possibly his illegitimate daughter. "What am I to do?" The act ends with him sitting silently alongside her.

When so many are lonely as seem to be lonely, it would be inexcusably selfish to be lonely alone."
(from *Camino Real*)

In theory you can hear me even though in fact you don't is all I need, just to feel you there within earshot and conceivably on the qui vive is all I ask...
(from *Happy Days*)

Both sum up the twentieth century's progression: mechanization, which seemed to promise so much happiness, turned out to be the means to accelerate murder and destruction, leaving in its wake bitter laughter overheard in a wasteland. Yet even if the best joke dries up, the itch to hear another fuels going to the theater and going to the theater remains necessary. Both men wrote for the stage, never just to be read. Their writing cannot be mistaken for other playwrights and certainly not for each other's. Yet Beckett and Williams are talking about the same thing.

> We're lonely. We're frightened. We hear the Streetcleaners' piping not far away. So now and then, although we've wounded each other time and again—we stretch out hands to each other in the dark that we can't escape from—we huddle together for some dim communal comfort—and that's what passes for love on this terminal stretch of the road that used to be royal. What is it, this feeling between us?
>
> (from *Camino Real*)

Chapter Twenty-Three

THEATER OF IDENTITY

Amiri Baraka (1934–2014)
Eve Ensler (b. 1953)
Larry Kramer (1935–2020)
August Wilson (1945–2005)

A ll theater, in some sense, affirms identity. The men of Athens, who roared outdoors in an amphitheater at the jokes written by Aristophanes about an ongoing war or the newest philosophy were trumpeting with their laughter that they were cultivated citizens of a democracy. In seventeenth century France or nineteenth century Russia, weeping or laughing while savoring the beauty of the French language in plays by Racine and Molière displayed an appreciation for the mastery of aristocratic traditions. English-speaking audiences have been flattered by Shakespeare's declarations of what it means to be English for five hundred years. Eighteenth-century English comedies, some of the best written by Irishmen, upheld courtesy rather than the court. Harold Pinter's savage twentieth century sitting-room plays confided to those who read or watched them that middle-class politesse masked feral survival tactics.

In Communist Russia, theater was a tool among the other arts used as tools—music, dance, literature, and cinema—to shape a common identity for disparate ethnic groups enrolled as comrades in the Soviet Union. As early as the 1930s, culture tsars in Moscow paid for plays to tour Central Asia and the Caucasus: plays in which women spoke up in public; plays, too, in which

young people talked back to their elders, deliberately overturn-
ing traditional roles by offering public examples to be applauded.
In Communist China, when Chairman Mao's wife, who had been
a B-movie actress, reformed the theater as part of the Cultural
Revolution, theatrical troupes who performed Chinese classics
were ordered to stand the traditional hierarchy of roles on its
head: Buddhist priests turned paragons into villains; landlords
were called out as enemies of the people. In the Chinese paradise
of the proletariat, factory workers and farmers were the heroes,
not feudal princes.

Whoever pays for theater expects in some way to determine
what happens on the stage. When the governments of Soviet Russia, Maoist China, Imperial France, or Elizabethan England paid
for theater, their goals were political and intended for the good of
audiences according to whatever passed at the time for social improvement. The same can be said for the American government
in the 1930s during the Great Depression. Congress justified
spending public money for the Federal Theatre Project (FTP),
part of the Works Progress Administration (WPA), because the
FTP provided jobs for unemployed theater professionals. As a
form of public education, a further good, plays were commissioned and produced by the FTP. America's Living Newspapers,
copying the template of dramatized journalism from the agitprop
plays of Russia and Germany, warned Americans about venereal
disease, called attention to housing shortages, and demonstrated
the usefulness of unions.

Hallie Flanagan, the director of the FTP, believed a democracy was meant to be inclusive, and communities excluded from
the professional stage by economic circumstances or social barriers deserved a share of the Federal largesse. Geographical dis-
tribution was also important for a national program. There was
a merit in authenticity if communities could write about themselves and be given opportunities to dramatize their own history
and experience. WPA units in Seattle and Kansas City, as well as
rural areas far from cities, received funds to originate new plays

and productions. Within cities, immigrant communities were helped to create plays in languages other than English: the WPA supported a Yiddish language theater, already flourishing, as well as German, Italian, and Spanish language theaters.

Black people of mixed descent were helped to create an African-American theater of original plays and adaptations. In 1936 the FTP's Negro Theater Unit—whose leadership was white—produced a "Voodoo" *Macbeth* set in Haiti, directed by Orson Welles. The production premiered in Harlem, moved to Broadway, and then toured American high schools. In 1937 the FTP's Negro Repertory Company in Seattle staged Theodore Browne's "African" version of Aristophanes' *Lysistrata* set in "Ebonia." The enforced submission of women in ancient Greece had unsubtle parallels with the enforced submission of black people in America. A "Committee Man" in the play says:

> A woman must be kept in her place! As I have always said, if you see a woman rising, pull her down. If you see a woman drowning, throw her an anchor. And if she comes to you for information, act dumb. Show them no mercy.

Lysistrata sold out its 1,100 seat house on opening night. The next afternoon, despite good reviews, the local chapter of the WPA closed the production. Too explicit.

Liberty Deferred (1938), written for the FTP by two black men, Abram Hill and John Silvera, dramatized the story of African Americans from slave ships to lynching. It was not produced. Of the three Living Newspapers the WPA proposed to produce in which the lives of African Americans were the subject of the news, none made it to a production on a stage. An outspoken black theater threatened American social order, especially in those states where people of color were denied a public voice and the right to vote. Senators from Mississippi and Texas led the fight to close the FTP down. They succeeded. Government funds in America were not to be spent advocating for political change.

With or without Federal support, the possibility of such subject matter in a theater inspired minority communities to continue to reconfigure their own identities onstage. Without Federal support the Yiddish theater played on, as did the African-American theater; each within its own ghetto where original plays were performed without the larger community or mainstream newspapers taking notice, the way immigrant communities stage plays today in Spanish and many other languages without much public notice in and around Los Angeles, New Orleans, and New York.

After the uplifting policies of the FTP were ended, censorship and the conventions of American movies and theater systematically demeaned certain identities. In mainstream American theater, films, and radio shows, people of color were performed (sometimes by white people) as dehumanizing caricatures such as the happy-go-lucky fool, the folksy old wise man, the noble sufferer, and the sacrificing mammy of melodrama and minstrel shows. Homosexuals of any kind were flamboyant freaks or self-loathing villains destined to meet unhappy ends. Women's roles were just as shaped as the roles of homosexuals by censors and convention. A woman's sexual desire, in particular, was mocked and punished in plotlines with disastrous conclusions, as was, often as not, a woman's desire for political power. Writers working within the commercial theater or Hollywood might pass off camouflaged acts of sabotage, but nothing overt was possible. It would not be financed, and if financed, it could not pass a censor.

Commercial theater, comedies especially, cheered on the social order. The social critic and sometime playwright Gore Vidal (1925–2012) pointed out that "Love, Love, Love" (the title of his 1959 essay on the subject), had settled on Broadway like a low-lying fog. Love, as Vidal defined it, "a warm druggedness, a surrender of the will to inchoate feelings of Togetherness," was the American theater's traditional way to avoid an argument, or serious consideration, of politics or social issues. To disagree and not fall in love onstage was to be, well, disagreeable and antisocial.

There had always been a dissident tradition in the American theater, of course. Arthur Miller continued to write criticisms of capitalism long after the WPA was closed down. In Miller's 1949 *Death of a Salesman*, now regarded as a classic of American theater, the audience is taught to mourn as the capitalist system spits out a sorry old worker like the pit of a swallowed fruit. One of Miller's most memorable lines is spoken by the salesman's wife Linda, who declares, "Attention must be paid." The audience, however, is not told how to pay attention, and more often than not, as Gore Vidal pointed out in his essay, attention is earned in Miller's plays based on sentimental appeals.

In the middle to late 1960s, a social revolution disrupted traditional American roles and rules offstage for people of color, women, and gay people demanding respect and power within America. Theater was again a revolutionary tool, and as Hallie Flanagan had hoped, dangerously so. The press, which had systematically suppressed or trivialized women, people of color, and homosexuals, began to advocate for their promotion, notice, and self-determination. American playwrights who wrote for black and women's theaters and openly gay theater had unprecedented opportunities to reach wider audiences and public awareness.

As audiences and critics refined their responses to such work, authenticity and self-definition were valued as they had been in the 1930s. Some playwrights were careful to remove themselves from their ghettos. Arthur Miller, at the height of his commercial success, strategically shied away from his identity as a Jew. Miller's early attempt to submit a script to a Federal Theater committee met with the condescending critique that his play was not that good, but suitable for Jewish immigrant audiences.

Even so, other playwrights have found it a source of power by calling attention to their differences from the mainstream. Consider, as examples of those who advocated for identity by writing plays: Eve Ensler, Larry Kramer, and August Wilson.

Eve Ensler's *The Vagina Monologues* (1996) is a play in which readers sitting on stools read index cards with text culled from interviews of women and girls describing their vaginas. To even say the word vagina in public was taboo in 1996. To put the ad in the newspaper, or have the title openly mentioned in a review, advanced a cause—that women should not be ashamed to speak of their bodies. The craft necessary to perform the play is minimal (no lights, no scenery, stools for the actors who read off cards rather than memorize lines) and so productions can be inexpensively produced, include celebrities who will generate headlines, and offer roles to performers who do not have the skills to memorize or move much on a stage. The aim is inclusion. Ensler's play has been performed in thousands of places and spawned V-Day, an international movement seeking to end violence toward women and girls. Ensler's monologues are now part of V-Day celebrations held on Valentine's Day around the world. The V in V-Day stands for vagina and also for Valentine, that is to say, love. After 2019, Ensler changed her name to V.

Larry Kramer's furious play *The Normal Heart* (1985) begins its action in 1981 as public knowledge of AIDS all too slowly unfolded. In 1981 the disease was still mysterious, untreatable, and relatively ignored by the mainstream press. Kramer demanded attention must be paid and dramatized how to pay attention by pitting those who worked within the system to accomplish gradual change against a man—an overt stand-in for the playwright—who rages against such restraint. In *The Normal Heart*, the one who accommodates dies of the disease, the one who rages lives on. In 1987 Kramer helped found Act Up, the civil disobedience group whose motto is *Silence=Death*, which might be said to be the moral of *The Normal Heart*.

The Normal Heart is latter-day agitprop, calling on audiences and readers to share righteous anger, break silence, and act up. If and when performances sting people to tears, those tears are meant to fuel political action, not pity. Gay identity in *The Normal Heart* is unapologetic, unlike previous flamboyance or hyper-masculinity in gay roles in American plays. As aggressive in demanding respect as *The Vagina Monologues*, *The Normal Heart* was written to appeal to and influence mainstream audiences. Neither Ensler nor Kramer needed similar success in subsequent writing for the stage. They'd had enough. Theater was a means for Kramer and Ensler, among other means—V-Day or Act-Up, *The Vagina Monologues* or *The Normal Heart*—to assert identity as part of a political process.

August Wilson was born in 1945 and named himself when he turned twenty. His father was a white German immigrant. His mother, Daisy Wilson, was African American and raised their six children by herself in a two-room cold-water apartment above a store in the Hill District of Pittsburgh, Pennsylvania. The boy who would name himself August and take his mother's family name, not his father's, was her fourth child. He dropped out of school at fifteen, accused of plagiarism because his teacher couldn't believe a black boy could write so well. He could. After educating himself at the public library and a stint in the army, he began his life's calling by taking down longhand notes in bars, often on napkins. He wrote plays that put the voices of African Americans—cabdrivers, jazz singers, ex-cons, and voodoo priestesses—into the repertory of the American theater.

In other countries and times, theater of identity had to do with language: Irishmen writing English comedies to be performed in London and what's written in French in Montreal, the capital of the Canadian province of Quebec. Identity has often been established in plays by dialect. Wilson's strategy was to use dialect selectively, unlike earlier African-American playwrights such as Zora Neale Hurston. He crafted singing texts infused with the beat of the blues, a beat he called his bedrock in a 2004 interview with Miles Marshall Lewis for *Believer* magazine.

Between 1983 and a few months before his death in 2005, Wilson wrote ten plays, nine of them set in Pittsburgh's Hill District. Each play takes place in a different decade of the 1900s. This epic play cycle of the twentieth century follows an African-American community, variously called colored, Negro, black, Black, and slurs that have become, for some people, unhealed

scars to be displayed proudly. Under many names, the protagonist over the century is the community made up of the characters
and families that repeat from play to play, a community in flux
in every decade of a century. Eugene O'Neill had a similar ambition: to depict an Irish-American family through the course
of eleven plays covering two centuries but, dissatisfied with the
results, O'Neill ordered the manuscripts burned before he died.

Wilson's completed cycle draws a dynamic from the same
insight that inspired, not O'Neill, but Arthur Miller: the doom—
or short-lived triumphs—of individuals in an oppressive society. For the people of color in August Wilson's plays to live, sing,
work—to endure in whatever ways they can—is itself heroic because the system, as Wilson understands it, is against them. That
they breathe is a confrontation with oppression and whatever
else they might do to survive is, for better or worse, valiant.

In *Ma Rainey's Black Bottom*, set in the late 1920s and written
in 1982, a blues diva insists during a Chicago recording session
on what seem to be capricious and petty demands, but because
she's not easy, the producers must recognize her as a person not
a performing animal.

> They don't care nothing about me. All they want is my voice.
> Well, I done learned that, and they gonna treat me like I want to
> be treated no matter how much it hurts them.
> (from *Ma Rainey's Black Bottom*)

In Wilson's play *Fences*, set in the 1957 and written in 1983,
the hero stands with a baseball bat in an empty backyard as if,
the stage directions say, "Death had pitched him a fastball in the
outside corner." Earlier he has declared:

> Alright…Mr. Death. See now…I'm gonna tell you what I'm gonna
> do. I'm gonna take and build me a fence around this yard. See?…
> You stay over there until you're ready for me. Then you come on.
> Bring your army. Bring your sickle. Bring your wrestling clothes.

I ain't gonna fall down on my vigilance this time.
(from *Fences*)

Along with first person announcements, theater of identity makes use of open diatribes and proclamations. Its messages need to be passed on as clearly as public service announcements and safety posters. For Wilson, memorable theater includes slogans, as much as dramatic situations. The man swinging a bat at death in *Fences* must declare in the first person who he is and what he is doing, just as Ma Rainey does. Almost every Wilson character declaims. There is a particular music to assertion, unlike sly inference or suggestion. In Arthur Miller's *Death of a Salesman*, the salesman's wife pleads, in a fruitless conversation with her sons, that attention must be paid. In theater of identity people come to the lip of the stage and announce *what* to pay attention to:

I hated my thighs, and I hated my vagina even more. I thought it was incredibly ugly. I was one of those women who had looked at it and, from that moment on, wished I hadn't. It made me sick. I pitied anyone who had to go down there. In order to survive, I began to pretend there was something else between my legs. I imagined furniture—cozy futons with light cotton comforters. (from *The Vagina Monologues*)

If you are a person of color or a woman or gay, as poet-playwright Amiri Baraka pointed out in a 2007 speech about Tennessee Williams, to be who you are requires action in a world that oppresses those identities. To take such action is a choice; the consequence of the choice is more likely punishment than reward. Such a situation is inherently theatrical. The dramatic setup is the pattern of the individual against the whole, which to the Greeks was Fate. In theater of identity, plays often follow the design of separate lives (the characters in *The Normal Heart* and *Fences*) within the dramatization of a struggle (the AIDS crisis and the Civil Rights movement) whose history is understood and therefore has a design. Often as not the power that crushes identity (or fails to) is unearned within the action of the play itself. For contemporary plays, we, the society being dramatized, are aware of the struggle and provide what's missing:

> NED. Hello. Hold on. (locating some pages and reading from them into the phone) "It is no secret that I consider the Mayor to be, along with the Times, the biggest enemy gay men and women must contend with in New York. Until the day I die I will never forgive this newspaper and this Mayor for ignoring this epidemic that is killing so many of my friends."
> (from *The Normal Heart*)

An audience often applauds here, cheering as truth speaks to power but little happens onstage to dramatize the newspaper's power or the mayor's heartlessness. We hear about such power, or already know of it. Kramer doesn't need or care to dramatize a meeting of the *New York Times* owners or the mayor's inner circle. Wilson never needs to explain the enormity of slavery on the stage or dramatize it. Listening and watching in the audience we know enough that the dramatic importance can be evoked by dance and song or speech or left to the resonance of history and our own experience. Wilson can drop names like Mellon as an emblematic rich man in Pittsburgh, Kramer can rail at his hometown newspaper and politicians, Ensler can mock futons as middle-class furniture, and inasmuch as audiences laugh, cry, cheer, or shout with shared understanding of these synecdoche (in which a part stands in for a greater whole), performances of the texts become rituals of affirmation.

In the theater of identity, although subject matter grows more diverse, more often than not the forms used to depict new subject matter are traditional because the assumed task is to change ideas of identity offstage, and a conventional form is the entrance point of understanding for an audience who thinks in conventions. Wilson's ten-play cycle, Kramer's *The Normal Heart*, and Ensler's *Vagina Monologues* have won international acclaim and consistent commercial success by repurposing theatrical traditions: realistic (as with Wilson) or agitprop (as with Ensler and Kramer), just as Madame Mao co-opted the Peking opera rather than create a new Chinese dramatic form to pass on revolutionary ideas.

If a conventional form is used though, adherence to its rules of craft need not be strict. Rough craft is just as good as facile finesse for these purposes, perhaps better, for virtuosity might distract from the message. Wilson's plays end abruptly—with a murder, with a song or a dance—leaving the issue in the audience's lap, like Odets's *Waiting for Lefty*. The lack of moral ambiguity in Kramer's *Normal Heart* is what sways its audiences, as the lack of moral ambiguity did the same for audiences who wept and cheered for *Uncle Tom's Cabin* in the nineteenth century. What seems to be a lack of literary intent in Ensler's *Vagina Monologues* is the crafted illusion of unedited reportage.

As in almost all theater, communion with the audience defines success. This is true for an audience laughing at Ensler's monologues, crying at Kramer's death toll, thrilling to Wilson's speeches, or rising to any playwright's call to action. Yet by defining themselves as tools of politics, the plays that construct identity risk being discarded or replaced as newer versions of identity inevitably develop. Such plays especially risk being discarded by the groups for whom they advocate. Ensler, for example, has been criticized by feminists with differing politics and divergent constructions of what a vagina means. Paradoxically, those in the avant-garde who advocate a theater of identity depend upon public acceptance in the here and now. Though of course there have been avant-garde theater movements unconcerned with identity or public acceptance or moral instruction. Such unconcern is risky. In Russia, those who practice avant-garde theater unconcerned with acceptance have been, for over a hundred years, murdered, imprisoned, and erased from—and sometimes returned to—official history.

Theater that serves as an example of how to lead one's life—as an individual or as a group—has a long history. The mainstream theatrical tradition dates back in the English-speaking theater to *Everyman* and other morality plays. Sometimes the artifice of a positive identity is a way for an older generation to maintain the illusion they'll have social control over a new generation's identity. In Soviet Russia, for example, Chekhov's ironic predictions about the future were portrayed as prophesy, the better to enfold the audience in a vision of progressive Marxist history. The potent ambiguity of Chekhov's scripts, however, has outlasted the certainties of Socialist Realism.

With the notable exception of Amiri Baraka's *Dutchman* (1964), set in a subway that turns out to be a route to Hell, not Harlem, the heat of a lot of political theater has cooled, as the stodginess of kitchen-sink realism has dampened the fire of what once seemed daring by virtue of its subject matter. Baraka is as concerned with identity as any playwright. In *Dutchman*, pale-white, red-haired Lula goads bookish, dark-skinned Clay until he cracks:

> If I'm a middle-class fake white man...Let me be who I feel like being. Uncle Tom. Thomas. Whoever. It's none of your business. You don't know anything except what's there for you to see. An act. Lies. Device. Not the pure heart, the pumping black heart. You don't ever know that. And I sit here in this buttoned-up suit to keep myself from cutting all your throats.
> (from *Dutchman*)

Having lured Clay to flaunt what he has called his "black heart," Lula stabs Clay fast twice, killing him. The other white people on the subway car quickly dispose of the body. This ritual of entrapment and ensuing knowledge of death is enacted every time the play is performed. The power of acceptance by white society to lure and erase black identity is an aspect of the ritual. Lula is eating an apple and offers it to Clay whom she recognizes at once as coming from New Jersey, the Garden State. Audiences may recognize or not this is the ancient story of Lilith tempting Adam. Or the audience may respond to nothing more than what's said and done in performance and the play will achieve a meaning.

What often dates other topical political plays is an inability to be reinterpreted, yet that does not discredit other values those plays carry. Newspapers are as important as novels; current events are no less important or inherently dramatic than history. If attention must be paid, the same questions apply: to what and why? Looked at historically, for how long? And why? A call for "positive role models" onstage from well-meaning priests, government censors, or advocacy groups, robs roles of their humanity, just as surely as any demeaning caricature does.

Raymond Chandler, the American crime writer, had this to say, in an essay titled "The Simple Art of Murder":

> There are no vital and significant forms of art; there is only art, and precious little of that. The growth of populations has in no way increased the adeptness with which substitutes can be produced and packaged.

A valid defense of political evaluation of plays is that values such as *vital* and *significant* are themselves political constructions. With this in mind, theater of identity proponents have rethought theater history. From a political point of view, artistic skill and craft are not inevitably applauded. Persuasive craft in the service of dubious politics is perverse, like effective advertising for poison. A search for authenticity has sometimes been advanced to mean that *only* women should write about women, or people of color about people of color. Ideas of inclusion have led to populist critics hurling charges of *elitism* as insults, but in doing so they are just as intolerant as aristocratic critics who used the word *common* to ignore or dismiss popular theater. Closed communities, whether aristocratic or populist, inevitably establish and evolve values independent of the outside world's values, but willful ignorance is not any nobler than ignorance due to lack of opportunity or exclusion. Ignorance of the outside world might sometimes be a virtue within a closed community.

There's nothing wrong with being ignorant. There's nothing right about it, either. Plays that educate, or set positive role models, or pass on moral lessons, or represent communities are not excused from aesthetic judgment any more than they are excused from being boring. To do so is to condescend to a community, not educate or represent it. Applying criteria to an artwork that diminishes artistry is like assessing a metal statue by estimating how many bullets could be manufactured if the statue was melted down. This has been done, literally and metaphorically, but it doesn't make it any less sad.

Theater of identity can ignite an audience. In 1900 Stanislavsky was playing Dr. Stockmann in Ibsen's *An Enemy of the People* on tour with the Moscow Art Theatre in St. Petersburg. A revolution, which would fail, was going on in the streets. Inside the theater, at a crucial point late in the play, when Stockmann readies himself to confront those who have thrown rocks at him, the audience cheered and shouted and ran forward to the lip of the stage to shake Dr. Stockmann's hand and embrace him. Such close identification of the audience with the character—as if he was one of them and spoke for them—returns the theater to its preliterate prime when shamans, priests and (in ancient Greece) politicians spoke for (and flew in imaginary dreams for) those who watched and listened. Such things still happen.

Chapter Twenty-Four

MISSING FROM HISTORY

Marita Bonner (1899–1971)
María Irene Fornés (1930–2018)
Adrienne Kennedy (b. 1931)
Maurice Polydore Marie Bernard Maeterlinck (1862–1949)

Any theater history is a snapshot taken while memory and gossip shuffle texts with whatever remains from live performances: drawings, sculptures, paintings, and in the modern era, still or moving photography. What is remembered changes, how it is remembered changes, as ideas about theater, gossip, and art change. The meaning and significance of the snapshot changes for the same reasons: ideas about theater and art change.

Georg Büchner died in 1837 at the age of twenty-four. His plays *Danton's Death* (published after stringent censoring in 1835) and *Woyzeck* (left unfinished in manuscript) are now esteemed for their intermittent realism, lower-class characters, and episodic structure. A high assessment of what Büchner wrote took time to rise.

In 1879 more than forty years after the playwright's death, Karl Emil Franzos arranged to have three plays by Büchner published (the third is a satirical romance, *Leonce and Lena*), after editing what was left of the manuscripts and completing *Woyzeck* himself. The Büchner's handwriting had faded so badly the ink, to be legible, was lifted from the paper with chemicals. It took a few more decades for the published plays to be produced.

Danton's Death premiered in 1902 in Berlin. *Woyzeck* premiered in 1913, when it was staged by the prestigious director Max Reinhardt in Munich.

Since then, *Danton's Death* and *Woyzeck* have become some of the most influential plays in history and among the most frequently performed. Büchner's reputation was assembled by scholars, critics, and theater artists and reinforced by the power of a live performances around the world over time.

Other playwrights have had their reputations disassembled over time. Beginning in the sixth century BC, there were tragedy contests every spring in the Greek city-state of Athens. For more than a hundred and fifty years—until the end of the fourth century—hundreds of writers competed, writing thousands of plays. Out of those thousands of plays, thirty-six full texts survive: seven written by Aeschylus (who won thirteen first prizes in Athens), eleven plays by Sophocles (who won first place twenty times), and eighteen plays by Euripides, who won only four first prizes in his lifetime, but so dominated the repertory after he died (he won a fifth prize posthumously), the judges stopped giving prizes to playwrights.

Despite any prestige they once held, tragedies by other classic Greek authors before, during, and after the classic period, aside from Aeschylus, Sophocles, and Euripides, are not a part of anyone's history, they are hearsay. The rest of those Greek competitors—from over a hundred years of contests—are now only names. From a very few of those names we know some very few lines, quoted by other people. Fragments written by Philocles, who was Aeschylus's nephew, can be read but not the tragedy that won Philocles first prize in the competition against Sophocles' *Oedipus Rex*. No texts survive from the one hundred-fifty tragedies written by Choerilus, though thirteen of them won first prize, according to the Suda, a tenth-century Byzantine encyclopedia. Astydamas, who in 372 BC won the last ivy wreath for tragedy, leaves behind only the gossip that he wanted his name immodestly carved onto the base of a statue.

There are no plays by Agathon to read, so famous in his day, that Aristophanes (from whom we have eleven ancient Greek comedies) could reliably make an audience laugh in 411 BC by depicting Agathon onstage wearing women's clothing while writing women's dialogue in a play called *The Thesmophoriazusae*. Someday, texts may be found written by Agathon or Philocles. Maybe.

Sometimes plays drop out of history—forgotten, abandoned, or erased deliberately. There is a play by Shakespeare we know by title alone, *Love's Labours Won*, mentioned in a list of plays by Shakespeare as early as 1598. Will that ever be found and become history? Maybe. Luck, rot, and mice contend.

Tastes change. Ideas of excellence change. After Maurice Polydore Marie Bernard Maeterlinck—let's call him Maeterlinck—won the Nobel Prize in 1911, it would have seemed a safe bet that the plays he wrote would survive at least a hundred years in the international theater repertory. Not so, though the Nobel Prize committee gave their award according to the citation "in appreciation of his many-sided literary activities, and especially of his dramatic works, which are distinguished by a wealth of imagination and by a poetic fancy, which reveals, sometimes in the guise of a fairy tale, a deep inspiration…"

Little more than a hundred years later, his work is mostly known as a source of a libretto for the opera *Pelléas and Mélisande* (written by Debussy in 1902) and because Chekhov made fun of Maeterlinck with the play within the play of *The Seagull*, written in 1895.

> All men and beasts, lions, eagles, and quails, horned stags, geese, spiders, silent fish that inhabit the waves, starfish from the sea, and creatures invisible to the eye—in one word, life—all, all life, completing the dreary round imposed upon it, has died out at last.
>
> (*The Seagull*, Act 1, Constance Garnett, trans.)

Maeterlinck's 1892 play *Pelléas and Mélisande*, set in an imaginary medieval kingdom, begins when a little maiden, Mélisande, is found weeping in the woods, a thin crown of gold lying nearby her. Asking her what happened prompts more weeping. Over the course of five acts, she's married to the prince who found her, she charms his father, fools around with his half-brother Pelléas, gets caught and—you've guessed it—dies unhappy, but not before giving birth to an undersized baby girl.

Act 4, scene 2 begins with this speech to Mélisande, translated by Richard Hovey in 1896 to simulate the archaic French with which Maeterlinck hoped to evoke the Middle Ages:

> Now that Pélléas's father is saved, and sickness, the old handmaid of Death, has left the castle, a little joy and a little sunlight will at last come into the house again...It was time!—For, since thy coming, we have only lived here whispering about a closed room... And truly I have pitied thee, Mélisande...Thou camest here all joyous, like a child seeking a gala-day, and at the moment thou enteredst in the vestibule I saw thy face change, and probably thy soul, as the face changes in spite of us when we enter at noon into a grotto too gloomy and too cold...

This is awful in translation. People who advocate for Maeterlinck claim this is better in French. It could hardly be worse. Might it return to the stage? For a while Maeterlinck's plays were performed, and not just in French or in France. Maeterlinck's *The Blue Bird* played Russian stages for almost a century. The plot? Two children search for the bluebird of happiness. Along the way they meet Sicknesses, Luxuries, Happinesses, Joys, Fire, Water, Sugar, and Bread—and a lot of other characters personified by their names and some stage business. Sugar, for instance, offers his fingers to the children to eat. Stanislavsky directed the premiere in 1908 at the Moscow Art Theatre. The costumes were spectacular. Here's a sample of the dialogue, translated in 1910 by Alexander Teixeira de Mattos, who was Dutch:

The Cat: Do you remember the time when, before the coming of the despot, we wandered at liberty upon the face of the earth?…Fire and Water were the sole masters of the world; and see what they have come to!…As for us puny descendants of the great wild animals…Look out!…Pretend to be doing nothing!…I see the Fairy and Light coming…Light has taken sides with Man; she is our worst enemy…

It's fascinating to consider that this was written more than ten years after Chekhov made fun of *Pelléas and Mélisande* in *The Seagull*. That fascination doesn't make the writing any less turgid. Two weeks after *The Blue Bird* opened at the Moscow Art Theatre, there was a parody of it at the Bat Cabaret on Ostozhenka Street where members of the Moscow Art Theatre performed for each other after hours.

There is a Spanish theory of literature that claims second-rate art works are more indicative of a culture than first-rate because first-rate art transcends its culture. If there ever is a Maeterlinck revival, perhaps it will be because a director or an ensemble finds a way to explore the texts as cultural artifacts, or as has been done, finds Maeterlinck's writing as an excuse for virtuosic direction and exuberant production values unencumbered by a text with dramatic action. Even so, the language will always be as static as Chekhov's parody. Maeterlinck believed in static drama. He thought performing Shakespeare's plays, or any plays, diminished their power. He didn't like live actors. He preferred marionettes. He aligned himself with the Symbolist movement of poets and painters, recoiling from the realism of Zola and Ibsen. The Symbolists rejected Freud's spoilsport theories of sexuality. "Art always uses a detour and does not act directly. Its mission is the supreme revelation of the infinite and the greatness and the secret beauty of Man," Maeterlinck wrote in an introduction to his plays.

The French director Lugné-Poe, who had championed Ibsen and Strindberg and hoped he had found something similar in Maeterlinck's work, veiled the proscenium opening in gauze for the premiere of *Pelléas and Mélisande*, the better to maintain the dreamy otherworld the play was thought to require. Dreamy otherworlds dispersed fast onstage and in poetry after the First World War erupted in 1914. As William Butler Yeats, the Irish poet who began as a Symbolist, wrote in a short poem titled "Three Movements," published in 1932:

> Shakespearean fish swam the sea, far away from land;
> Romantic fish swam in nets coming to the hand;
> What are all those fish that lie gasping on the strand?

Fancy fairy tales no longer provided much pleasure in the twentieth century world of killing machines and poison gas.

Maeterlinck's reputation was punctured by a scandal. Among his many interests, he was fascinated by insects, about which he wrote three different books. In 1926 it was discovered he had plagiarized large sections of a book about termites (!) he claimed to have written himself. Maeterlinck, who could read Dutch, seems to have translated a South African termite book from the original Afrikaans into French. Perhaps he thought no one would notice. Many aspects of Maeterlinck's life are theatrical, often more interesting than the scenes in his plays. According to Bettina Liebowitz Knapp's 1975 biography of Maeterlinck, he used to dress up in the full skirts and headdress of an abbess and roller skate in the abbey he rented in southwestern France. He sometimes wrote in a dark blue room in which white paper butterflies with notes written on them were pinned to the walls.

In 1890, reviewing Maeterlinck's *La Princesse Maleine* for the reputation-making newspaper, *Le Figaro*, the French critic Octave Mirbeau, wrote:

> Maeterlinck has given us the most brilliant work of our time,... superior in beauty to what is most beautiful in Shakespeare.

A vision of Maeterlinck's beauties has faded (for the time being). What seemed in 1890 as an advance of the avant garde curled into a cul-de-sac. Glowing assessments of Symbolism, like the brilliance of the late nineteenth century international design movement called Art Nouveau, grew dimmer and dissipated during the First World War.

Symbolism is hardly the only or last movement in the theater to exhaust itself within thirty years, say the 1890s to the 1920s. Naturalism in the theater barely lasted longer, the 1880s to say, 1919. Socialist Realism made it without irony from the 1930s to the 1980s. Now it endures in China as kitsch. Expressionism in the theater had its thirty years from 1900 to the 1930s before it shut up shop. In America and Germany, Expressionism inspired some playwrights, including Eugene O'Neill and Brecht, who moved on to other ideas about theater for various reasons. One good reason: the lack of audiences or appreciative critics for Expressionist plays.

Consider Marita Bonner, a black woman from the Boston area, Radcliffe class of 1922, whose Expressionist play *The Purple Flower*, published in *Crisis* magazine in 1927, opens with this stage direction.

> Scene: An open plain. It is bounded distantly on one side by Nowhere and faced by a high hill—Somewhere...The White Devils live on the side of the hill. Somewhere. On top of the hill grows the purple Flower-of-Life-at-Its-Fullest. This flower is as tall as a pine and stands alone on top of the hill. The Us's live in the valley that lies between Nowhere and Somewhere and spend their time trying to devise means of getting up the hill. The White Devils live all over the sides of the hill and try every trick, known and unknown, to keep the Us's from getting to the hill.

People Maria Bonner respected strongly recommended her to write realistic plays advancing the cause of equality, plays that were easier for more people to understand. Bonner switched from writing plays in which the White Devils sang,

You stay where you are!
We don't want you up here!
If you come you'll be on par
With all we hold dear.
So stay—stay—stay! Yes stay where you are!

to writing a series of sharply observed and detailed realistic short stories set in a mixed-race Chicago neighborhood. In 1941 she stopped writing entirely and chose to raise a family. She taught English for many years in the Chicago public school system. Her plays appear in anthologies, but there have been no professional productions so far; interest in producing plays written by women of color focuses, for now, on who is writing now, and the social concerns of now. Unlike Maeterlinck's plays, though, Marita Bonner's work is not dated, nor will it ever be dated. It is, like the plays by Euripides, forever modern in the sense of new, fresh, and despite Bonner's origins in Expressionism, unclassifiable. If her writing doesn't match the interests of our times, it might someday. Her adult life doesn't make for memorable gossip; the wildness of her early writing is contagious.

Texts make it possible for Marita Bonner to be "rediscovered." Texts make it possible for Maeterlinck to be reexamined. The innovative actors or directors who did not match the aesthetics of their time had no such opportunities before the invention of video and film. Consider the dismissive contemporary reviews of films directed by Federico Fellini or Orson Welles, films that have become standards of excellence in the history of cinema. Happily, like misunderstood films, the texts of plays unappreciated in their time can be preserved and passed on with the hope that later generations will understand, as happened with *Danton's Death*.

The circle of attention in American theater history has recently widened to include reassessment of the plays written by María Irene Fornés and Adrienne Kennedy, decades after their avant-garde work premiered Off-Broadway. Unlike Thornton

Wilder's *Our Town*, the plays proposed for performance by the Cuban-American Fornés and the African-American Kennedy dramatize the plurality, rather than the unity, of American identity and experience. The text of *Fefu and Her Friends*, written by Fornés in 1977, specifies the audience be split into four groups who watch four different scenes performed simultaneously in different parts of the theater. The four groups rotate from scene to scene, each group sees all four scenes, each group experiences a different order of scenes. Kennedy's *Funnyhouse of a Negro*, written in 1964, splits up the consciousness of its protagonist, a woman of mixed race who identifies with Queen Victoria, the Duchess of Hapsburg, Jesus Christ, and Patrice Lumumba, the Congolese spokesman for African solidarity. These plays have taken on historical importance as their deconstruction of theatrical conventions is increasingly understood as the dramatic action of the performance, important social advocacy, not simply formal innovation.

When we read theater history, or we are told something is important in theater history, questions follow. Why is this history? How did it become history? Artistic excellence? Defined how? Cultural importance? Defined how? Influence? Influence on whom? Gossipy interest? For whom? Moral example? Political lesson? Again, for whom?

What comes and goes into the history of the theater we would like to think is due to timeless excellence. It is also due to whims and personal decisions. Büchner's widow, who survived him by forty years, destroyed the pages of *Woyzeck* she thought were too scandalous. Tennessee Williams' estate was controlled for ten years after his death by a conservative Russian woman (she had lived a wild life before she settled down), who kept much of Williams' later experimental work suppressed until she died. Eugene O'Neill burned the eleven plays of his history cycle, and if the terms of O'Neill's will had been respected his masterpiece, *Long Day's Journey Into Night*, would not have been made public until 1978. His wife and publisher, who had sworn to him they would wait twenty-five years after his death to break the wax seal on the manuscript, broke their promise and restored O'Neill's waning reputation within a year of his death.

Political power and the power of the purse effect history, too. When Stalin took over control of the arts in the Soviet Union, experimental theater was shut down in favor of Socialist Realism. Stanislavsky, who was continuing to experiment beyond realism, was kept under a gentle house arrest. His nurses, we now know, were government spies. The director Meyerhold, who protested the monopoly of realism at a meeting of the Director's Union, was put up against a wall and shot dead in 1940. Mention of Meyerhold in Russian theater history was forbidden until 1955, two years after Stalin died. Not until English and German translations popped up in the 1970s did Meyerhold's theoretical writing reenter Russian theater history.

In thinking about theater history, consider what is not there and why it isn't. Why is something missing from history? The corruption of time, as for the ancient Greeks we know only by name? Opportunity, as with Marita Bonner? Moral example? There were no positive gay characters in the American commercial theater because the Wales Padlock law made such things illegal until 1967. Political lesson, as with Meyerhold? So new it defies genres, as was so for *Ubu Roi*, *A Month in the Country*, and *Hedda Gabler*? So new it will take time to change history?

A truly original work of theater recognizes some connection between people we hadn't understood or noticed or hadn't felt before. Once we do understand, we recognize such connections when we next encounter them. When we look back, we recognize that we had, perhaps, felt something when we encountered such connections before, but had not yet a way to identify what it was we felt.

The French novelist Marcel Proust (1871–1922), who changed the action of the novel from a developing plot to the development of a point of view, wrote:

...the world around us (which was not created once and for all, but is created afresh as often as an original artist is born) appears to us entirely different from the old world, but perfectly clear...It will last until the next geological catastrophe is precipitated by a new painter or writer of original talent.

(Proust, *The Guermantes Way*, F. Scott Moncrieff, trans.)

Every time we go to the theatre or read a play, there is an opportunity to reshuffle another version of theater history, adding, omitting, rethinking.

BIBLIOGRAPHY

Aeschylus. *Aeschylus: The Oresteia*. Translated by Robert Fagles. New York: Viking Press, 1975.

———. *Agamemnon*. Translated by Robert Browning. London: Smith, Elder, & Co., 1877.

———. *Agamemnon*. Translated by Gilbert Murray. New York: Oxford University Press, 1920.

———. *Agamemnon*. Translated by Robert Potter. Norwich, UK: John Crouse in the Marketplace, 1777.

———. *An Oresteia*. Translated by Anne Carson. New York: Farrar, Straus and Giroux, 2010.

———. *The Oresteia*. Translated by Ted Hughes. New York: Farrar, Straus and Giroux, 1999.

———. *Oresteia: Agamemnon, The Libation Bearers, The Eumenides*. Translated by Richmond Lattimore. Chicago: University of Chicago Press, 1953.

———. *The Persians*. Translated by Janet Lembke and C.J. Herington. New York: Oxford University Press, 1991.

Aiken, George S. *Uncle Tom's Cabin or, Life Among the Lowly, A Domestic Drama in Six Acts*. New York: Samuel French, 1858.

Annenkov, Pavel Vaselivich. "Rachel in Russia: The Shchepkin-Annenkov Correspondence." Translated by Laurence Senelick. *Theatre Research International* 3, no. 2 (May 1978), 93–114.

Anonymous. "The Brome play of Abraham and Isaac." In *Medieval and Tudor Drama: Twenty-Four Plays*. Edited by John Gassner. New York: Applause Books, 2000.

———. *Castle of Perseverance*. Edited by David N. Klausner. Kalamazoo, Michigan: Medieval Institute Publications, 2010.

———. "Everyman." Edited by John Skot. In *Medieval and Tudor Drama: Twenty-Four Plays*. Edited by John Gassner. New York: Applause Books, 2000.

———. "Quem Quaeritis." In *Medieval and Tudor Drama: Twenty-Four Plays*. Edited by John Gassner. New York: Applause Books, 2000.

Antoine, André. *Memories of the Théâtre-Libre* (Books of the Theatre Series, No. 5). Translated by Marvin Carlson. Coral Gables, Florida: University of Miami Press, 1964.

Appia, Adolphe. *The Work of Living Art: A Theory of the Theatre*. Translated by H.D. Albright. Coral Gables, Florida: University of Miami Press, 1960.

Aristophanes. *Aristophanes, The Complete Plays*. Translated by Paul Roche. New York: New American Library, 2005.

———. *Frogs and Other Plays*. Translated by David Barrett. Revised translation with an introduction and notes by Shomit Dutta. London: Penguin Classics, 2007.

Aristotle. *Poetics (Norton Critical Editions)*. Edited by David Gorman and Michelle Zerba. Translated by James Hutton. New York: W.W. Norton & Company, Inc, 2018.

Artaud, Antonin. *Theater and Its Double*. New York: Grove Press, 1958.

Baraka, Amiri (Leroi Jones). *Dutchman*. New York: William Morrow, 1964.

Barras, Charles M. *The Black Crook*. Buffalo, New York: Rockwell, Backer & Hill, 1866.

Beckett, Samuel. *Complete Dramatic Works of Samuel Beckett*. London: Faber & Faber, 2006.

———. *The Unnamable*. New York: Grove Press, 1958.

Bonner, Marita. "Exit—An Illusion." *The Crisis*, 36 (Oct 1929).

———. "The Purple Flower." *The Crisis*, 35 (Jan 1928).

Borges, Jorge Luis. "Blindness." In *Seven Nights*. Translated by Eliot Weinberger. New York: New Directions, 1984.

Brecht, Bertolt. *Bertolt Brecht Collected Plays, Volume One*. London: Methuen, 1970.

———. *Bertolt Brecht Collected Plays, Volume Two*. Edited by John Willett and Ralph Manheim. London: Methuen Drama, 2007.

———. *Bertolt Brecht Collected Plays, Volume Five*. Edited by John Willett and Ralph Manheim. London: Methuen Drama, 1999.

———. *Bertolt Brecht Collected Plays, Volume Six, part one*. Edited by John Willett and Ralph Manheim. London: Methuen Drama, 1985.

———. *Bertolt Brecht Collected Plays, Volume Seven, part two*. Edited by Tania and James Stern with W.H. Auden. London: Methuen Drama, 1988.

———. *Brecht on Theatre: The Development of an Aesthetic*. Edited and translated by John Willett. New York: Hill and Wang, 1964.

———. *Galileo*. Adapted and translated by Charles Laughton. New York: Grove Press, 1966.

Breton, André. *The Surrealist Manifesto*. Translated by Richard Seaver and Helen R. Lane. In *Manifestoes of Surrealism*. Ann Arbor: University of Michigan, 1969.

Büchner, Georg. *Danton's Death, Leonce and Lena and Woyzeck*. Translated by Victor Price. Oxford: Oxford University Press, 1971.

Calderón de la Barca, Pedro. *Life is a Dream*. Translated by Roy Campbell. In *The Classic Theatre III: Six Spanish Plays*. Edited by Eric Russell Bentley. Garden City: Doubleday and Co., Inc., 1959.

Camus, Albert. *The Myth of Sisyphus*. Translated by Justin O'Brien. New York: Alfred A. Knopf, 1955.

Chandler, Raymond. "The Simple Art of Murder." *The Atlantic Monthly*, December 1944.

Chekhov, Anton. *Cherry Orchard*. Translated by Julian West. In *Plays of Anton Tchekoff*. New York: Scribner's, 1917.

———. *The Complete Plays: Anton Chekhov*. Edited and translated by Laurence Senelick. New York: W.W. Norton & Company, 2007.

———. *The Seagull*. Translated by Constance Garnett. London: Chatto & Windus, 1923.

Chikamatsu Monzaemon. *Four Major Plays of Chikamatsu*. Translated by Donald Keene. New York: Columbia University Press, 1998.

Clurman, Harold. *The Fervent Years*. New York: Alfred A. Knopf, 1945.

Cocteau, Jean. *The Infernal Machine and Other Plays*. New York: New Directions, 1967.

———. "Preface" to *The Eiffel Tower Wedding*. Translated by Michael Benedikt & George E. Wellwarth. In *Modern French plays: An Anthology from Jarry to Ionesco*. London: Faber & Faber, 1964.

Craig, Edward Gordon. *On the Art of the Theatre*. Edinburgh & London: T.N. Foulis, 1905.

Delacroix, Eugène. *The Journal of Eugène Delacroix*. Edited with an introduction by Hubert Wellington. Translated by Lucy Norton. London: Phaidon Press Limited, 1951.

Dickinson, Emily. *Further Poems of Emily Dickinson*. Edited by Martha Dickinson Bianchi. Boston: Little, Brown and Company, 1929.

Dryden, John. *All for Love, or The World Well Lost*. London: Methuen Drama, 2004.

Eliot, T.S. *The Sacred Wood: Essays on Poetry and Criticism*. London: Methuen & Co., Ltd., 1920.

Ensler, Eve. *The Vagina Monologues*, 10th Anniversary Edition. New York: Villard, 2007.

Euripides. *The Bacchae*. Translated by Robert Bagg. Amherst: University of Massachusetts Press, 1978.

———. *The Cyclops*. Translated by Heather McHugh. New York: Oxford University Press, 2001.

———. *Hippolytus*. Translated by Gilbert Murray. London: Allen Unwin, 1902.

———. *Iphigenia in Aulis*, revised edition. Translated by M.S. Merwin. Oxford: Oxford University Press, 1992.

———. *Iphigenia in Tauris*. Translated by Witter Bynner. New York: Mitchell Kennerley, 1915.

———. *Medea*. Translated by Gilbert Murray. New York: Oxford University Press, 1907.

———. *Trojan Women*. Translated by Alan Shapiro. New York: Oxford University Press, 2009.

FitzGerald, Edward. *The Rubáiyát of Omar Khayyám*. London: Macmillan & Company, 1899.

Flanagan, Hallie. *Arena*. New York: Duell, Sloan and Pearce, 1940.

———. *Dynamo*. New York: Duell, Sloan and Pearce, 1943.

Fornés, María Irene. *Fefu and Her Friends*. New York: Broadway Play Publishing, 2017.

Freud, Sigmund. *The Interpretation of Dreams,* third edition. Translated by A.A. Brill. New York: The Macmillan Company, 1913.

Gelbart, Larry and Burt Shevelove, and Stephen Sondheim. *A Funny Thing*

Happened on the Way to the Forum. New York: Applause Theatre & Cinema Books, 2000.

Genet, Jean. *The Balcony*. Translated by Bernard Frechtman. London: Faber & Faber, 1957.

———. *The Blacks*. Translated by Bernard Frechtman. London: Faber and Faber, 1960.

———. *The Maids*. Translated by Bernard Frechtman. London: Faber and Faber, 1953.

———. *Our Lady of the Flowers*. Translated by Bernard Frechtman. New York: Grove Press, 1963.

———. *The Screens*. Translated by Bernard Frechtman. New York: Grove Press, 1962.

Glaspell, Susan. *Trifles*. New York: Frank Shay, 1916.

Goethe, Johann Wolfgang von. *Iphigenia in Tauris*. Translated by Anna Swanwick. New York: Arthur Hinds & Company, 1850.

Goldoni, Carlo. *The Servant of Two Masters*. Translated by Edward J. Dent. Cambridge: Cambridge University Press, 1928.

Gorky, Maxim. *The Lower Depths*. Translated by Jenny Covan. New York: Brentano's Publishers, 1922.

———. *The Lower Depths*. Translated by Kitty Hunter-Blair and Jeremy Brooks. London: Eyre Methuen, 1973.

Haigh, A.E. *The Tragic Drama of Greeks*. Oxford: Clarendon Press, 1896.

Hazelton, George C. and J. Harry Benrimo. *The Yellow Jacket*. Indianapolis, Indiana: Bobbs-Merrill Company, 1913.

Herondas. *Mimiamboi*. Translated by Guy Davenport. In *The Mimes of Herondas*. San Francisco: Grey Fox Press, 1981.

Heyward, Du Bose and Ira Gershwin. *Porgy and Bess*. New York: Random House, 1935.

Hill, Abram and John Silvera. *Liberty Deferred and Other Living Newspapers of the 1930s*. Fairfax, Virginia: George Mason University Press, 1989.

Hroswitha. *Dulcitus*. Translated by Sister Mary Margaret Butler. In *Medieval and Tudor Drama: Twenty-Four Plays*. Edited by John Gassner. New York: Applause Books, 2000.

Ibsen, Henrik. *Hedda Gabler*. Translated by Edmund Gosse and William Archer. London: William Heinemann, 1891.

———. "Letter to Bjørnstjerne Bjørnson." In *Ibsen: A Biography*. Michael Meyer. New York: Doubleday, 1971.

———. *Peer Gynt*. Translated by William and Charles Archer. London: Walter Scott, 1904.

———. *Peer Gynt*. Translated by Jerry Bamman and Irene B. Berman. New York: Theatre Communications Group, 1993.

Ionesco, Eugène. *Four Plays by Eugène Ionesco*. Translated by Donald M. Allen. New York: Grove Press, 1958.

———. *Rhinoceros*. Translated by Derek Prouse. New York: Grove Press, 1960.

Jarry, Alfred. *Ubu Roi*. Translated by Barbara Wright. New York: New Directions, 1961.

Kaufman, George S. and Edna Ferber. *Dinner at Eight*. New York: Double-day, Doran & Company, 1932.

Kennedy, Adrienne. *The Adrienne Kennedy Reader*. Minneapolis: University of Minnesota Press, 2001.

Kharms, Daniil. *Daniil Kharms and the Poetics of the Absurd: Essays and Materials*. Edited by Neil Cornwell. London: Palgrave Macmillan, 1991.

———. *Today I Wrote Nothing: The Selected Writings of Daniil Kharms*. Translated by Matvei Yankelevich. New York: Overlook Press, 2009.

Kramer, Larry. *The Normal Heart*. New York: Plume, 1985.

Li Syau Chan. *The Wild Boar Forest*. Translated by J. D. Mitchell and D. Chang. In *The Red Pear Garden: Three Great Dramas of Revolutionary China*. Edited by John D. Mitchell. Introduction by Richard E. Strassberg. Boston: D.R. Godine, 1973.

Lope de Vega. *The Classic Theatre III: Six Spanish Plays*. Translated by Roy Campbell. Garden City, NY: Doubleday and Co., Inc., 1959.

Lorca, Federico Garcia. *Five plays of Federico Garcia Lorca*. Translated by James Graham-Luján and Richard L. O'Connell. New York: C. Scribner's Sons, 1941.

———. *Three Tragedies*. Translated by James Graham-Luján and Richard L. O'Connell. New York: New Directions, 1947.

Luce, Clare Booth. *The Women*. New York: Random House, 1937.

Machiavelli, Niccolò. *The Mandrake*. Translated by Wallace Shawn. New York: Dramatists Play Service, Inc., 1998.

Maeterlinck, Maurice. *The Blue Bird*. Translated by Alexander Teixeira de Mattos. New York: Dodd, Mead and Company, 1911.

———. *The Plays of Maurice Maeterlinck*. Translated by Richard Hovey. Chicago: Stone & Kimball, 1896.

Marshall, Frank Albert. "Preface." *Hamlet: A Tragedy in Five Acts*. London: Chiswick Press, 1879.

Martin, John. *The Modern Dance*. New York: S. Barnes and Company, 1963.

Menander of Athens. *Menander*. Edited by David R. Slavitt and Palmer Bovie. Philadelphia: University of Pennsylvania Press, 1998.

Meyer, Michael. *Ibsen: A Biography*. New York: Doubleday, 1971.

Meyerhold, Vsevolod. *Meyerhold on Theatre*. Translated by Edward Braun. New York: Hill & Wang, 1969.

Miller, Arthur. *Collected Plays 1944–1961*. New York: Library of America, 2006.

Mishima, Yukio (Kimitake Hiraoka). *Five Modern Nō Plays*. Translated by Donald Keene. New York: Alfred A. Knopf, 1957.

———. *Madame de Sade*. Translated by Donald Keene. New York: Grove Press, 1967.

———. *Mishima Onstage: The Black Lizard and Other Plays*. Translated by Laurence Kominz. Ann Arbor: University of Michigan Press, 2007.

———. *My Friend Hitler and Other Plays*. Translated by Hiroaki Sato. New York: Columbia University Press, 2002.

Molière (Jean-Baptiste Poquelin). *The Imaginary Invalid*. Translated by Henri van Laun. Mineola, NY: Dover Press, 2004.

———. *The Misanthrope*. Translated by Richard Wilbur. New York: Harcourt, Brace & Company, 1955.

———. *Molière: the Misanthrope and Other Plays*. Translated by James Wood and David Coward. New York: Penguin Books, 2000.

———. *The School for Wives*. Translated by Richard Wilbur. New York: Dramatists Play Service, 1971.

———. *Sganarelle, or the Imaginary Cuckold*. Translated by Richard Wilbur. New York: Dramatists Play Service, 1993.

———. *Tartuffe, or, the Impostor*. Translated by Richard Wilbur. New York: Harcourt, Brace & Company, 1963.

Mowatt, Anna Cora. *Fashion*. Marrickville, New South Wales: Wentworth Press, 2016.

Odets, Clifford. *Awake and Sing!* New York: Random House, 1935.

———. *Paradise Lost*. New York: Random House, 1936.

———. *Waiting for Lefty. New Theatre*, February 1935.

O'Neill, Eugene. *Eugene O'Neill: Complete Plays 1913–1920*. New York: Library of America, 1988.

———. *Eugene O'Neill: Complete Plays 1920–1931*. New York: Library of America, 1988.

———. *Eugene O'Neill: Complete Plays 1932–1943*. New York: Library of America, 1988.

Peking Opera Troupe in Shanghai. *Taking Tiger Mountain by Strategy* (1970 script). Collectively written and revised by members of the Peking Opera Troupe in Shanghai. Translated by R. E. Strassberg. In *The Red Pear Garden: Three Great Dramas of Revolutionary China*. Edited by John D. Mitchell. Introduction by Richard E. Strassberg. Boston: D.R. Godine, 1973.

Plautus (Titus Maccius Plautus). *The Menaechmi*. Translated by Palmer Bovie. In *Classical Comedy: Greek and Roman*. Edited by Robert W. Corrigan. New York: Applause Theatre & Cinema Books, 2000.

Plutarch. *Plutarch's Lives*. Translated by Sir Thomas North. London: J.M. Dent, 1910.

Poel, William. *Shakespeare in the Theatre*. London: Sidgwick and Jackson Ltd., 1913.

Pope, Alexander. *An Essay on Criticism*. London: W. Lewis, 1711.

Proust, Marcel. *The Guermantes Way,* volume 2. Translated by F. Scott Moncrieff. London: Chatto and Windus, 1925.

Racine, Jean. *Phèdre*. Translated by Ted Hughes. New York: Farrar, Straus and Giroux, 2000.

———. *Phaedra by Racine*. Translated by Richard Wilbur. New York: Harcourt, Brace Jovanovich, 1987.

Rice, Elmer. *The Adding Machine*. New York: Doubleday, Page & Company, 1923.

Robeson, Paul. "Testimony of Paul Robeson before the House Committee on Un-American Activities, June 12, 1956." In *Thirty Years of Treason: Excerpts from Hearings Before the House Committee on Un-Ameri-*

can Activities, 1938–1968. Edited by Eric Bentley. New York: Viking Press, 1971.

Schiller, Friedrich von. *Love and Intrigue.* Translated by Laurence Senelick. New York: Broadway Play Publishers, 2008.

Schopenhauer, Arthur. *The World as Will and Representation,* vol. I, fourth book, seventh edition. Translated by R.B. Haldane, M.A. and J. Kemp. London: Kegan Paul, Trench, Trübner & Co., 1909.

Seneca (Lucius Annaeus Seneca, Seneca the Younger). *Seneca: His Tenne Tragedies.* Edited by Thomas Newton. Indianapolis: Indiana University Press, 1964.

———. *Seneca. Six Tragedies.* Translated by Emily Wilson. New York: Oxford University Press, 2010.

———. *Seneca's Oedipus.* Translated by Ted Hughes. London: Faber & Faber, 1969.

———. *Seneca's Tragedies: volume 1.* Translated by Frank Justus Miller. Cambridge, Mass.: Harvard University Press, 1917.

Shakespeare, William. *William Shakespeare: The Complete Works, Original Spelling edition.* Edited by Gary Taylor, John Jowett, William Montgomery, and S. Schoenbaum. Oxford: Clarendon Press, 1986.

Sophocles. *The Complete Sophocles: The Thebian Plays, volume 1.* Edited by Peter Burian and Alan Shapiro. New York: Oxford University Press, 2003.

———. *The Complete Sophocles: Electra and other plays, volume 2.* Edited by Peter Burian and Alan Shapiro. New York: Oxford University Press, 2010.

Stanislavsky, Konstantin. *My Life in the Theater.* Translated by J.J. Robbins. Boston: Little, Brown & Company, 1924.

Stein, Gertrude. *Four Saints in Three Acts.* New York: Random House, 1934.

———. *Last Operas and Plays.* New York: Rinehart & Co., 1949.

Stone, John Augustus. *Metamora; or, The Last of the Wampanoags.* In *Metamora and Other Plays.* Bloomington, Indiana: Indiana University Press, 1965.

Strindberg, August. *The Chamber Plays.* Translated by Evert Sprinchorn, Seabury Quinn, Jr., and Kenneth Petersen. Minneapolis: University of Minnesota Press, 1962.

———. "Preface" to *Miss Julie.* In *Eight Famous Plays by August Strindberg.* Translated by Edwin Björkman. New York: Scribner's, 1949.

———. *Miss Julie.* Translated by Edith and Warner Oland. Boston: John W. Luce and Co., 1912.

———. *Plays, Two: The Dance of Death, A Dream Play, The Stronger.* Translated by Michael Levinson Meyer. London: Methuen, 1982.

———. *Twelve Plays.* Translated by Elizabeth Sprigge. London: Constable, 1963.

Terence (Publius Terentius Afer). *The Mother-in-Law.* Translated by Stanley Ireland. Liverpool: Liverpool University Press, 1990.

Terry, Walter. *Dance in America.* New York: Harper Row, 1971.

Theophrastus. *Characters, an Ancient Take on Bad Behavior.* Translated by

Pamela Mensch. New York: Callaway Arts & Entertainment, 2018.

Thurber, James. "The Wolf Who Went Places," *The New Yorker*. May 19, 1956.

Treadwell, Sophie. *Machinal*. London: Nick Hern Books, 1995.

Turgenev, Ivan. *A Month in the Country*. Translated by Isaiah Berlin. London: The Hogarth Press, London, 1981.

———. *A Month in the Country*. Translated by Constance Garnett. In *Three Plays*. London: Cassell & Company, 1934.

Tyan Han. *The White Snake*. Translated by D. Chang. English verse adaptation by W. Packard. In *The Red Pear Garden: Three Great Dramas of Revolutionary China*. Edited by John D. Mitchell. Introduction by Richard E. Strassberg. Boston: D.R. Godine, 1973.

Tyler, Royall and Cynthia A. Kierner. *The Contrast: Manners, Morals, and Authority in the Early American Republic*. New York: New York University Press, 2007.

Vidal, Gore. "Love, Love, Love." *Partisan Review*, Spring 1959.

Whitman, Walt. *Leaves of Grass*. Brooklyn, NY: Walt Whitman, 1855.

Wilde, Oscar. *The Importance of Being Earnest*. London: Leonard Smithers, 1899.

Wilder, Thornton. *Our Town: A Play in Three Acts*. New York: Harper Perennial Modern Classics, 2003.

———. *Thornton Wilder: Collected Plays and Writings on Theater*. New York: Library of America, 2007.

Williams, Tennessee. *Clothes for a Summer Hotel*. New York: New Directions, 1983.

———. *Something Cloudy, Something Clear*. New York: New Directions, 1995.

———. *A Streetcar Named Desire*. New York: New Directions, 1947.

———. *Tennessee Williams: Plays 1937–1955*. New York: Library of America, 2000.

———. *Tennessee Williams: Plays 1957–1980*. New York: Library of America, 2000.

———. *The Traveling Companion and other Plays*. New York: New Directions, 2008.

Wilson, August. *August Wilson Century Cycle*. New York: Theatre Communications Group, 2007.

Wu Zuguang, Huang Zaolin, and Mei Shaowu. *Peking Opera and Mei Lanfang*. Beijing: New World Press, 1981.

Yeats, William Butler. *The Death of Cuchulain*. Ithaca, New York: Cornell University Press, 1939.

———. *Eleven Plays of William Butler Yeats*. New York: Collier Books, 1966.

———. *Four Plays for Dancers*. London: Macmillan and Company, Ltd., 1921.

———. *The Tower*. London: Macmillan, 1928.

———. *The Winding Stair*. London: Macmillan and Co., 1933.

Zeami (Zeami Motokiyo). *The Kadensho*. Translated by Sakurai Chuichi, Hayashi Shuseki, Satoi Rokuro, and Miyai Bin. Kyoto: Sumiya Shinobe Publishing Institute, 1968.

Zola, Émile. "Naturalism on the Stage." Translated by Samuel Draper. In *Playwrights on Playwriting: from Ibsen to Ionesco*. Edited by Toby Cole. New York: Cooper Square Press, 2001.

ABOUT THE AUTHOR

 **DAVID KAPLAN** is the author of *Five Approaches to Acting* (2001, 2007) which describes the provenance and practice of onstage performance. In his own practice, he directs plays and teaches classes around the world. He pursues projects over decades. In 1997 he began research on what would become, in 2016, a concert-party version in Ghana of Tennessee Williams' *Ten Blocks on the Camino Real*. As part of the process in 2012, he staged a marketplace version in Paysandu, Uruguay in Rioplatanese Spanish.

Other texts directed by David Kaplan putting theory into practice that refines theory include a Sufi *King Lear* in Tashkent, Uzbekistan, performed in the Uzbek language; Genet's *The Maids* in Ulaan Baator, Mongolia, performed in Mongolian; *A Midsummer Night's Dream* in Buryatia, performed in the Buryat language with shamans. In Russia, Mr. Kaplan staged the first Russian-language productions of *Auntie Mame* and Tennessee Williams' *Suddenly Last Summer*. Also in Russia, in Russian: *Macbeth* and Eugene O'Neill's *Ah, Wilderness!* At the Hong Kong Repertory Theatre, he has staged Tennessee Williams' *The Eccentricities of a Nightingale* and Edward Albee's *Three Tall Women*, both in Cantonese. He has directed performances seen in forty of the fifty United States.

He has taught at Clark, Hofstra, NYU, Columbia, Rutgers, The University of New Mexico, The University of the South, Mississippi State University, The Siberian Academy of Fine Arts (in Russian), the Hong Kong Academy of Performing Arts, Bilkent University in Ankara Turkey, Actuando sin Actuar in Mexico, the Metodi Festival in Italy, the William Esper Studio, and the Lee Strasberg Institute.